Masterpieces (

The Best Speeche

from the days of Slavery to the Present Time

Editor

Alice Moore Dunbar-Nelson

Alpha Editions

This edition published in 2022

ISBN : 9789356902268

Design and Setting By
Alpha Editions
www.alphaedis.com
Email - info@alphaedis.com

Contents

PREFACE

It seems eminently fitting and proper in this year, the fiftieth anniversary of the Proclamation of Emancipation that the Negro should give pause and look around him at the things which he has done, those which he might have done, and those which he intends to do. We pause, just at the beginning of another half century, taking stock of past achievements, present conditions, future possibilities.

In considering the literary work of the Negro, his pre-eminence in the field of oratory is striking. Since the early nineteenth century until the present time, he is found giving eloquent voice to the story of his wrongs and his proscriptions. Crude though the earlier efforts may be, there is a certain grim eloquence in them that is touching, there must be, because of the intensity of feeling behind the words.

Therefore, it seems appropriate in putting forth a volume commemorating the birth of the Negro into manhood, to collect some few of the speeches he made to help win his manhood, his place in the economy of the nation, his right to stand with his face to the sun. The present volume does not aim to be a complete collection of Negro Eloquence; it does not even aim to present the best that the Negro has done on the platform, it merely aims to present to the public some few of the best speeches made within the past hundred years. Much of the best is lost; much of it is hidden away in forgotten places. We have not always appreciated our own work sufficiently to preserve it, and thus much valuable material is wasted. Sometimes it has been difficult to obtain good speeches from those who are living because of their innate modesty, either in not desiring to appear in print, or in having thought so little of their efforts as to have lost them.

The Editor is conscious that many names not in the table of contents will suggest themselves to the most casual reader, but the omissions are not intentional nor yet of ignorance always, but due to the difficulty of procuring the matter in time for the publication of the volume before the golden year shall have closed.

In collecting and arranging the matter, for the volume, I am deeply indebted first to the living contributors who were so gracious and generous in their responses to the request for their help, and to the relatives of those who have passed into silence, for the loan of valuable books and manuscripts. I cannot adequately express my gratitude to Mr. John E. Bruce and Mr. Arthur A. Schomburg, President and Secretary of the Negro Society for Historical Research, for advice, suggestion, and best of all, for help in lending priceless books and manuscripts and for aid in copying therefrom.

Again, we repeat, this volume is not a complete anthology; not the final word in Negro eloquence of to-day, nor yet a collection of all the best; it is merely a suggestion, a guide-post, pointing the way to a fuller work, a slight memorial of the birth-year of the race.

THE EDITOR.

October, 1913.

THE PEOPLE OF HAYTI AND A PLAN OF EMIGRATION[1]

BY PRINCE SAUNDERS

Respected Gentlemen and Friends:

At a period so momentous as the present, when the friends of abolition and emancipation, as well as those whom observation and experience might teach us to beware to whom we should apply the endearing appellations, are professedly concerned for the establishment of an Asylum for those Free Persons of Color, who may be disposed to remove to it, and for such persons as shall hereafter be emancipated from slavery, a careful examination of this subject is imposed upon us.

So large a number of abolitionists, convened from different sections of the country, is at all times and under any circumstances, an interesting spectacle to the eye of the philanthropist, how doubly delightful then is it, to me, whose interests and feelings so largely partake in the object you have in view, to behold this convention engaged in solemn deliberation upon those subjects employed to promote the improvement of the condition of the African race.

* * * * *

Assembled as this convention is, for the promotion and extension of its beneficent and humane views and principles, I would respectfully beg leave to lay before it a few remarks upon the character, condition, and wants of the afflicted and divided people of Hayti, as they, and that island, may be connected with plans for the emigration of the free people of color of the United States.

God in the mysterious operation of his providence has seen fit to permit the most astonishing changes to transpire upon that naturally beautiful and (as to soil and productions) astonishingly luxuriant island.

The abominable principles, both of action and belief, which pervaded France during the long series of vicissitudes which until recently she has experienced, extended to Hayti, or Santo Domingo have undoubtedly had an extensive influence upon the character, sentiments, and feelings of all descriptions of its present inhabitants.

This magnificent and extensive island which has by travellers and historians been often denominated the "paradise of the New World," seems from its situation, extent, climate, and fertility peculiarly suited to become an object of interest and attention to the many distinguished and enlightened philanthropists whom God has been graciously pleased to inspire with a zeal for the promotion of the best interests of the descendants of Africa. The recent proceedings in several of the slave States toward the free population of color in those States seem to render it highly probable that that oppressed class of the community will soon be obliged to flee to the free States for protection. If the two rival Governments of Hayti were consolidated into one well-balanced pacific power, there are many hundred of the free people in the New England and Middle States who would be glad to repair there immediately to settle, and believing that the period has arrived, when many zealous friends to abolition and emancipation are of opinion that it is time for them to act in relation to an asylum for such persons as shall be emancipated from slavery, or for such portion of the free colored population at present existing in the United States, as shall feel disposed to emigrate, and being aware that the authorities of Hayti are themselves desirous of receiving emigrants from this country, are among the considerations which have induced me to lay this subject before the convention.

The present spirit of rivalry which exists between the two chiefs in the French part of the island, and the consequent belligerent aspect and character of the country, may at first sight appear somewhat discouraging to the beneficent views and labors of the friends of peace; but these I am inclined to think are by no means to be considered as insurmountable barriers against the benevolent exertions of those Christian philanthropists whose sincere and hearty desire it is to reunite and pacify them.

There seems to be no probability of their ever being reconciled to each other without the philanthropic interposition and mediation of those who have the welfare of the African race at heart. And where, in the whole circle of practical Christian philanthropy and active beneficence, is there so ample a field for the exertion of those heaven-born virtues as in that hitherto distracted region? In those unhappy divisions which exist in Hayti is strikingly exemplified the saying which is written in the sacred oracles, "that when men forsake the true worship and service of the only true God, and bow down to images of silver, and gold, and four-footed beasts and creeping things, and become contentious with each other," says the inspired writer, "in such a state of things trust ye not a friend, put ye not confidence in a guide; keep the doors of thy mouth from her that lieth in thy bosom; for there the son dishonoreth the father, and the daughter riseth up against her mother, the daughter-in-law against her mother-in-law, and a man's enemies shall be those of his own house."

Had the venerable prophet in the foregoing predictions alluded expressly and entirely to the actual moral, political, and above all, to the religious character and condition of the Haytians, he could scarcely have given a more correct description of it.

For there is scarcely a family whose members are not separated from each other, and arrayed under the banners of the rival chiefs, in virtual hostility against each other. In many instances the husband is with Henry, and the wife and children with Boyer, and there are other instances in which the heads of the family are with Boyer, and the other members with Henry.

Let it be distinctly remembered, that these divided and distressed individuals are not permitted to hold any intercourse with each other; so that it is only when some very extraordinary occurrence transpires, that persons in the different sections of the country receive any kind of information from their nearest relatives and friends.

"Blessed are the peacemakers," is the language of that celestial law-giver, who taught as never man taught; and his religion uniformly assures the obedient recipients of his spirit, that they shall be rewarded according to the extent, fidelity, and sincerity of their works of piety and beneficence.

And if, according to the magnitude of the object in all its political, benevolent, humane, and Christian relations, the quantum of recompense is to be awarded and apprised to the just, to how large a share of the benediction of our blessed Savior to the promoters of peace shall those be authorized to expect who may be made the instruments of the pacification and reunion of the Haytian people? Surely the blessings of thousands who are, as it were, ready to perish, must inevitably come upon them.

When I reflect that it was in this city that the first abolition society that was formed in the world was established, I am strongly encouraged to hope, that here also there may originate a plan, which shall be the means of restoring many of our fellow beings to the embraces of their families and friends, and place that whole country upon the basis of unanimity and perpetual peace.

If the American Convention should in their wisdom think it expedient to adopt measures for attempting to affect a pacification of the Haytians, it is most heartily believed, that their benevolent views would be hailed and concurred in with alacrity and delight by the English philanthropists.

It is moreover believed that a concern so stupendous in its relations, and bearing upon the cause of universal abolition and emancipation, and to the consequent improvement and elevation of the African race, would tend to awaken an active and a universally deep and active interest in the minds of that numerous host of abolitionists in Great Britain, whom we trust have the best interests of the descendants of Africa deeply at heart.

TOUSSAINT L'OUVERTURE AND THE HAYTIAN REVOLUTIONS[2]

BY JAMES MCCUNE SMITH, M. A., M. D.

Ladies and Gentlemen:

Whilst the orgies of the French revolution thrust forward a being whose path was by rivers of blood, the horrors of Santo Domingo produced one who was pre-eminently a peacemaker—TOUSSAINT L'OUVERTURE.

In estimating the character of Toussaint L'Ouverture, regard must be paid, not to the enlightened age in which he lived, but to the rank in society from which he sprang—a rank which must be classed with a remote and elementary age of mankind.

Born forty-seven years before the commencement of the revolt, he had reached the prime of manhood, a slave, with a soul uncontaminated by the degradation which surrounded him. Living in a state of society where worse than polygamy was actually urged, we find him at this period faithful to one wife—the wife of his youth—and the father of an interesting family. Linked with such tender ties, and enlightened with some degree of education, which his indulgent master, M. Bayou, had given him, he fulfilled, up to the moment of the revolt, the duties of a Christian man in slavery.

At the time of the insurrection—in which he took no part—he continued in the peaceable discharge of his duties as coachman; and when the insurgents approached the estate whereon he lived, he accomplished the flight of M. Bayou, whose kind treatment (part of this kindness was teaching this slave to read and write) he repaid by forwarding to him produce for his maintenance while in exile in these United States.

Having thus faithfully acquitted himself as a slave, he turned towards the higher destinies which awaited him as a freeman. With a mind stored with patient reflection upon the biographies of men, the most eminent in civil and military affairs; and deeply versed in the history of the most remarkable revolutions that had yet occurred amongst mankind, he entered the army of the insurgents under Jean François. This chief rapidly promoted him to the offices of physician to the forces, aid-de-camp, and colonel. Jean François, in alliance with the Spaniards, maintained war at this time for the cause of royalty.

Whilst serving under this chief, Toussaint beheld another civil war agitating the French colony. On one side, the French Commissioners, who had acknowledged the emancipation of the slaves, maintained war for the Republic; on the other side, the old noblesse, or planters, fought under the royal banner, having called in the aid of the British forces in order to re-establish slavery and the ancient regime.

In this conflict, unmindful of their solemn oaths against the decree of the 15th of May, 1791, the whites of both parties, including the planters, hesitated not to fight in the same ranks, shoulder to shoulder, with the blacks. Caste was forgotten in the struggle for principles!

At this juncture Jean François, accompanied by his principal officers, and possessed of all the honors and emoluments of a captain-general in the service of his Catholic Majesty, retired to Spain, leaving Toussaint at liberty to choose his party. Almost immediately joining that standard which acknowledged and battled for equal rights to all men, he soon rendered signal service to the Commissioners, by driving the Spaniards from the northern, and by holding the British at bay in the eastern part of the island. For these services he was raised to the rank of general by the French commander at Porte-aux-Paix, General Laveaux, a promotion which he soon repaid by saving that veteran's life under the following circumstances: Villate, a mulatto general, envious of the honors bestowed on Toussaint, treacherously imprisoned General Laveaux in Cape François. Immediately upon hearing this fact, Toussaint hastened to the Cape at the head of 10,000 men and liberated his benefactor. And, at the very moment of his liberation, a commission arrived from France appointing General Laveaux Governor of the Colony; his first official act was to proclaim Toussaint his lieutenant. "This is the black," said Laveaux, "predicted by Raynal, and who is destined to avenge the outrages committed against his whole race." A remark soon verified, for on his attainment of the supreme power, Toussaint avenged those injuries—by forgiveness!

As an acknowledgment for his eminent services against the British, and against the mulattoes, who, inflamed with all the bitterness of *caste*, had maintained a sanguinary war under their great leader Rigaud, in the southern part of the colony, the Commissioners invested Toussaint with the office and dignity of general-in-chief of Santo Domingo.

From that moment began the full development of the vast and versatile genius of this extraordinary man. Standing amid the terrible, because hostile, fragments of two revolutions, harassed by the rapacious greed of commissioners upon commissioners, who, successively dispatched from France, hid beneath a republican exterior a longing after the spoils; with an army in the field accustomed by five years' experience to all the license of civil war, Toussaint, with a giant hand, seized the reins of government, reduced these conflicting elements to harmony and order, and raised the colony to nearly its former prosperity, his lofty intellect always delighting to effect its object rather by the tangled mazes of diplomacy than by the strong arm of physical force, yet maintaining a steadfast and unimpeached adherence to truth, his word, and his honor.

General Maitland, commander of the British forces, finding the reduction of the island to be utterly hopeless, signed a treaty with Toussaint for the evacuation of all the posts which he held. "Toussaint then paid him a visit, and was received with military honors. After partaking of a grand entertainment, he was presented by General Maitland, in the name of His Majesty, with a splendid service of plate, and put in possession of the government-house which had been built and furnished by the English."

* * * * *

Buonaparte, on becoming First Consul, sent out the confirmation of Toussaint as commander-in-chief, who, with views infinitely beyond the short-sighted and selfish vision of the Commissioners, proclaimed a general amnesty to the planters who had fled during the revolutions, earnestly invited their return to the possession of their estates, and, with a delicate regard to their feelings, decreed that the epithet "emigrant" should not be applied to them. Many of the planters accepted the invitation, and returned to the peaceful possession of their estates.

In regard to the army of Toussaint, General Lacroix, one of the planters who returned, affirms "that never was a European army subjected to a more rigid discipline than that which was observed by the troops of Toussaint." Yet this army was converted by the commander-in-chief into industrious laborers, by the simple expedient of *paying them for their labor.* "When he restored many of the planters to their estates, there was no restoration of their former property in human beings. No human being was to be bought or sold. Severe tasks, flagellations, and scanty food were no longer to be endured. The planters were obliged to employ their laborers on the footing of hired servants." "And under this system," says Lacroix, "the colony advanced, as if by enchantment towards its ancient splendor; cultivation was extended with such rapidity that every day made its progress more perceptible. All appeared to be happy, and regarded Toussaint as their guardian angel. In making a tour of the island, he was hailed by the blacks with universal joy, nor was he less a favorite of the whites."

Toussaint, having effected a bloodless conquest of the Spanish territory, had now become commander of the entire island. Performing all the executive duties, he made laws to suit the exigency of the times. His Egeria was temperance accompanied with a constant activity of body and mind.

The best proof of the entire success of his government is contained in the comparative views of the exports of the island, before the revolutions, and during the administration of Toussaint. Bear in mind that, "before the revolution there were 450,000 slave laborers working with a capital in the shape of buildings, mills, fixtures, and implements, which had been accumulating during a century. Under Toussaint there were 290,000 free laborers, many of them just from the army or the mountains, working on plantations that had undergone the devastation of insurrection and a seven years' war."

* * * * *

In consequence of the almost entire cessation of official communication with France, and for other reasons equally good, Toussaint thought it necessary for the public welfare to frame a new constitution for the government of the island. With the aid of M. Pascal, Abbe Moliere, and Marinit, he drew up a constitution, and submitted the same to a General Assembly convened from every district, and by that assembly the constitution was adopted. It was subsequently promulgated in the name of the people. And, on the 1st of July, 1801, the island was declared to be an independent State, in which *all men*, without regard to complexion or creed, possessed *equal rights*.

This proceeding was subsequently sanctioned by Napoleon Buonaparte, whilst First Consul. In a letter to Toussaint, he says, "We have conceived for you esteem, and we wish to recognize and proclaim the great services you have rendered the French people. If their colors fly on Santo Domingo, it is to you and your brave blacks that we owe it. Called by your talents and the force of circumstances to the chief command, you have terminated the civil war, put a stop to the persecutions of some ferocious men, and restored to honor the religion and the worship of God, from whom all things come. The situation in which you were placed, surrounded on all sides by enemies, and without the mother country being able to succor or sustain you, has rendered legitimate the articles of that constitution."

Although Toussaint enforced the duties of religion, he entirely severed the connection between Church and State. He rigidly enforced all the duties of morality, and would not suffer in his presence even the approach to indecency of dress or manner. "Modesty," said he, "is the defense of woman."

The chief, nay the idol of an army of 100,000 well-trained and acclimated troops ready to march or sail where he wist, Toussaint refrained from raising the standard of liberty in any one of the neighboring island, at a time when, had he been fired with what men term ambition, he could easily have revolutionized the entire archipelago of the west. But his thoughts were bent on conquest of another kind; he was determined to overthrow an *error* which designing and interested men had craftily instilled into the civilized world,—a belief in the natural inferiority of the Negro race. It was the glory and the warrantable boast of Toussaint that he had been the instrument of demonstrating that, even with the worst odds against them, this race is entirely capable of achieving liberty and of self-government. He did more: by abolishing caste he proved the artificial nature of such distinctions, and further demonstrated that even slavery cannot unfit men for the full exercise of all the functions which belong to free citizens.

"Some situations of trust were filled by free Negroes and mulattoes, who had been in respectable circumstances under the old Government; but others were occupied by Negroes, and even by Africans, who had recently emerged from the lowest condition of slavery."

But the bright and happy state of things which the genius of Toussaint had almost created out of elements the most discordant was doomed to be of short duration. For the dark spirit of Napoleon, glutted, but not satiated with the glory banquet afforded at the expense of Europe and Africa, seized upon this, the most beautiful and happy of the Hesperides, as the next victim of its remorseless rapacity.

With the double intention of getting rid of the republican army, and reducing back to slavery the island of Hayti, he sent out his brother-in-law, General Leclerc, with 26 ships of war and 25,000 men.

Like Leonidas at Thermopylæ, or the Bruce at Bannockburn, Toussaint determined to defend from thraldom his sea-girt isle, made sacred to liberty by the baptism of blood.

On the 28th of January, 1802, Leclerc arrived off the bay of Samana, from the promontory of which Toussaint, in anxious alarm, beheld for the first time in his life so large an armament. "We must all perish," said he, "all France has come to Santo Domingo!" But this despondency passed away in a moment, and then this man, who had been a kindly-treated slave, prepared to oppose to the last that system which he now considered worse than death.

It is impossible, after so long a tax on your patience, to enter on a detailed narration of the conflict which ensued. The hour of trial served only to develop and ennoble the character of Toussaint, who rose, with misfortune, above the allurements of rank and wealth which were offered as the price of his submission; and the very ties of parental love he yielded to the loftier sentiment of patriotism.

On the 2d of February, a division of Leclerc's army, commanded by General Rochambeau, an old planter, landed at Fort Dauphin, and ruthlessly murdered many of the inhabitants (freedmen) who, unarmed, had been led by curiosity to the beach, in order to witness the disembarkation of the troops.

Christophe, one of the generals of Toussaint, commanding at Cape François, having resisted the menaces and the flattery of Leclerc, reduced that ill-fated town to ashes, and retired with his troops into the mountains, carrying with him 2,000 of the white inhabitants of the Cape, who were protected from injury during the fierce war which ensued.

Having full possession of the plain of the Cape, Leclerc, with a proclamation of liberty in his hand, in March following re-established slavery with all its former cruelties.

This treacherous movement thickened the ranks of Toussaint, who thenceforward so vigorously pressed his opponent, that as a last resort, Leclerc broke the shackles of the slave, and proclaimed "Liberty and equality to all the inhabitants of Santo Domingo."

This proclamation terminated the conflict for the time. Christophe and Dessalines, general officers, and at length Toussaint himself, capitulated, and, giving up the command of the island to Leclerc, he retired, at the suggestion of that officer, to enjoy rest and the sweet endearments of his family circle, on one of his estates near Gonaives. At this place he had remained about one month, when, without any adequate cause, Leclerc caused him to be seized, and to be placed on board of a ship of war, in which he was conveyed to France, where, without trial or condemnation, he was imprisoned in a loathsome and unhealthy dungeon. Unaccustomed to the chill and damp of this prison-house, the aged frame of Toussaint gave way, and he died.

In this meagre outline of his life I have presented simply facts, gleaned, for the most part, from the unwilling testimony of his foes, and therefore resting on good authority. The highest encomium on his character is contained in the fact that Napoleon believed that by capturing him he would be able to re-enslave Hayti; and even this encomium is, if possible, rendered higher by the circumstances which afterward transpired, which showed that his principles were so thoroughly disseminated among his brethren, that, without the presence of Toussaint, they achieved that liberty which he had taught them so rightly to estimate.

The capture of Toussaint spread like wild-fire through the island, and his principal officers again took the field. A fierce and sanguinary war ensued, in which the French gratuitously inflicted the most awful cruelties on their prisoners, many of whom having been hunted with bloodhounds, were carried in ships to some distance from the shore, murdered in cold blood, and cast into the sea; their corpses were thrown by the waves back upon the beach, and filled the air with pestilence, by which the French troops perished in large numbers. Leclerc having perished by pestilence, his successor, Rochambeau, when the conquest of the island was beyond possibility, became the cruel perpetrator of these bloody deeds.

Thus it will be perceived that treachery and massacre were begun on the side of the French. I place emphasis on these facts in order to endeavor to disabuse the public mind of an attempt to attribute to emancipation the acts of retaliation resorted to by the Haytians in *imitation* of what the enlightened French had taught them. In two daily papers of this city there were published, a year since, a series of articles entitled the "Massacres of Santo Domingo."

The "massacres" are not attributable to emancipation, for we have proved otherwise in regard to the first of them. The other occurred in 1804, twelve years after the slaves had disenthralled themselves. Fearful as the latter may have been, it did not equal the atrocities previously committed on the Haytians by the French. And the massacre was restricted to the white French inhabitants, whom Dessalines, the Robespierre of the island, suspected of an attempt to bring back slavery, with the aid of a French force yet hovering in the neighborhood.

And if we search for the cause of this massacre, we may trace it to the following source: Nations which are pleased to term themselves civilized have one sort of faith which they hold to one another, and another sort which they entertain towards people less advanced in refinement. The faith which they entertain towards the latter is, very often, treachery, in the vocabulary of the civilized. It was treachery towards Toussaint that caused the massacre of Santo Domingo; it was treachery towards Osceola that brought bloodhounds into Florida!

General Rochambeau, with the remnant of the French army, having been reduced to the dread necessity of striving "to appease the calls of hunger by feeding on horses, mules, and the very dogs that had been employed in hunting down and devouring the Negroes," evacuated the island in the autumn of 1803, and Hayti thenceforward became an independent State.

Ladies and Gentlemen, I have now laid before you a concise view of the revolutions of Hayti in the relation of cause and effect; and I trust you will now think, that, so far from being scenes of indiscriminate massacre from which we should turn our eyes in horror, these revolutions constitute an epoch worthy of the anxious study of every American citizen.

Among the many lessons that may be drawn from this portion of history is one not unconnected with the present occasion. From causes to which I need not give a name, there is gradually creeping into our otherwise prosperous state the incongruous and undermining influence of *caste*. One of the local manifestations of this unrepublican sentiment is, that while 800 children, chiefly of foreign parents, are educated and taught trades at the expense of all the citizens, colored children are excluded from these privileges.

With the view to obviate the evils of such an unreasonable proscription, a few ladies of this city, by their untiring exertions, have organized an "Asylum for Colored Orphans." Their zeal in this cause is infinitely beyond all praise of mine, for their deeds of mercy are smiled on by Him who has declared, that "Whosoever shall give to drink unto one of these little ones a cup of cold water, shall in no wise lose her reward." Were any further argument needed to urge them on in their blessed work, I would point out to them the revolutions of Hayti, where, in the midst of the orgies and incantations of civil war, there appeared, as a spirit of peace, the patriot, the father, the benefactor of mankind—Toussaint L'Ouverture, a freedman, who had been taught to read while in slavery!

LIBERIA: ITS STRUGGLES AND ITS PROMISES[3]

BY HON. HILARY TEAGUE

Senator at Monrovia, Liberia

As far back towards the infancy of our race as history and tradition are able to conduct us, we have found the custom everywhere prevailing among mankind, to mark by some striking exhibition, those events which were important and interesting, either in their immediate bearing or in their remote consequences upon the destiny of those among whom they occurred. These events are epochs in the history of man; they mark the rise and fall of kingdoms and of dynasties; they record the movements of the human mind, and the influence of those movements upon the destinies of the race; and whilst they frequently disclose to us the sad and sickening spectacle of innocence bending under the yoke of injustice, and of weakness robbed and despoiled by the hand of an unscrupulous oppression, they occasionally display, as a theme for admiring contemplation, the sublime spectacle of the human mind, roused by a concurrence of circumstances, to vigorous advances in the career of improvement.

The utility of thus marking the progress of time—of recording the occurrence of events, and of holding up remarkable personages to the contemplation of mankind—is too obvious to need remark. It arises from the instincts of mankind, the irrepressible spirit of emulation, and the ardent longings after immortality; and this restless passion to perpetuate their existence which they find it impossible to suppress, impels them to secure the admiration of succeeding generations in the performance of deeds, by which, although dead, they may yet speak. In commemorating events thus powerful in forming the manners and sentiments of mankind, and in rousing them to strenuous exertion and to high and sustained emulation, it is obvious that such, and such only, should be selected as virtue and humanity would approve; and that, if any of an opposite character be held up, they should be displayed only as beacons, or as towering Pharos throwing a strong but lurid light to mark the melancholy grave of mad ambition, and to warn the inexperienced voyager of the existing danger.

Thanks to the improved and humanized spirit—or should I not rather say, the chastened and pacific civilization of the age in which we live?—that laurels gathered upon the field of mortal strife, and bedewed with the tears of the widow and the orphan, are regarded now, not with admiration, but with horror; that the armed warrior, reeking in the gore of murdered thousands, who, in the age that is just passing away, would have been hailed with noisy acclamation by the senseless crowd, is now regarded only as the savage commissioner of an unsparing oppression, or at best, as the ghostly executioner of an unpitying justice. He who would embalm his name in the grateful remembrance of coming generations; he who would secure for himself a niche in the temple of undying fame; he who would hew out for himself a monument of which his country may boast; he who would entail upon heirs a name which they may be proud to wear, must seek some other field than that of battle as the theatre of his exploits.

We have not yet numbered twenty-six years since he who is the oldest colonist amongst us was the inhabitant—not the citizen—of a country, and that, too, the country of his birth, where the prevailing sentiment is, that he and his race are incapacitated by an inherent defect in their mental constitution, to enjoy that greatest of all blessings, and to exercise that greatest of all rights, bestowed by a beneficent God upon his rational creatures, namely, the government of themselves by themselves. Acting upon this opinion, an opinion as false as it is foul—acting upon this opinion, as upon a self-evident proposition, those who held it proceeded with a fiendish consistency to deny the rights of citizens to those whom they had declared incapable of performing the duties of citizens. It is not necessary, and therefore I will not disgust you with the hideous picture of that state of things which followed upon the prevalence of this blasphemous theory. The bare mention that such an opinion prevailed would be sufficient to call up in the mind, even of those who had never witnessed its operation, images of the most sickening and revolting character. Under the iron reign of this crushing sentiment, most of us who are assembled here to-day drew our first breath, and sighed away the years of our youth. No hope cheered us; no noble object looming in the dim and distant future kindled our ambition. Oppression—cold, cheerless oppression, like the dreary region of eternal winter,—chilled every noble passion and fettered and paralyzed every arm. And if among the oppressed millions there were found here and there one in whose bosom the last glimmer of a generous passion was not yet extinguished—one, who, from the midst of inglorious slumberers in the deep degradation around him, would lift up his voice and demand those rights which the God of nature hath bestowed in equal gift upon all His rational creatures, he was met at once, by those who had at first denied and then enforced, with the stern reply that for him and for all his race, liberty and expatriation are inseparable.

Dreadful as the alternative was, fearful as was the experiment now proposed to be tried, there were hearts equal to the task; hearts which quailed not at the dangers which loomed and frowned in the distance, but calm, cool, and fixed in their purpose, prepared to meet them with the watchword, "Give me liberty or give me death."

Passing by intermediate events, which, did the time allow, it would be interesting to notice, we hasten to the grand event—the era of our separate existence, when the American flag first flung out its graceful folds to the breeze on the heights of Mesurado, and the pilgrims, relying upon the protection of Heaven and the moral grandeur of their cause, took solemn possession of the land in the name of Virtue, Humanity, and Religion.

It would discover an unpardonable apathy were we to pass on without pausing a moment to reflect upon the emotions which heaved the bosoms of the pilgrims, when they stood for the first time where we now stand. What a prospect spread out before them! They stood in the midst of an ancient wilderness, rank and compacted with the growth of a thousand years, unthinned and unreclaimed by a single stroke of the woodman's axe. Few and far between might be found inconsiderable openings, where the ignorant native erected his rude habitation, or savage as his patrimonial wilderness, celebrated his bloody rites, and presented his votive gifts to demons. The rainy season—that terrible ordeal of foreign constitutions—was about setting in; the lurid lightning shot its fiery bolts into the forest around them, the thunder muttered its angry tones over their head, and the frail tenements, the best which their circumstances could afford, to shield them from a scorching sun by day and drenching rains at night, had not yet been completed. To suppose that at this time, when all things above and around them seemed to combine their influence against them; to suppose they did not perceive the full danger and magnitude of the enterprise they had embarked in, would be to suppose, not that they were heroes, but that they had lost the sensibility of men. True courage is equally remote from blind recklessness and unmanning timidity; and true heroism does not consist in insensibility to danger. He is a hero who calmly meets, and fearlessly grapples with the dangers which duty and honor forbid him to decline. The pilgrims rose to a full perception of all the circumstances of their condition. But when they looked back to that country from which they had come, and remembered the degradations in that house of bondage out of which they had been so fortunate as to escape, they bethought themselves; and, recollecting the high satisfaction with which they knew success would gladden their hearts, the rich inheritance they would entail upon their children, and the powerful aid it would lend to the cause of universal humanity, they yielded to the noble inspiration and girded them to the battle either for doing or for suffering.

Let it not be supposed, because I have laid universal humanity under a tribute of gratitude to the founders of Liberia, that I have attached to their humble achievements too important an influence in that grand system of agencies which is now at work, renovating human society, and purifying and enlarging the sources of its enjoyment. In the system of that Almighty Being, without whose notice not a sparrow falls to the ground,

"Who sees, with equal eye as God of all,
A hero perish, or a sparrow fall,
Atoms or systems into ruin hurled,
And now a bubble-burst, and now a world."

"Righteousness exalteth a nation, but sin is a reproach to any people." All attempts to correct the depravity of man, to stay the headlong propensity to vice, to abate the madness of ambition, will be found deplorably inefficient, unless we apply the restrictions and the tremendous sanctions of religion. A profound regard and deference for religion, a constant recognition of our dependence upon God, and of our obligation and accountability to Him; an ever-present, ever-pressing sense of His universal and all-controlling providence, this, and only this, can give energy to the arm of law, cool the raging fever of the passions, and abate the lofty pretensions of mad ambition. In prosperity, let us bring out our thank-offering, and present it with cheerful hearts in orderly, virtuous, and religious conduct. In adversity, let us consider, confess our sins, and abase ourselves before the throne of God. In danger, let us go to Him, whose prerogative it is to deliver; let us go to Him, with the humility and confidence which a deep conviction that the battle is not to the strong nor the race to the swift, is calculated to inspire.

Fellow citizens! we stand now on ground never occupied by a people before. However insignificant we may regard ourselves, the eyes of Europe and America are upon us, as a germ, destined to burst from its enclosure in the earth, unfold its petals to the genial air, rise to the height and swell to the dimensions of the full-grown tree, or (inglorious fate) to shrivel, to die, and to be buried in oblivion. Rise, fellow citizens, rise to a clear and full perception of your tremendous responsibilities! Upon you, rely upon it, depends in a measure you can hardly conceive the future destiny of your race. You—you are to give the answer, whether the African race is doomed to unterminable degradation, a hideous blot on the fair face of Creation, a libel upon the dignity of human nature, or whether it is capable to take an honorable rank amongst the great family of nations! The friends of the colony are trembling: The enemies of the colored man are hoping. Say, fellow citizens, will you palsy the hands of your friends and sicken their hearts, and gladden the souls of your enemies, by a base refusal to enter upon a career of glory which is now opening so propitiously before you? The genius of universal emancipation, bending from her lofty seat, invites you to accept the wreath of national independence. The voice of your friends, swelling upon the breeze, cries to you from afar—Raise your standard! Assert your independence! throw out your banners to the wind! And will the descendants of the mighty Pharaohs, that awed the world; will the sons of him who drove back the serried legions of Rome and laid siege to the "eternal city"—will they, the achievements of whose fathers are yet the wonder and admiration of the world—will they refuse the proffered boon? Never! never!! never!!! Shades of the mighty dead! spirits of departed great ones! inspire us, animate us to the task; nerve us for the battle! Pour into our bosom a portion of that ardor and patriotism which bore you on to battle, to victory, and to conquest. Shall Liberia live? Yes; in the generous emotions now swelling in your bosom; in the high and noble purpose—now fixing itself in your mind, and referring into the unyieldingness of indomitable principle, we hear the inspiring response—Liberia shall live before God and before the nations of the earth!

The night is passing away; the dusky shades are fleeing and even now

"Jocund day stands tiptoe
On the misty mountain top."

WHAT TO THE SLAVE IS THE FOURTH OF JULY?[4] [4]

BY FREDERICK DOUGLASS

FREDERICK DOUGLASS, *the greatest of Negro orators, though born and reared a slave, attained great eminence in the world. After a successful career as lecturer and editor and author, he held successively the positions of Secretary to the Santo Domingo Commission, 1871; Presidential Elector for the State of New York, 1872; United States Marshal for the District of Columbia, 1876-81; Recorder of Deeds for the District, 1881-86; Minister to Hayti, 1889-91.*

Fellow Citizens:

Pardon me, and allow me to ask, why am I called upon to speak here today? What have I or those I represent to do with your national independence? Are the great principles of political freedom and of natural justice, embodied in that Declaration of Independence, extended to us? and am I, therefore, called upon to bring our humble offering to the national altar, and to confess the benefits, and express devout gratitude for the blessings resulting from your independence to us?

Would to God, both for your sakes and ours, that an affirmative answer could be truthfully returned to these questions. Then would my task be light, and my burden easy and delightful. For who is there so cold that a nation's sympathy could not warm him? Who so obdurate and dead to the claims of gratitude, that would not thankfully acknowledge such priceless benefits? Who so stolid and selfish that would not give his voice to swell the halleluiahs of a nation's jubilee, when the chains of servitude had been torn from his limbs? I am not that man. In a case like that, the dumb might eloquently speak, and the "lame man leap like a hart."

But such is not the state of the case. I say it with a sad sense of disparity between us. I am not included within the pale of this glorious anniversary! Your high independence only reveals the immeasurable distance between us. The blessings in which you this day rejoice are not enjoyed in common. The rich inheritance of justice, liberty, prosperity, and independence bequeathed by your fathers is shared by you, not by me. The sunlight that brought life and healing to you has brought stripes and death to me. This Fourth of July is *yours*, not *mine. You* may rejoice, *I* must mourn. To drag a man in fetters into the grand illuminated temple of liberty, and call upon him to join you in joyous anthems, were inhuman mockery and sacrilegious irony. Do you mean, citizens, to mock me, by asking me to speak today? If so, there is a parallel to your conduct. And let me warn you, that it is dangerous to copy the example of a nation whose crimes, towering up to heaven, were thrown down by the breath of the Almighty, burying that nation in irrecoverable ruin. I can to-day take up the lament of a peeled and woe-smitten people.

"By the rivers of Babylon, there we sat down. Yes! We wept when we remembered Zion. We hanged our harps upon the willows in the midst thereof. For there they that carried us away captive, required of us a song; and they who wasted us, required of us mirth, saying, Sing us one of the songs of Zion. How can we sing the Lord's song in a strange land? If I forget thee, O Jerusalem, let my right hand forget her cunning. If I do not remember thee, let my tongue cleave to the roof of my mouth."

Fellow citizens, above your national, tumultuous joy, I hear the mournful wail of millions, whose chains, heavy and grievous yesterday, are to-day rendered more intolerable by the jubilant shouts that reach them. If I do forget, if I do not remember those bleeding children of sorrow this day, "may my right hand forget her cunning, and may my tongue cleave to the roof of my mouth!" To forget them, to pass lightly over their wrongs, and to chime in with the popular theme, would be treason most scandalous and shocking, and would make me a reproach before God and the world. My subject, then, fellow citizens, is "American Slavery." I shall see this day and its popular characteristics from the slave's point of view. Standing here, identified with the American bondman, making his wrongs mine, I do not hesitate to declare, with all my soul, that the character and conduct of this nation never looked blacker to me than on this Fourth of July. Whether we turn to the declarations of the past, or to the professions of the present, the conduct of the nation seems equally hideous and revolting. America is false to the past, false to the present, and solemnly binds herself to be false to the future. Standing with God and the crushed and bleeding slave on this occasion, I will, in the name of humanity, which is outraged, in the name of liberty, which is fettered, in the name of the Constitution and the Bible, which are disregarded and trampled upon, dare to call in question and to denounce, with all the emphasis I can command, everything that serves to perpetuate slavery—the great sin and shame of America! "I will not equivocate; I will not excuse;" I will use the severest language I can command, and yet not one word shall escape me that any man, whose judgment is not blinded by prejudice, or who is not at heart a slave-holder, shall not confess to be right and just.

But I fancy I hear some one of my audience say it is just in this circumstance that you and your brother abolitionists fail to make a favorable impression on the public mind. Would you argue more and denounce less, would you persuade more and rebuke less, your cause would be much more likely to succeed. But, I submit, where all is plain there is nothing to be argued. What point in the anti-slavery creed would you have me argue? On what branch of the subject do the people of this country need light? Must I undertake to prove that the slave is a man? That point is conceded already. Nobody doubts it. The slave-holders themselves acknowledge it in the enactment of laws for their government. They acknowledge it when they punish disobedience on the part of the slave. There are seventy-two crimes in the State of Virginia, which, if committed by a black man (no matter how ignorant he be), subject him to the punishment of death; while only two of these same crimes will subject a white man to like punishment. What is this but the acknowledgment that the slave is a moral, intellectual, and responsible being? The manhood of the slave is conceded. It is admitted in the fact that Southern statute-books are covered with enactments, forbidding, under severe fines and penalties, the teaching of the slave to read or write. When you can point to any such laws in reference to the beasts of the field, then I may consent to argue the manhood of the slave. When the dogs in your streets, when the fowls of the air, when the cattle on your hills, when the fish of the sea, and the reptiles that crawl, shall be unable to distinguish the slave from a brute, then will I argue with you that the slave is a man!

For the present it is enough to affirm the equal manhood of the Negro race. Is it not astonishing that, while we are plowing, planting, and reaping, using all kinds of mechanical tools, erecting houses, constructing bridges, building ships, working in metals of brass, iron, copper, silver, and gold; that while we are reading, writing, and cyphering, acting as clerks, merchants, and secretaries, having among us lawyers, doctors, ministers, poets, authors, editors, orators, and teachers; that while we are engaged in all manner of enterprises common to other men—digging gold in California, capturing the whale in the Pacific, feeding sheep and cattle on the hillside, living, moving, acting, thinking, planning, living in families as husbands, wives, and children, and above all, confessing and worshiping the Christian God, and looking hopefully for life and immortality beyond the grave—we are called upon to prove that we are men?

Would you have me argue that man is entitled to liberty? That he is the rightful owner of his own body? You have already declared it. Must I argue the wrongfulness of slavery? Is that a question for republicans? Is it to be settled by the rules of logic and argumentation, as a matter beset with great difficulty, involving a doubtful application of the principle of justice, hard to be understood? How should I look to-day in the presence of Americans, dividing and subdividing a discourse, to show that men have a natural right to freedom, speaking of it relatively and positively, negatively and affirmatively? To do so would be to make myself ridiculous, and to offer an insult to your understanding. There is not a man beneath the canopy of heaven who does not know that slavery is wrong *for him.*

What! Am I to argue that it is wrong to make men brutes, to rob them of their liberty, to work them without wages, to keep them ignorant of their relations to their fellow men, to beat them with sticks, to flay their flesh with the lash, to load their limbs with irons, to hunt them with dogs, to sell them at auction, to sunder their families, to knock out their teeth, to burn their flesh, to starve them into obedience and submission to their masters? Must I argue that a system thus marked with blood and stained with pollution is wrong? No; I will not. I have better employment for my time and strength that such arguments would imply.

What, then, remains to be argued? Is it that slavery is not divine; that God did not establish it; that our doctors of divinity are mistaken? There is blasphemy in the thought. That which is inhuman cannot be divine. Who can reason on such a proposition? They that can, may; I cannot. The time for such argument is past.

At a time like this, scorching irony, not convincing argument, is needed. Oh! had I the ability, and could I reach the nation's ear, I would to-day pour out a fiery streak of biting ridicule, blasting reproach, withering sarcasm, and stern rebuke. For it is not light that is needed, but fire; it is not the gentle shower, but thunder. We need the storm, the whirlwind, and the earthquake. The feeling of the nation must be quickened; the conscience of the nation must be roused; the propriety of the nation must be startled; the hypocrisy of the nation must be exposed; and its crimes against God and man must be denounced.

What to the American slave is your Fourth of July? I answer, a day that reveals to him, more than all other days of the year, the gross injustice and cruelty to which he is the constant victim. To him your celebration is a sham; your boasted liberty an unholy license; your national greatness, swelling vanity; your sounds of rejoicing are empty and heartless; your denunciations of tyrants, brass-fronted impudence; your shouts of liberty and equality, hollow mockery; your prayers and hymns, your sermons and thanksgivings, with all your religious parade and solemnity, are to him mere bombast, fraud, deception, impiety, and hypocrisy—a thin veil to cover up crimes which would disgrace a nation of savages. There is not a nation on the earth guilty of practises more shocking and bloody than are the people of these United States at this very hour.

Go where you may, search where you will, roam through all the monarchies and despotisms of the Old World, travel through South America, search out every abuse and when you have found the last, lay your facts by the side of the every-day practises of this nation, and you will say with me that, for revolting barbarity and shameless hypocrisy, America reigns without a rival.

SHOULD COLORED MEN BE SUBJECT TO THE PAINS AND PENALTIES OF THE FUGITIVE SLAVE LAW?[5]

BY CHARLES H. LANGSTON

CHARLES H. LANGSTON, *a native of Ohio, was the first to counsel resistance to the Fugitive Slave Act, and lost no opportunity himself to disobey it. He was found guilty of violating the law in rescuing John Price, an alleged fugitive from service in Kentucky. This speech is his answer to the question of the judge why the sentence should not be pronounced upon him. He was sentenced to one hundred and twenty days' imprisonment, and fined $100.00 and costs, amounting to $872.72.*

After a trial of twenty-three days in the United States District Court for the Northern District of Ohio, Hiram V. Willson presiding, and at a cost to the United States Government of more than two thousand dollars, C. H. Langston was found guilty of violating the Fugitive Slave Law, by rescuing John Price, an alleged fugitive from service in Kentucky, from the custody of one, Anderson Jennings, at Wellington, on the 13th day of September, 1858.

Mr. Langston was sentenced to twenty days' imprisonment in the jail of Cuyahoga county, and also to pay a fine of one hundred dollars and a portion of the costs of prosecution, amounting to nine hundred and seventy-two dollars and seventy cents.

BILL OF COSTS

Fine and bill of costs as copied from the Journal of the Court:

Fine	$100.00
Clerk's fees	32.10
Marshal's fees	30.40
United States' witnesses	131.10
Docket fees	20.00
	——
Total	$972.70

On the morning of the 12th of May, 1859, C. H. Langston was brought into court to receive his sentence.

The judge, having entered the "oyez, oyez" of the crier, announced the opening of the court, and the rattling of the gavel of the bailiff soon brought the immense crowd to silence. The business then proceeded as follows:

THE COURT.—Mr. Langston, you will stand up, sir.

Mr. Langston arose.

THE COURT.—You have been tried, Mr. Langston, by a jury, and convicted of a violation of the criminal laws of the United States. Have you or your counsel anything to say why the sentence of the law should not be pronounced upon you?

MR. LANGSTON.—I am for the first time in my life before a court of justice, charged with the violation of law, and am now about to be sentenced. But before receiving that sentence I propose to say one or two words in regard to the mitigation of that sentence, if it may be so construed. I can not, of course, and do not expect that what I may say will in any way change your predetermined line of action. I ask no such favor at your hands.

I know that the courts of this country, that the laws of this country, that the governmental machinery of this country are so constituted as to oppress and outrage colored men, men of my complexion. I cannot then, of course, expect, judging from the past history of the country, any mercy from the laws, from the Constitution, or from the courts of the country.

Some days prior to the 13th of September, 1858, happening to be in Oberlin on a visit, I found the country round about there, and the village itself, filled with alarming rumors as to the fact that slave-catchers, kidnappers, and Negro stealers were lying hidden and skulking about, awaiting some opportunity to get their bloody hands on some helpless creature, to drag him back,—or for the first time,—into helpless and lifelong bondage.

These reports becoming current all over that neighborhood, old men and innocent women and children became exceedingly alarmed for their safety. It was not uncommon to hear mothers say that they dare not send their children to school, for fear that they would be caught up and carried off by the way. Some of these people had become free by long and patient toil at night, after working the long, long day for cruel masters, and thus at length getting money enough to buy their liberty.

Others had become free by means of the good will of their masters. And there were others who had become free—to their everlasting honor, I say it—by the intensest exercise of their own God-given powers;—by escaping from the plantations of their masters, eluding the blood-thirsty patrols and sentinels so thickly scattered all along their path, outrunning blood-hounds and horses, swimming rivers and fording swamps, and reaching at last, through incredible difficulties, what they, in their delusion, supposed to be free soil. These three classes were in Oberlin, trembling alike for their safety because they well knew their fate should these men-hunters get their hands on them.

In the midst of such excitement, the 13th day of September was ushered in—a day ever memorable in the history of Oberlin, and I presume also, in the history of this court. These men-hunters had, by lying devices, decoyed into a place, where they could get their hands on him—I will not say a slave, for I do not know that—but a *man*, *a brother*, who had the right to his liberty under the laws of God, under the laws of nature, and under the Declaration of American Independence.

In the midst of all this excitement the news came to us like a flash of lightning that an actual seizure under and by means of fraudulent pretenses, had been made! Being identified with that man by color, by race, by manhood, by sympathies, such as God has implanted in us all, I felt it my duty to go and do what I could towards liberating him. I had been taught by my Revolutionary father—and I say this with all due respect to him—and by his honored associates, that the fundamental doctrine of this Government was, that *all* men have a right to life and liberty, and coming from the Old Dominion I had brought into Ohio these sentiments deeply impressed upon my heart. I went to Wellington, and hearing from the parties themselves by what authority the boy was held in custody, I conceived from what little knowledge I had of law that they had no right to hold him. And as your Honor has repeatedly laid down the law in this court, a man is free until he is proven to be legally restrained of his liberty. I believed that upon that principle of law those men were bound to take their prisoner before the very first magistrate they found and there establish the facts set forth in their warrant, and that until they did this every man should presume that their claim was unfounded, and to institute such proceedings for the purpose of securing an investigation as they might find warranted by the laws of this State.

Now, sir, if that is not the plain common sense and correct view of the law, then I have been misled, both by your Honor and by the prevalent received opinion. It is said that they had a warrant. Why then, should they not establish its validity before the proper officers? And I stand here to-day, sir, to say that with an exception, of which I shall soon speak, *to procure such a lawful investigation of the authority under which they claimed to act, was the part I took in that day's proceedings, and the only part.* I supposed it to be my duty as a citizen of Ohio—excuse me for saying that, sir,—as an *outlaw of the United States*, (much sensation) to do what I could to secure at least this form of justice to my brother, whose liberty was at peril.—*Whatever more than that has been sworn to on this trial, as act of mine, is false, ridiculously false.* When I found these men refusing to go, according to the law, as I apprehended it, and subject their claim to an official inspection, and that nothing short of a *habeas corpus* would oblige such an inspection, I was willing to go even thus far, supposing in that county a sheriff might, perhaps, be found with nerve enough to serve it. In this again, I failed. Nothing then was left to me, nothing to the boy in custody, but the confirmation of my first belief that the pretended authority was worthless, and the employment of those means of liberation which belong to us. With regard to the part I took in the forcible rescue, which followed, I have nothing to say, further than I have already said. The evidence is before you. It is alleged that I said "*We* will have him anyhow." *This I NEVER said.* I did say to Mr. Lowe, what I honestly believe to be the truth, that the crowd was very much excited, many of them averse to longer delay and bent upon a rescue at all hazards; and that he being an old acquaintance and friend of mine, I was anxious to extricate him from the dangerous position he occupied, and therefore advised Jennings to give the boy up. Further than this I did not say, either to him or to anyone else.

The law under which I am arraigned is an unjust one, one made to crush the colored man, and one that outrages every feeling of humanity, as well as every rule of Right.

With its constitutionality I have nothing to do; about that I know but little and care much less. But suppose it is constitutional, what then? To tell me a law is constitutional which robs me of my *liberty* is simply ridiculous. I would curse the constitution that authorized the enactment of such a law; I would trample the provisions of such a law under my feet and defy its pains and penalties. I would respect and obey such an inhuman law no more than OUR revolutionary fathers did the odious and absurd doctrine that kings and tyrants reign and rule by divine *right.* But it has often been said by learned and good men that this law is unconstitutional. I remember the excitement that prevailed throughout all the free States when it was passed; I remember, too, how often it has been said by individuals, conventions, legislatures, and even *Judges* that it is not only unconstitutional, but that it never could be, never should be, and never was meant to be enforced. I had always believed, until the contrary appeared in the actual institution of proceedings, that the provisions of this odious statute would never be enforced within the bounds of this State.

But I have another reason to offer why I should not be sentenced, and one that I think pertinent to the case. The common law of England—and you will excuse me for referring to that, since I am not a lawyer, but a private man—was that every man should be tried by a jury of men occupying the same political and legal status *with himself.* Lords should be tried before a jury of lords; peers of the realm should be tried before peers of the realm; vassals before vassals. And even "where an *alien* was indicted, the jury *shall be demenietate*, or *half foreigners*"; and a jury thus constituted were sworn "well and truly to try and true deliverance make between the sovereign lord, the king, and the prisoner whom they have in charge; and a true verdict to give according to the evidence and without prejudice." The Constitution of the United States guarantees—not merely to its citizens, but to *all persons*—a trial before an impartial jury. I have had no such trial.

The colored man is oppressed by certain universal and deeply fixed prejudices. Those jurors are well known to have shared largely in these prejudices, and I therefore consider that they were neither impartial, nor were they a jury of my peers. Politically and legally they are not my equals. They have aided to form a State constitution which denies to colored men citizenship, and under that constitution laws have been enacted withholding from us many of our most valuable rights. These unjust laws exclude colored men from the jury box and force us to be tried in every case by jurors, not only filled with prejudices against us, but far above us politically and legally, made so both by the statute laws and by the Constitution. The prejudices which white people have against colored men grow out of the fact that we have, as a people, *consented* for two hundred years to be *slaves* of the whites. We have been scourged, crushed, and cruelly oppressed, and have submitted to it all tamely, meekly, peaceably; I mean, as a people, with rare individual exceptions,—and to-day you see us thus meekly submitting to the penalties of an infamous law. Now the Americans have this feeling, and it is an honorable one, that they will respect those who rebel at oppression, but despise those who tamely submit to outrage and wrong; and while our people as a people submit, they will as a people be despised. Why, they will hardly meet on terms of equality with us in a whiskey shop, in a car, at a table, or even at the altar of God, so thorough and hearty a contempt have they for those who *lie still* under the heel of the oppressor. The jury came into the box with that feeling. They knew that they had that feeling, and so the Court knows now, and knew then. The gentlemen who prosecuted me, the Court itself, and even the counsel who defended me, have that feeling.

I was tried by a jury which was prejudiced; before a Court that was prejudiced; prosecuted by an officer who was prejudiced, and defended, though ably, by counsel who were prejudiced. And therefore it is, your Honor, that I urge by all that is good and great in manhood, that I should not be subjected to the pains and penalties of this oppressive law, when I have not been tried, either by a jury of my peers, according to the principles of the common law, or by an impartial jury according to the Constitution of the United States.

One more word, sir, and I have done. I went to Wellington, knowing that colored men have no rights in the United States which white men are bound to respect; that the Courts had so decided; that Congress had so enacted; that the people had so decreed.

There is not a spot in this wide country, not even by the altars of God, nor in the shadow of the shafts that tell the imperishable fame and glory of the heroes of the Revolution; no, nor in the old Philadelphia Hall, where any colored man may dare to ask mercy of a white man. Let me stand in that Hall and tell a United States marshal that my father was a Revolutionary soldier; that he served under Lafayette, and fought through the whole war, and that he fought for my freedom as much as for his own; and he would sneer at me, and clutch me with his bloody fingers, and say he has a *right* to make me a slave! and when I appeal to Congress, they say he has a right to make me a slave, and when I appeal to your Honor, *your Honor* says he has a right to make me a slave. And if any man, white or black, seeks an investigation of that claim, he makes himself amenable to the pains and penalties of the Fugitive Slave Act, for BLACK MEN HAVE NO RIGHTS WHICH WHITE MEN ARE BOUND TO RESPECT. (Great applause.) I, going to Wellington with the full knowledge of all this, knew that if that man was taken to Columbus he was hopelessly gone, no matter whether he had ever been in slavery before or not. I knew that I was in the same situation myself, and that by the decision of your Honor, if any man whatever were to claim me as his slave and seize me, and my brother, being a lawyer, should seek to get out a writ of *habeas corpus* to expose the falsity of the claim, he would be thrust into prison under one provision of the Fugitive Slave Law, for interfering with the man claiming to be in pursuit of a fugitive, and I, by the perjury of a solitary wretch, would by another of its provisions be helplessly doomed to lifelong bondage, without the possibility of escape.

Some may say that there is no danger of free persons being seized and carried off as slaves. No one need labor under such a delusion. Sir, *four* of the eight persons who were first carried back under the act of 1850 were afterwards proved to be *free men*. They were free persons, but wholly at the mercy of the oath of one man. And but last Sabbath afternoon a letter came to me from a gentleman in St. Louis informing me that a young lady, who was formerly under my instructions at Columbus, a free person, is now lying in jail at that place, claimed as the slave of some wretch who never saw her before, and waiting for testimony of relatives at Columbus to establish her freedom. I could stand here by the hour and relate such instances. In the very nature of the case, they must be constantly occurring. A letter was not long since found upon the person of a counterfeiter, when arrested, addressed to him by some Southern gentleman, in which the writer says:

"Go among the niggers, find out their marks and scars; make good descriptions and send to me, and I'll find masters for 'em."

That is the way men are carried *back* to slavery.

But in view of all the facts, I say that, if ever again a man is seized near me, and is about to be carried southward as a slave before any legal investigation has been had, I shall hold it to be my duty, as I held it that day, to secure for him, if possible, a legal inquiry into the character of the claim by which he is held. And I go farther; I say that if it is adjudged illegal to procure even such an investigation, then we are thrown back upon those last defenses of our rights which cannot be taken from us, and which God gave us that we need not be slaves. I ask your Honor, while I say this, to place yourself in my situation, and you will say with me that, if your brother, if your friend, if your wife, if your child, had been seized by men who claimed them as fugitives, and the law of the land forbade you to ask any investigation, and precluded the possibility of any legal protection or redress—then you will say with me that you would not only demand the protection of the law, but you would call in your neighbors and your friends, and would ask them to say with you, that, these, your friends, *could not* be taken into slavery.

And now, I thank you for this leniency, this indulgence, in giving a man unjustly condemned, by a tribunal before which he is declared to have no rights, the privilege of speaking in his own behalf. I know that it will do nothing toward mitigating your sentence, but it is a privilege to be allowed to speak, and I thank you for it. I shall submit to the penalty, be it what it may. But I stand up here to say that if for doing what I did on that day at Wellington, I am to go to jail for six months, and pay a fine of a thousand dollars, according to the Fugitive Slave Law, and if such is the protection the laws of this country afford me, I must take upon myself the responsibility of self-protection; when I come to be claimed by some perjured wretch as his slave, I shall never be taken into slavery. And in that trying hour, I would have others do to me, as I would call upon my friends to help me; as I would call upon you, your Honor, to help me, as I would call upon you (to the District Attorney) to help me, and upon you (to Judge Bliss), and you (his counsel) *so help me God*! I stand here to say that I will do all I can for any man thus seized and held, though the inevitable penalty of six months' imprisonment and one thousand dollars fine for each offense hang over me! We have all a common humanity, and that humanity will, if rightly exercised, compel us to aid each other when our rights are invaded. The man who can see a fellow man wronged and outraged without assisting him must have lost all the manly feelings of his nature. You would all assist any man under such circumstances; your manhood would require it; and no matter what the laws might be, you would honor yourself for doing it, while your friends and your children to all generations would honor you for doing it, and every good and honest man would say you had done *right*! (Great and prolonged applause, in spite of the efforts of the Court and marshal.)

Judge Willson remarked: Mr. Langston, you do the Court injustice in supposing the remarks were called out as a mere idle form, or would not get a respectful consideration from the Court.

It is not the duty of the Court to make the laws—that is left to other tribunals; but our duty, under an official oath, is to administer the laws, good or bad, as we find them.

I find many mitigating circumstances in your case, and the sentence will therefore be, that you pay a fine of one hundred dollars and the costs of suit, and be imprisoned in jail for twenty days, and it shall be the duty of the Marshal to see the imprisonment carried out in this or some other county jail in this district.

YOUNG MEN, TO THE FRONT!

BY HON. RICHARD T. GREENER, LL. D.

RICHARD T. GREENER, *as far as is known, was the first Negro to be graduated from Harvard University with the degree of Bachelor of Arts. He received the degree of LL.D. both from Howard University and from Liberia College, Monrovia, of which he was the dean for some time. In 1897 he was appointed United States Consul to Vladivostok, and served through the Russian-Japanese War. While in this official capacity he was decorated by the Chinese Government with the order of the "Double Dragon," the only Negro ever so honored.*

The adage which was once so common, if not so thoroughly axiomatic as to gain universal credence—"Old men for council and young men for war"—assumes additional notoriety to-day, when the old men are quarreling in the council chamber and the young men are kept outside the door. While the young men are willing to allow much to the school of experience, many of them are the followers of Locke, and believe in the doctrine of innate ideas. They believe, to continue the comparison, that experience and wisdom do not always spring from length of years, nor does ignorance appertain to youth as a necessity. They dare assert that, as there are those who would never be men, lived they to be as old as Methuselah, so there are some whose minds are as well filled, whose judgments are as mature at twenty-five and eight, and their energy as decisive as though they were in their tenth lustrum. Conscious of this fact, it is the absurdity of folly for the young colored men of the country to sit idly by and see the grandest opportunities slipping away, the best cases lost by default because of the lack of energy displayed by many of our so-called leaders who have been longer on the field. With some very few exceptions, honorable as they are rare, they have done well for their day and generation; but with regard to the needs and policy of the Negroes of the present hour they are as innocent as babes. Men for the most part of excellent temper and good working capacity, they lack that which is the handmaid and often the indispensable auxiliary of knowledge and all effective work—judgment. Unconscious puppets often, they dance to unseen music, moved themselves by hidden wires.

The convention was the favorite resort of the leading Negro of ten years ago. He convened and resolved, resolved and unconvened—read his own speeches, was delighted with his own frothy rhetoric, and really imagined himself a great man. He talked eloquently then, it must be granted, because he spoke of his wrongs; but when the war overturned the edifice of slavery "Othello's occupation" was "gone," indeed. The number who have survived and held their own under the new order of things may be counted upon one hand. They survive through that grand old law so much combated but ever true—the survival of the fittest. They alone give character and reputation to the Negro. They make for him a fame which begets respect where his wrongs only excited pity. The field is comparatively clear now some of the older hacks have fallen by the way or lie spavined at the roadside. The question is, Will the young men of color throughout the country resolve to begin now to take part in public affairs, asserting their claim wherever it is denied, maintaining it wherever contested, and show that the young may be safe in counsel as well as good for war?

There are some who arrogate to themselves wisdom because of their years, just as some equally absurd people think they are wise because they never went to a high school or an academy—men, Heaven save the mark! who pride themselves on having never slaked their thirst at the fount of knowledge. It is not our purpose to disparage age. We remember what Cicero has written, so delightfully, of its pleasures; what Cephalus and Socrates thought of it in the Republic. We look "toward sunset" with reverence and respect; but it is with a reverence that makes us conscious of our own duty. The young men are now studying, working, some, alas! idling away their time who ought to be the active, earnest men in the next Presidential campaign; young men who are to control the destinies of the race. Many of them are of marked ability and decidedly energetic in character. Not so fluent, perhaps, as their fathers, they are more thoughtful. They are found throughout the country. We feel that, if like Roderick Dhu, we should put the whistle to our lips and blow a stirring blast, they would spring up in every part of the country ready with voice, pen, or muscle to do their share in any honorable work. In spirit we do this, as young men ourselves, willing to blow a blast which, would that the young men of the country would hear and heed! Young men, to the front! Young men, rouse yourselves! Take the opportunities; make them where they are denied! "Quit you like men; be strong."

Young men, to the front!

THE CIVIL RIGHTS' BELL[6]

BY ROBERT BROWNE ELLIOT

Representative from South Carolina

Mr. Speaker:

While I am sincerely grateful for this high mark of courtesy that has been accorded to me by this House, it is a matter of regret to me that it is necessary at this day that I should rise in the presence of an American Congress to advocate a bill which simply asserts equal rights and equal public privileges for all classes of American citizens. I regret, sir, that the dark hue of my skin may lend a color to the imputation that I am controlled by motives personal to myself in my advocacy of this great measure of national justice. Sir, the motive that impels me is restricted by no such narrow boundary, but is as broad as your Constitution. I advocate it, sir, because it is right. The bill, however, not only appeals to your justice, but it demands a response from your gratitude.

In the events that led to the achievement of American independence the Negro was not an inactive or unconcerned spectator. He bore his part bravely upon many battlefields, although uncheered by that certain hope of political elevation which victory would secure to the white man. The tall granite shaft, which a grateful State has reared above its sons who fell in defending Fort Griswold against the attack of Benedict Arnold, bears the name of Jordan, Freeman, and other brave men of the African race, who there cemented with their blood the corner-stone of the Republic. In the State which I have the honor in part to represent (South Carolina) the rifle of the black man rang out against the troops of the British Crown in the darkest days of the American Revolution. Said General Greene, who has been justly termed the "Washington of the North," in a letter written by him to Alexander Hamilton, on the 10th of January, 1781, from the vicinity of Camden, South Carolina: "There is no such thing as national character or national sentiment. The inhabitants are numerous, but they would be rather formidable abroad than at home. There is a great spirit of enterprise among the black people, and those that come out as volunteers are not a little formidable to the enemy."

At the battle of New Orleans under the immortal Jackson, a colored regiment held the extreme right of the American line unflinchingly, and drove back the British column that pressed upon them at the point of the bayonet. So marked was their valor on that occasion that it evoked from their great commander the warmest encomiums, as will be seen from his dispatch announcing the brilliant victory.

As the gentleman from Kentucky (Mr. Beck), who seems to be the leading exponent on this floor of the party that is arrayed against the principle of this bill, has been pleased, in season and out of season, to cast odium upon the Negro and to vaunt the chivalry of his State, I may be pardoned for calling attention to another portion of the same dispatch. Referring to the various regiments under his command, and their conduct on that field which terminated the second war of American Independence, General Jackson says. "At the very moment when the entire discomfiture of the enemy was looked for with a confidence amounting to certainty, the Kentucky reinforcements, in whom so much reliance had been placed, ingloriously fled."

In quoting this indisputable piece of history, I do so only by way of admonition and not to question the well-attested gallantly of the true Kentuckian, and to the gentleman that it would be well that he should not flaunt his heraldry so proudly while he bears this bar-sinister on the military escutcheon of his State—a State which answered the call of the Republic in 1861, when treason thundered at the very gates of the Capital, by coldly declaring her neutrality in the impending struggle. The Negro, true to that patriotism and love of country that have ever marked and characterized his history on this continent, came to the aid of the Government in its efforts to maintain the Constitution. To that Government he now appeals; that Constitution he now invokes for protection against outrage and unjust prejudices founded upon caste.

But, sir, we are told by the distinguished gentleman from Georgia (Mr. Stephens) that Congress has no power under the Constitution to pass such a law, and that the passage of such an act is in direct contravention of the rights of the States. I cannot assent to any such proposition. The Constitution of a free government ought always to be construed in favor of human rights. Indeed, the thirteenth, fourteenth, and fifteenth amendments, in positive words, invest Congress with the power to protect the citizen in his civil and political rights. Now, sir, what are civil rights? Rights natural, modified by civil society. Mr. Lieber says: "By civil liberty is meant, not only the absence of individual restraint, but liberty within the social system and political organism—a combination of principles, and laws which acknowledge, protect, and favor the dignity of man * * * civil liberty is the result of man's two fold character as an individual and social being, so soon as both are equally respected."[7]

Alexander Hamilton, the right-hand man of Washington in the perilous days of the then infant Republic; the great interpreter and expounder of the Constitution, says: "Natural liberty is the gift of a beneficent Creator to the whole human race; civil liberty is founded on it, civil liberty is only natural liberty modified and secured by civil society."[8]

* * * * *

Are we then, sir, with the amendments to our constitution staring us in the face; with these grand truths of history before our eyes; with innumerable wrongs daily inflicted upon five million citizens demanding redress, to commit this question to the diversity of legislation? In the words of Hamilton—"Is it the interest of the Government to sacrifice individual rights to the preservation of the rights of an artificial being called the States? There can be no truer principle than this, that every individual of the community at large has an equal right to the protection of Government. Can this be a free Government if partial distinctions are tolerated or maintained?"

The rights contended for in this bill are among "the sacred rights of mankind, which are not to be rummaged for among old parchments or musty records; they are written as with a sunbeam in the whole volume of human nature, by the hand of the Divinity itself, and can never be erased or obscured by mortal power."

But the Slaughter-house cases!—The Slaughter-house cases!

The honorable gentleman from Kentucky, always swift to sustain the failing and dishonored cause of proscription, rushes forward and flaunts in our faces the decision of the Supreme Court of the United States in the Slaughter-house cases, and in that act he has been willingly aided by the gentleman from Georgia. Hitherto, in the contests which have marked the progress of the cause of equal civil rights, our opponents have appealed sometimes to custom, sometimes to prejudice, more often to pride of race, but they have never sought to shield themselves behind the Supreme Court. But now for the first time, we are told that we are barred by a decision of that court, from which there is no appeal. If this be true we must stay our hands. The cause of equal civil rights must pause at the command of a power whose edicts must be obeyed till the fundamental law of our country is changed.

Has the honorable gentleman from Kentucky considered well the claim he now advances? If it were not disrespectful I would ask, has he ever read the decision which he now tells us is an insuperable barrier to the adoption of this great measure of justice?

In the consideration of this subject, has not the judgment of the gentleman from Georgia been warped by the ghost of the dead doctrines of States-rights? Has he been altogether free from prejudices engendered by long training in that school of politics that well-nigh destroyed this Government?

Mr. Speaker, I venture to say here in the presence of the gentleman from Kentucky, and the gentleman from Georgia, and in the presence of the whole country, that there is not a line or word, not a thought or dictum even, in the decision of the Supreme Court in the great Slaughter-house cases, which casts a shadow of doubt on the right of Congress to pass the pending bill, or to adopt such other legislation as it may judge proper and necessary to secure perfect equality before the law to every citizen of the Republic. Sir, I protest against the dishonor now cast upon our Supreme Court by both the gentleman from Kentucky and the gentleman from Georgia. In other days, when the whole country was bowing beneath the yoke of slavery, when press, pulpit, platform, Congress and courts felt the fatal power of the slave oligarchy, I remember a decision of that court which no American now reads without shame and humiliation. But those days are past; the Supreme Court of to-day is a tribunal as true to freedom as any department of this Government, and I am honored with the opportunity of repelling a deep disgrace which the gentleman from Kentucky, backed and sustained as he is by the gentleman from Georgia, seeks to put upon it.

* * * * *

The amendments in the Slaughter-house cases one and all, are thus declared to have as their all-pervading design and ends the security of the recently enslaved race, not only their nominal freedom, but their complete protection from those who had formerly exercised unlimited dominion over them. It is in this broad light that all these amendments must be read, the purpose to secure the perfect equality before the law of all citizens of the United States. What you give to one class you must give to all, what you deny to one class you shall deny to all, unless in the exercise of the common and universal police power of the State, you find it needful to confer exclusive privileges on certain citizens, to be held and exercised still for the common good of all.

Such are the doctrines of the Slaughter-house cases—doctrines worthy of the Republic, worthy of the age, worthy of the great tribunal which thus loftily and impressively enunciates them. Do they—I put it to any man, be he lawyer or not; I put it to the gentleman from Georgia—do they give color even to the claim that this Congress may not now legislate against a plain discrimination made by State laws or State customs against that very race for whose complete freedom and protection these great amendments were elaborated and adopted? Is it pretended, I ask the honorable gentleman from Kentucky or the honorable gentleman from Georgia—is it pretended anywhere that the evils of which we complain, our exclusion from the public inn, from the saloon and table of the steamboat, from the sleeping-coach on the railway, from the right of sepulture in the public burial-ground, are an exercise of the police power of the State? Is such oppression and injustice nothing but the exercise by the State of the right to make regulations for the health, comfort, and security of all her citizens? Is it merely enacting that one man shall so use his own as not to injure anothers? Is the colored race to be assimilated to an unwholesome trade or to combustible materials, to be interdicted, to be shut up within prescribed limits? Let the gentleman from Kentucky or the gentleman from Georgia answer. Let the country know to what extent even the audacious prejudice of the gentleman from Kentucky will drive him, and how far even the gentleman from Georgia will permit himself to be led captive by the unrighteous teachings of a false political faith.

If we are to be likened in legal view to "unwholesome trades," to "large and offensive collections of animals" to "noxious slaughter-houses," to "the offal and stench which attend on certain manufactures" let it be avowed. If that is still the doctrine of the political party, to which the gentlemen belong, let it be put upon record. If State laws which deny us the common rights and privileges of other citizens, upon no possible or conceivable ground save one of prejudice, or of "taste" as the gentleman from Texas termed it, and as I suppose the gentlemen will prefer to call it, are to be placed under the protection of a decision which affirms the right of a State to regulate the police power of her great cities, then the decision is in conflict with the bill before us. No man will dare maintain such a doctrine. It is as shocking to the legal mind as it is offensive to the heart and conscience of all who love justice or respect manhood. I am astonished that the gentleman from Kentucky or the gentleman from Georgia should have been so grossly misled as to rise here and assert that the decision of the Supreme Court in these cases was a denial to Congress of the power to legislate against discriminations on account of race, color, or previous conditions of servitude because that Court has decided that exclusive privileges conferred for the common protection of the lives and health of the whole community are not in violation of the recent amendments. The only ground upon which the grant of exclusive privileges to a portion of the community is ever defended is that the substantial good of all is promoted; that in truth it is for the welfare of the whole community that certain persons should alone pursue certain occupations. It is not the special benefit conferred on the few that moves the legislature, but the ultimate and real benefit of all, even of those who are denied the right to pursue those specified occupations. Does the gentleman from Kentucky say that my good is promoted when I am excluded from the public inn? Is the health or safety of the community promoted? Doubtless his prejudice is gratified. Doubtless his democratic instincts are pleased; but will he or his able coadjutor say that such exclusion is a lawful exercise of the police power of the State, or that it is not a denial to me of the equal protection of the laws? They will not so say.

But each of these gentlemen quote at some length from the decision of the court to show that the court recognizes a difference between citizenship of the United States and citizenship of the States. That is true and no man here who supports this bill questions or overlooks the difference. There are privileges and immunities which belong to me as a citizen of the United States, and there are other privileges and immunities which belong to me as a citizen of my State. The former are under the protection of the Constitution and laws of the United States, and the latter are under the protection of the Constitution and laws of my State. But what of that? Are the rights which I now claim—the right to enjoy the common public conveniences of travel on public highways, of rest and refreshment at public inns, of education in public schools, of burial in public cemeteries—rights which I hold as a citizen of the United States or of my State? Or, to state the question more exactly, is not the denial of such privileges to me a denial to me of the equal protection of the laws? For it is under this clause of the fourteenth amendment that we place the present bill, no State shall "deny to any person within its jurisdiction the equal protection of the laws." No matter, therefore, whether his rights are held under the United States or under his particular State he is equally protected by this amendment. He is always and everywhere entitled to the equal protection of the laws. All discrimination is forbidden; and while the rights of citizens of a State as such are not defined or conferred by the Constitution of the United States, yet all discrimination, all denial of equality before the law, all denial of equal protection of the laws whether State or national laws, is forbidden.

The distinction between the two kinds of citizenship is clear, and the Supreme Court has clearly pointed out this distinction, but it has nowhere written a word or line which denies to Congress the power to prevent a denial of equality of rights whether those rights exist by virtue of citizenship of the United States or of a State. Let honorable members mark well this distinction. There are rights which are conferred on us by the United States. There are other rights conferred on us by the states of which we are individually the citizens. The fourteenth amendment does not forbid a state to deny to all its citizens any of those rights which the state itself has conferred with certain exceptions which are pointed out in the decision which we are examining. What it does forbid is inequality, is discrimination or, to use the words of the amendment itself, is the denial "to any person within its jurisdiction, the equal protection of the laws." If a State denies to me rights which are common to all her other citizens, she violates this amendment, unless she can show, as was shown in the Slaughter-house cases, that she does it in the legitimate exercise of her police power. If she abridges the rights of all her citizens equally, unless those rights are specifically guarded by the Constitution of the United States, she does not violate this amendment. This is not to put the rights which I hold by virtue of my citizenship of South Carolina under the protection of the national Government; it is not to blot out or overlook in the slightest particular the distinction between rights held under the United States and rights held under the States; but it seeks to secure equality to prevent discrimination, to confer as complete and ample protection on the humblest as on the highest.

The gentleman from Kentucky, in the course of the speech to which I am now replying, made a reference to the State of Massachusetts which betrays again the confusion which exists in his mind on this precise point. He tells us that Massachusetts excludes from the ballot-box all who cannot read and write, and points to that fact as the exercise of a right which this bill would abridge or impair. The honorable gentleman from Massachusetts (Mr. Dawes) answered him truly and well, but I submit that he did not make the best reply, why did he not ask the gentleman from Kentucky if Massachusetts had ever discriminated against any of her citizens on account of color, or race, or previous condition of servitude? When did Massachusetts sully her proud record by placing on her statute-book any law which admitted to the ballot the white man and shut out the black man. She has never done it; she will not do it; she cannot do it so long as we have a Supreme Court which reads the Constitution of our country with the eyes of Justice; nor can Massachusetts or Kentucky deny to any man on account of his race, color, or previous condition of servitude, that perfect equality of protection under the laws so long as Congress shall exercise the power to enforce by appropriate legislation the great and unquestionable securities embodied in the fourteenth amendment to the Constitution.

* * * * *

Now, sir, having spoken of the prohibition imposed by Massachusetts, I may be pardoned for a slight inquiry as to the effect of this prohibition. First, it did not in any way abridge or curtail the exercise of the suffrage by any person who enjoyed such right. Nor did it discriminate against the illiterate native and the illiterate foreigner. Being enacted for the good of the entire commonwealth, like all just laws, its obligations fell equally and impartially on all its citizens. And as a justification for such a measure, it is a fact too well known almost for mention here that Massachusetts had, from the beginning of her history, recognized the inestimable value of an educated ballot, by not only maintaining a system of free schools, but also enforcing an attendance thereupon, as one of the safeguards for the preservation of a real republican form of government. Recurring then, sir, to the possible contingency alluded to by the gentleman from Kentucky, should the State of Kentucky, having first established a system of common schools whose doors shall swing open freely to all, as contemplated by the provisions of this bill, adopt a provision similar to that of Massachusetts, no one would have cause justly to complain. And if in the coming years the result of such legislation should produce a constituency rivaling that of the Old Bay State, no one would be more highly gratified than I. Mr. Speaker, I have neither the time nor the inclination to notice the many illogical and forced conclusions, the numerous transfers of terms, or the vulgar insinuations which further encumber the argument of the gentleman from Kentucky. Reason and argument are worse than wasted upon those who meet every demand for political and civil liberty by such ribaldry as this—extracted from the speech of the gentleman from Kentucky: "I suppose there are gentlemen on this floor who would arrest, imprison, and fine a young woman in any State of the South if she were to refuse to marry a Negro man on account of color, race, or previous condition of servitude, in the event of his making her a proposal of marriage, and her refusing on that ground. That would be depriving him of a right he had under the amendment, and Congress would be asked to take it up and say, 'This insolent white woman must be taught to know that it is a misdemeanor to deny a man marriage because of race, color, or previous condition of servitude,' and Congress will be urged to say after a while that that sort of thing must be put a stop to, and your conventions of colored men will come here asking you to enforce that right."

Now, sir, recurring to the venerable and distinguished gentleman from Georgia (Mr. Stephens) who has added his remonstrance against the passage of this bill, permit me to say that I share in the feeling of high personal regard for that gentleman which pervades this House. His years, his ability, and his long experience in public affairs entitle him to the measure of consideration which has been accorded to him on this floor. But in this discussion I cannot and will not forget that the welfare and rights of my whole race in this country are involved. When, therefore, the honorable gentleman from Georgia lends his voice and influence to defeat this measure, I do not shrink from saying that it is not from him that the American House of Representatives should take lessons in matters touching human rights or the joint relations of the State and national governments. While the honorable gentleman contented himself with harmless speculations in his study, or in the columns of a newspaper, we might well smile at the impotence of his efforts to turn back the advancing tide of opinion and progress; but, when he comes again upon this national arena, and throws himself with all his power and influence across the path which leads to the full enfranchisement of my race, I meet him only as an adversary; nor shall age or any other consideration restrain me from saying that he now offers this Government which he has done his utmost to destroy, a very poor return for its magnanimous treatment, to come here and seek to continue, by the assertion of doctrines obnoxious to the true principles of our Government, the burdens and oppressions which rest upon five millions of his countrymen who never failed to lift their earnest prayers for the success of this Government when the gentleman was seeking to break up the union of these States and to blot the American Republic from the galaxy of nations.

Sir, it is scarcely twelve years since that gentleman shocked the civilized world by announcing the birth of a government which rested on human slavery as its corner-stone. The progress of events has swept away that pseudo-government which rested on greed, pride, and tyranny; and the race whom he then ruthlessly spurned and trampled on is here to meet him in debate, and to demand that the rights which are enjoyed by its former oppressors—who vainly sought to overthrow a Government which they could not prostitute to the base uses of slavery—shall be accorded to those who even in the darkness of slavery kept their allegiance true to freedom and the Union. Sir, the gentleman from Georgia has learned much since 1861; but he is still a laggard. Let him put away entirely the false and fatal theories which have so greatly marred an otherwise enviable record. Let him accept, in its fullness and beneficence, the great doctrine that American citizenship carries with it every civil and political right which manhood can confer. Let him lend his influence with all his masterly ability, to complete the proud structure of legislation which makes this nation worthy of the great declaration which heralded its birth and he will have done that which will most nearly redeem his reputation in the eyes of the world, and best vindicate the wisdom of that policy which has permitted him to regain his seat upon this floor.

To the diatribe of the gentleman from Virginia (Mr. Harris) who spoke yesterday, and who so far transcended the limits of decency and propriety as to announce upon this floor that his remarks were addressed to white men alone, I shall have no word of reply. Let him feel that a Negro was not only too magnanimous to smite him in his weakness, but was even charitable enough to grant him the mercy of his silence. I shall, sir, leave to others less charitable the unenviable and fatiguing task of sifting out of that mass of chaff the few grains of sense that may, perchance deserve notice. Assuring the gentleman that the Negro in this country aims at a higher degree of intellect than that exhibited by him in this debate, I cheerfully commend him to the commiseration of all intelligent men the world over—black men as well as white men.

Sir, equality before the law is now the broad, universal, glorious rule and mandate of the Republic. No State can violate that. Kentucky and Georgia may crowd their statute-books with retrograde and barbarous legislation; they may rejoice in the odious eminence of their consistent hostility to all the great steps of human progress which have marked our national history since slavery tore down the stars and stripes on Fort Sumter; but, if Congress shall do its duty, if Congress shall enforce the great guarantees which the Supreme Court has declared to be the one pervading purpose of all the recent amendments, then their unwise and unenlightened conduct will fall with the same weight upon the gentlemen from those States who now lend their influence to defeat this bill, as upon the poorest slave who once had no rights which the honorable gentlemen were bound to respect.

But, sir, not only does the decision in the Slaughter-house cases contain nothing which suggests a doubt of the power of Congress to pass the pending bill, but it contains an express recognition and affirmance of such power. I quote from page 81 of the volume: "Nor shall any State deny to any person within its jurisdiction the equal protection of the laws."

In the light of the history of these amendments, and the pervading purpose of them which we have already discussed, it is not difficult to give a meaning to this clause. The existence of laws in the States where the newly emancipated Negroes resided, which discriminated with gross injustice and hardship against them as a class, was the evil to be remedied by this clause, and by it such laws are forbidden.

If, however, the States did not conform their views to its requirements, then, by the fifth section of the article of amendment, Congress was authorized to enforce it by suitable legislation. We doubt very much whether any action of a State not directed by way of discrimination against the Negroes as a class, or on account of their race, will ever be held to come within the purview of this provision. It is so clearly a provision for that race and that emergency, that a strong case would be necessary for its application to any other. But as it is a State that is to be dealt with, and not alone the validity of its laws, we may safely leave that matter until Congress shall have exercised its power, or some case of State oppression, by denial of equal justice in its courts, shall have claimed a decision at our hands.

No language could convey a more complete assertion of the power of Congress over the subject embraced in the present bill than is here expressed. If the States do not conform to the requirements of this clause, if they continue to deny to any person within their jurisdiction the equal protection of the laws, or as the Supreme Court had said "deny equal justice in its Courts" then Congress is here said to have power to enforce the Constitutional guarantee by appropriate legislation. That is the power which this bill now seeks to put in exercise.

It proposes to enforce the Constitutional guarantee against inequality and discrimination by appropriate legislation. It does not seek to confer new rights, nor to place rights conferred by State citizenship under the protection of the United States, but simply to prevent and forbid inequality and discrimination on account of race, color, or previous condition of servitude. Never was there a bill which appealed for support more strongly to that sense of justice and fair play which has been said, and in the main with justice, to be a characteristic of the Anglo-Saxon race. The Constitution warrants it; the Supreme Court sanctions it; justice demands it.

Sir, I have replied to the extent of my ability to the arguments which have been presented by the opponents of this measure. I have replied also to some of the legal propositions advanced by gentlemen on the other side; and now that I am about to conclude, I am deeply sensible of the imperfect manner in which I have performed the task. Technically, this bill is to decide upon the civil status of the colored American citizen; a point disputed at the very formation of our present form of government, when by a short-sighted policy, a policy repugnant to true republican government, one Negro counted as three-fifth of a man. The logical result of this mistake of the framers of the Constitution strengthened the cancer of slavery, which finally spread its poisonous tentacles over the southern portion of the body politic. To arrest its growth and save the nation we have passed through the harrowing operation of intestine war, dreaded at all times, resorted to at the last extremity, like the surgeon's knife, but absolutely necessary to extirpate the disease which threatened with the life of the nation the overthrow of civil and political liberty on this continent. In that dire extremity the members of the race which I have the honor in part to represent—the race which pleads for justice at your hands to-day,—forgetful of their inhuman and brutalizing servitude at the South, their degradation and ostracism at the North, flew willingly and gallantly to the support of the national Government.

Their sufferings, assistance, privations, and trials in the swamps and in the rice-fields, their valor on the land and on the sea, form a part of the ever-glorious record which makes up the history of a nation preserved, and might, should I urge the claim, incline you to respect and guarantee their rights and privileges as citizens of our common Republic. But I remember that valor, devotion, and loyalty are not always rewarded according to their just deserts, and that after the battle some who have borne the brunt of the fray may, through neglect or contempt, be assigned to a subordinate place, while the enemies in war may be preferred to the sufferers.

The results of the war, as seen in reconstruction, have settled forever the political status of my race. The passage of this bill will determine the civil status, not only of the Negro, but of any other class of citizens who may feel themselves discriminated against. It will form the cap-stone of that temple of liberty, begun on this continent under discouraging circumstances, carried on in spite of the sneers of monarchists and the cavils of pretended friends of freedom, until at last it stands, in all its beautiful symmetry and proportions, a building the grandest which the world has ever seen, realizing the most sanguine expectations and the highest hopes of those who, in the name of equal, impartial, and universal liberty, laid the foundation-stone.

The Holy Scriptures tell us of an humble handmaiden who long, faithfully, and patiently gleaned in the rich fields of her wealthy kinsman, and we are told further that at last, in spite of her humble antecedents she found favor in his sight. For over two centuries our race has "reaped down your fields," the cries and woes which we have uttered have "entered into the ears of the Lord of Sabaoth" and we are at last politically free. The last vestiture only is needed—civil rights. Having gained this, we may, with hearts overflowing with gratitude and thankful that our prayer has been answered, repeat the prayer of Ruth: "Entreat me not to leave thee, or to return from following after thee; for whither thou goest, I will go; and where thou lodgest, I will lodge; thy people shall be my people, and thy God my God; where thou diest I will die, and there will I be buried; the Lord do so to me, and more also, if ought but death part thee and me."

CIVIL RIGHTS AND SOCIAL EQUALITY[9]

BY HON. JOHN R. LYNCH

The House having under consideration the civil-rights bill, Mr. Lynch said:

Mr. Speaker:

I will now endeavor to answer the arguments of those who have been contending that the passage of this bill is an effort to bring about social equality between the races. That the passage of this bill can in any manner affect the social status of any one seems to me to be absurd and ridiculous. I have never believed for a moment that social equality could be brought about even between persons of the same race. I have always believed that social distinctions existed among white people the same as among colored people. But those who contend that the passage of this bill will have a tendency to bring about social equality between the races virtually and substantially admit that there are no social distinctions among white people whatever, but that all white persons, regardless of their moral character, are the social equals of each other; for if by conferring upon colored people the same rights and privileges that are now exercised and enjoyed by whites indiscriminately will result in bringing about social equality between the races, then the same process of reasoning must necessarily bring us to the conclusion that there are no social distinctions among whites, because all white persons, regardless of their social standing, are permitted to enjoy these rights. See then how unreasonable, unjust, and false is the assertion that social equality is involved in this legislation. I cannot believe that gentlemen on the other side of the House mean what they say when they admit as they do that the immoral, the ignorant, and the degraded of their own race are the social equals of themselves and their families. If they do, then I can only assure them that they do not put as high an estimate upon their own social standing as respectable and intelligent colored people place upon theirs; for there are hundreds and thousands of white people of both sexes whom I know to be the social inferiors of respectable and intelligent colored people. I can then assure that portion of my Democratic friends on the other side of the House whom I regard as my social inferiors that if at any time I should meet any one of you at a hotel and occupy a seat at the same table with you, or the same seat in a car with you, do not think that I have thereby accepted you as my social equal. Not at all. But if any one should attempt to discriminate against you for no other reason than because you are identified with a particular race or religious sect, I would regard it as an outrage; as a violation of the principles of republicanism; and I would be in favor of protecting you in the exercise and enjoyment of your rights by suitable and appropriate legislation.

No, Mr. Speaker, it is not social rights that we desire. We have enough of that already. What we ask is protection in the enjoyment of *public* rights. Rights which are or should be accorded to every citizen alike. Under our present system of race distinctions a white woman of a questionable social standing, yea, I may say, of an admitted immoral character, can go to any public place or upon any public conveyance and be the recipient of the same treatment, the same courtesy, and the same respect that is usually accorded to the most refined and virtuous; but let an intelligent, modest, refined colored lady present herself and ask that the same privileges be accorded to her that have just been accorded to her social inferior of the white race, and in nine cases out of ten, except in certain portions of the country, she will not only be refused, but insulted for making the request.

Mr. Speaker, I ask the members of this House in all candor, is this right? I appeal to your sensitive feelings as husbands, fathers, and brothers, is this just? You who have affectionate companions, attractive daughters, and loving sisters, is this just? If you have any of the ingredients of manhood in your composition you will answer the question most emphatically, No! What a sad commentary upon our system of government, our religion, and our civilization! Think of it for a moment; here am I, a member of your honorable body, representing one of the largest and wealthiest districts in the State of Mississippi, and possibly in the South; a district composed of persons of different races, religions, and nationalities and yet, when I leave my home to come to the capital of the nation, to take part in the deliberations of the House and to participate with you in making laws for the government of this great Republic, in coming through the God-forsaken States of Kentucky and Tennessee, if I come by the way of Louisville or Chattanooga, I am treated, not as an American citizen, but as a brute. Forced to occupy a filthy smoking-car both night and day, with drunkards, gamblers, and criminals; and for what? Not that I am unable or unwilling to pay my way; not that I am obnoxious in my personal appearance or disrespectful in my conduct; but simply because I happen to be of a darker complexion. If this treatment was confined to persons of our own sex we could possibly afford to endure it. But such is not the case. Our wives and our daughters, our sisters and our mothers, are subjected to the same insults and to the same uncivilized treatment. You may ask why we do not institute civil suits in the State courts. What a farce! Talk about instituting a civil-rights suit in the State courts of Kentucky, for instance, where decision of the judge is virtually rendered before he enters the court-house, and the verdict of the jury substantially rendered before it is impaneled. The only moments of my life when I am necessarily compelled to question my loyalty to my Government or my devotion to the flag of my country is when I read of outrages having been committed upon innocent colored people and the perpetrators go unwhipped of justice, and when I leave my home to go traveling.

Mr. Speaker, if this unjust discrimination is to be longer tolerated by the American people, which I do not, cannot, and will not believe until I am forced to do so, then I can only say with sorrow and regret that our boasted civilization is a fraud; our republican institutions a failure; our social system a disgrace; and our religion a complete hypocrisy. But I have an abiding confidence—(though I must confess that that confidence was seriously shaken a little over two months ago)—but still I have an abiding confidence in the patriotism of this people, in their devotion to the cause of human rights, and in the stability of our republican institutions. I hope that I will not be deceived. I love the land that gave me birth; I love the Stars and Stripes. This country is where I intend to live, where I expect to die. To preserve the honor of the national flag and to maintain perpetually the Union of the States hundreds, and I may say thousands, of noble, brave, and true-hearted colored men have fought, bled, and died. And now, Mr. Speaker, I ask, can it be possible that that flag under which they fought is to be a shield and a protection to all races and classes of persons except the colored race? God forbid!

* * * * *

In conclusion, Mr. Speaker, I say to the Republican members of the House that the passage of this bill is expected of you. If any of our Democratic friends will vote for it, we will be agreeably surprised. But if Republicans should vote against it, we will be sorely disappointed; it will be to us a source of deep mortification as well as profound regret. We will feel as though we are deserted in the house of our friends. But I have no fears whatever in this respect. You have stood by the colored people of this country when it was more unpopular to do so than it is to pass this bill. You have fulfilled every promise thus far, and I have no reason to believe that you will not fulfill this one. Then give us this bill. The white man's government Negro-hating democracy will, in my judgment, soon pass out of existence. The progressive spirit of the American people will not much longer tolerate the existence of an organization that lives upon the passions and prejudices of the hour.

I appeal to all the members of the House—Republicans and Democrats, conservatives and liberals—to join with us in the passage of this bill, which has its object the protection of human rights. And when every man, woman, and child can feel and know that his, her, and their rights are fully protected by the strong arm of a generous and grateful Republic, then we can all truthfully say that this beautiful land of ours, over which the "Star-Spangled Banner" so triumphantly waves, is, in truth and in fact, the "land of the free and the home of the brave."

ALEXANDER DUMAS, FILS[10]

The following public tribute was paid to his father by the younger Dumas on the occasion of taking his seat in the French Academy (February 11, 1875).

"The fact," said he, "that so many men superior to me have had to knock many times at your door before it was opened to them would fill me with pride, did I not know the real reason of your sympathy. In order to reach my place among you, gentlemen, I have employed magical spells, I have used witchcraft. Standing on my own merits alone I should not have dared to face your judgment, but I knew that a good genius—that is the right word—was fighting on my behalf, and that you were determined to offer no defense. I have sheltered myself under a name which you would have wished long ago to honor in itself, and which you are now able to honor only in me. Believe me, gentlemen, it is with the greatest modesty that I come to-day to accept a reward which has been so easily granted to me only because it was reserved for another. I cannot—I may not—receive it except in trust; allow me then, at once and publicly, to make restitution of it to the man who, unhappily, can no longer receive it himself. Thus you will be granting me the highest honor which I can covet, and the only one *to which* I have any real right."

AN ADDRESS DELIVERED AT THE CENTENNIAL ANNIVERSARY OF THE PENNSYLVANIA SOCIETY FOR PROMOTING THE ABOLITION OF SLAVERY[11]

BY JOHN MERCER LANGSTON

Ladies and Gentlemen:

The history of this Association, owing to its objects and achievements, sweep in an interest that is not confined to any class: an interest that is not confined to any people, and whose scope and consequences cannot be foretold by human inspiration. It affects the emancipation of a whole race; and in that it touches the progress and character of all who are brought in contact with that race, the forms of government over the world and the world's progress in all departments. There was a recent time in American history when no man, in all its length and breadth, could read the Declaration of Independence and say that he possessed all of his civil and political liberties. Garrison could not speak in New Orleans, nor could the silver-tongued Phillips address an audience south of Mason and Dixon's line. Nor was it expedient for John C. Calhoun to address his arguments in Independence Hall, or for Davis and Yulee and Mason to propound theirs in Faneuil Hall. Speech was itself in thrall, and bound to the section in which it found voice. When Garrison and Phillips had been invited to speak in Cincinnati, they were counseled by their friends not to do so. There was danger that the mobs of Covington and Cincinnati would assassinate them publicly; and it is notorious that the opposing arguments that reached Washington from the North and from the South advanced no further in either direction. This impugned and belied the very freedom declared in the Declaration and Constitution; and made both the mockery of Europe. The contradiction is reconciled; the taunt is silenced; speech is legally free and protected over all the Union, and the Pennsylvania Abolition Society has done more than any other agency—more than all other agencies combined—to vitalize the Constitution and give being to the Declaration. This society fought for the glowing assertion of all the centuries: That men are born free and equal, and are endowed with inalienable right to life, liberty, and the pursuit of happiness. It kept the contrast between the declaration and its practise in a clear light. It repeated the assertion and reasserted it. It argued the justice with the very facts and reasons that had been presented to the Congress by whom the Declaration was framed. Undisturbed by ridicule, unchecked by hostility, undaunted by persecution, it has kept the law in the van of the fight; sustained it by reserves of humane reason; by appeals to national strength and welfare, and growth, and influence, and wealth; it disseminated the truth in churches, at the polls, in lyceums, by the press; it was unanswerable because its claim was founded in equity, and recognized in religion, and had ineradicable place in the great muniment of national being. It appealed to the individual conscience as well as to pride, patriotism, piety, and interest, and it won, and now celebrates a victory immeasurably greater than that of Yorktown or Waterloo or Marathon. Those were the victories of nation over nation, or at the utmost of a principle of limited application. We celebrate the successful battle of the grandest principle in human organization; that is confined to no race, limited to no country, cramped by no restriction, but is as broad as the world, as applicable as humanity itself and as enduring as time. The sentiment which elected Abraham Lincoln was contained in an address delivered before the Pennsylvania Abolition Society by Benjamin Rush, one of its earliest and most honored members. It was: "Freedom and slavery cannot long exist together!"

Ladies and Gentlemen of the Abolition Society, those who see the American citizens of African descent one hundred years hence will be proud of them, and convinced that the great century struggle that won their enfranchisement was worth infinitely more than it cost. We are now leaving politics. We have gained through them the rights and opportunities they conferred, that could be secured in no other way. We are devoting ourselves to learning and industry; the attainment of wealth and manufacture of character. We shall never leave our home. There are but two facts to be recognized. We are here. The white race is here. Both share the same rights; make and obey the same laws; struggle for progress under the same conditions. The logical conclusion of our birthright and of our proclaimed and perfected equality before the law is that we shall remain, and remaining strive with equal advantages with our white fellow citizens for our own good and the nation's welfare.

AN ADDRESS DELIVERED AT THE CENTENNIAL ANNIVERSARY OF THE PENNSYLVANIA SOCIETY FOR PROMOTING THE ABOLITION OF SLAVERY[12]

BY MRS. FRANCES ELLEN WATKINS HARPER

FRANCES ELLEN WATKINS HARPER *was a distinguished anti-slavery lecturer, writer and poet, born in Baltimore, Maryland, in 1825, of free parents. After the close of the Civil War she went South and worked as a teacher and lecturer, but later returned to Philadelphia, where she devoted her time to lecturing and writing for the temperance cause, having charge, for a number of years, of the W. C. T. U. work among Negroes. "Iola Leroy, or the Shadows Uplifted," is her best-known work, besides which she published a number of small books of verses.*

Ladies and Gentlemen:

The great problem to be solved by the American people, if I understand it, is this: Whether or not there is strength enough in democracy, virtue enough in our civilization, and power enough in our religion to have mercy and deal justly with four millions of people but lately translated from the old oligarchy of slavery to the new commonwealth of freedom; and upon the right solution of this question depends in a large measure the future strength, progress, and durability of our nation. The most important question before us colored people is not simply what the Democratic party may do against us or the Republican party do for us; but what are we going to do for ourselves? What shall we do towards developing our character, adding our quota to the civilization and strength of the country, diversifying our industry, and practising those lordly virtues that conquer success, and turn the world's dread laugh into admiring recognition? The white race has yet work to do in making practical the political axiom of equal rights, and the Christian idea of human brotherhood; but while I lift mine eyes to the future I would not ungratefully ignore the past. One hundred years ago and Africa was the privileged hunting-ground of Europe and America, and the flag of different nations hung a sign of death on the coasts of Congo and Guinea, and for years unbroken silence had hung around the horrors of the African slave-trade. Since then Great Britain and other nations have wiped the bloody traffic from their hands, and shaken the gory merchandise from their fingers, and the brand of piracy has been placed upon the African slave-trade. Less than fifty years ago mob violence belched out its wrath against the men who dared to arraign the slaveholder before the bar of conscience and Christendom. Instead of golden showers upon his head, he who garrisoned the front had a halter around his neck. Since, if I may borrow the idea, the nation has caught the old inspiration from his lips and written it in the new organic world. Less than twenty-five years ago slavery clasped hands with King Cotton, and said slavery fights and cotton conquers for American slavery. Since then slavery is dead, the colored man has exchanged the fetters on his wrist for the ballot in his hand. Freedom is king, and Cotton a subject.

It may not seem to be a gracious thing to mingle complaint in a season of general rejoicing. It may appear like the ancient Egyptians seating a corpse at their festal board to avenge the Americans for their shortcomings when so much has been accomplished. And yet with all the victories and triumphs which freedom and justice have won in this country, I do not believe there is another civilized nation under Heaven where there are half so many people who have been brutally and shamefully murdered, with or without impunity, as in this Republic within the last ten years. And who cares? Where is the public opinion that has scorched with red-hot indignation the cowardly murderers of Vicksburg and Louisiana? Sheridan lifts up the vail from Southern society, and behind it is the smell of blood, and our bones scattered at the grave's mouth; murdered people; a White League with its "covenant of death and agreement with hell." And who cares? What city pauses one hour to drop a pitying tear over these mangled corpses, or has forged against the perpetrator one thunderbolt of furious protest? But let there be a supposed or real invasion of Southern rights by our soldiers, and our great commercial emporium will rally its forces from the old man in his classic shades, to clasp hands with "dead rabbits" and "plug-uglies" in protesting against military interference. What we need to-day in the onward march of humanity is a public sentiment in favor of common justice and simple mercy. We have a civilization which has produced grand and magnificent results, diffused knowledge, overthrown slavery, made constant conquests over nature, and built up a wonderful material prosperity. But two things are wanting in American civilization—a keener and deeper, broader and tenderer sense of justice—a sense of humanity, which shall crystallize into the life of the nation the sentiment that justice, simple justice, is the right, not simply of the strong and powerful, but of the weakest and feeblest of all God's children; a deeper and broader humanity, which will teach men to look upon their feeble brethren not as vermin to be crushed out, or beasts of burden to be bridled and bitted, but as the children of the living God; of that God whom we may earnestly hope is in perfect wisdom and in perfect love working for the best good of all. Ethnologists may differ about the origin of the human race. Huxley may search for it in protoplasms, and Darwin send for the missing links, but there is one thing of which we may rest assured,—that we all come from the living God and that He is the common Father. The nation that has no reverence for man is also lacking in reverence for God and needs to be instructed.

As fellow citizens, leaving out all humanitarian views—as a mere matter of political economy it is better to have the colored race a living force animated and strengthened by self-reliance and self-respect, than a stagnant mass, degraded and self-condemned. Instead of the North relaxing its efforts to diffuse education in the South, it behooves us for our national life, to throw into the South all the healthful reconstructing influences we can command. Our work in this country is grandly constructive. Some races have come into this world and overthrown and destroyed. But if it is glory to destroy, it is happiness to save; and Oh! what a noble work there is before our nation! Where is there a young man who would consent to lead an aimless life when there are such glorious opportunities before him? Before our young men is another battle—not a battle of flashing swords and clashing steel—but a moral warfare, a battle against ignorance, poverty, and low social condition. In physical warfare the keenest swords may be blunted and the loudest batteries hushed; but in the great conflict of moral and spiritual progress your weapons shall be brighter for their service and better for their use. In fighting truly and nobly for others you win the victory for yourselves.

Give power and significance to your own life, and in the great work of upbuilding there is room for woman's work and woman's heart. Oh, that our hearts were alive and our vision quickened, to see the grandeur of the work that lies before. We have some culture among us, but I think our culture lacks enthusiasm. We need a deep earnestness and a lofty unselfishness to round out our lives. It is the inner life that develops the outer, and if we are in earnest the precious things lie all around our feet, and we need not waste our strength in striving after the dim and unattainable. Women, in your golden youth; mother, binding around your heart all the precious ties of life,—let no magnificence of culture, or amplitude of fortune, or refinement of sensibilities, repel you from helping the weaker and less favored. If you have ampler gifts, hold them as larger opportunities with which you can benefit others. Oh, it is better to feel that the weaker and feebler our race the closer we will cling to them, than it is to isolate ourselves from them in selfish, or careless unconcern, saying there is a lion without. Inviting you to this work I do not promise you fair sailing and unclouded skies. You may meet with coolness where you expect sympathy; disappointment where you feel sure of success; isolation and loneliness instead of heart-support and co-operation. But if your lives are based and built upon these divine certitudes, which are the only enduring strength of humanity, then whatever defeat and discomfiture may overshadow your plans or frustrate your schemes, for a life that is in harmony with God and sympathy for man there is no such word as fail. And in conclusion, permit me to say, let no misfortunes crush you; no hostility of enemies or failure of friends discourage you. Apparent failure may hold in its rough shell the germs of a success that will blossom in time, and bear fruit throughout eternity. What seemed to be a failure around the Cross of Calvary and in the garden has been the grandest recorded success.

A MEMORIAL DISCOURSE[13]

BY REV. HENRY HIGHLAND GARNET

HENRY HIGHLAND GARNET, *who at the time of the delivery of this speech was in charge of the Fifteenth Street Presbyterian Church in Washington, D. C., was one of the foremost figures in the great anti-slavery movement in New York. He was the first colored man to speak in the National Capitol.*

Matthew xxiii-4. "For they bind heavy burdens, and grievous to be borne, and lay them on men's shoulders, but they themselves will not move them with one of their fingers."

In this chapter, of which my text is a sentence, the Lord Jesus addressed his disciples, and the multitude that hung spell-bound upon the words that fell from his lips. He admonished them to beware of the religion of the Scribes and Pharisees, which was distinguished for great professions, while it succeeded in urging them to do but a little, or nothing that accorded with the law of righteousness.

In theory they were right; but their practices were inconsistent and wrong. They were learned in the law of Moses, and in the traditions of their fathers, but the principles of righteousness failed to affect their hearts. They knew their duty but did it not. The demands which they made upon others proved that they themselves knew what things men ought to do. In condemning others they pronounced themselves guilty. They demanded that others should be just, merciful, pure, peaceable, and righteous. But they were unjust, impure, unmerciful—they hated and wronged a portion of their fellowmen, and waged a continual war against the government of God.

* * * * *

Such was their conduct in the Church and in the State. We have modern Scribes and Pharisees, who are faithful to their prototypes of ancient times.

With sincere respect and reverence for the instruction, and the warning given by our Lord, and in humble dependence upon him for his assistance, I shall speak this morning of the Scribes and Pharisees of our times who rule the State. In discharging this duty, I shall keep my eyes upon the picture which is painted so faithfully and life-like by the hand of the Saviour.

Allow me to describe them. They are intelligent and well-informed, and can never say, either before an earthly tribunal or at the bar of God, "We knew not of ourselves what was right." They are acquainted with the principles of the law of nations. They are proficient in the knowledge of Constitutional law. They are teachers of common law, and frame and execute statute law. They acknowledge that there is a just and impartial God, and are not altogether unacquainted with the law of Christian love and kindness. They claim for themselves the broadest freedom. Boastfully they tell us that they have received from the court of heaven the Magna Charta of human rights that was handed down through the clouds, and amid the lightnings of Sinai, and given again by the Son of God on the Mount of Beatitudes, while the glory of the Father shone around him. They tell us that from the Declaration of Independence and the Constitution they have obtained a guaranty of their political freedom, and from the Bible they derive their claim to all the blessings of religious liberty. With just pride they tell us that they are descended from the Pilgrims, who threw themselves upon the bosom of the treacherous sea, and braved storms and tempests, that they might find in a strange land, and among savages, free homes, where they might build their altars that should blaze with acceptable sacrifice unto God. Yes! they boast that their fathers heroically turned away from the precious light of Eastern civilization, and taking their lamps with oil in their vessels, joyfully went forth to illuminate this land, that then dwelt in the darkness of the valley of the shadow of death. With hearts strengthened by faith they spread out their standard to the winds of heaven, near Plymouth rock; and whether it was stiffened in the sleet and frosts of winter, or floated on the breeze of summer, it ever bore the motto, "Freedom to worship God."

But others, their fellow-men, equal before the Almighty, and made by him of the same blood, and glowing with immortality, they doom to life-long servitude and chains. Yes, they stand in the most sacred places on earth, and beneath the gaze of the piercing eye of Jehovah, the universal Father of all men, and declare, "that the best possible condition of the Negro is slavery."

In the name of the Triune God I denounce the sentiment as unrighteous beyond measure, and the holy and the just of the whole earth say in regard to it, Anathema-maranatha.

What is slavery? Too well do I know what it is. I will present to you a bird's-eye view of it; and it shall be no fancy picture, but one that is sketched by painful experience. I was born among the cherished institutions of slavery. My earliest recollections of parents, friends, and the home of my childhood are clouded with its wrongs. The first sight that met my eyes was a Christian mother enslaved by professed Christians, but, thank God, now a saint in heaven. The first sounds that startled my ear, and sent a shudder through my soul, were the cracking of the whip and the clanking of chains. These sad memories mar the beauties of my native shores, and darken all the slave-land, which, but for the reign of despotism, had been a paradise. But those shores are fairer now. The mists have left my native valleys, and the clouds have rolled away from the hills, and Maryland, the unhonored grave of my fathers, is now the free home of their liberated and happier children.

Let us view this demon, which the people have worshiped as a God. Come forth, thou grim monster, that thou mayest be critically examined! There he stands. Behold him, one and all. Its work is to chattelize man; to hold property in human beings. Great God! I would as soon attempt to enslave Gabriel or Michael as to enslave a man made in the image of God, and for whom Christ died. Slavery is snatching man from the high place to which he was lifted by the hand of God, and dragging him down to the level of the brute creation, where he is made to be the companion of the horse and the fellow of the ox.

It tears the crown of glory from his head, and as far as possible obliterates the image of God that is in him. Slavery preys upon man, and man only. A brute cannot be made a slave. Why? Because a brute has not reason, faith, nor an undying spirit, nor conscience. It does not look forward to the future with joy or fear, nor reflect upon the past with satisfaction or regret. But who in this vast assembly, who in all this broad land, will say that the poorest and most unhappy brother in chains and servitude has not every one of these high endowments? Who denies it? Is there one? If so, let him speak. There is not one; no, not one.

But slavery attempts to make a man a brute. It treats him as a beast. Its terrible work is not finished until the ruined victim of its lusts, and pride, and avarice, and hatred, is reduced so low that with tearful eyes and feeble voice he faintly cries, "I am happy and contented—I love this condition."

"Proud Nimrod first the bloody chase began,
A mighty hunter he; his prey was man."

The caged lion may cease to roar, and try no longer the strength of the bars of his prison, and lie with his head between his mighty paws and snuff the polluted air as though he heeded not. But is he contented? Does he not instinctively long for the freedom of the forest and the plain? Yes, he is a lion still. Our poor and forlorn brother whom thou hast labelled "slave," is also a man. He may be unfortunate, weak, helpless, and despised, and hated, nevertheless he is a man. His God and thine has stamped on his forehead his title to his inalienable rights in characters that can be read by every intelligent being. Pitiless storms of outrage may have beaten upon his defenseless head and he may have descended through ages of oppression, yet he is a man. God made him such, and his brother cannot unmake him. Woe, woe to him who attempts to commit the accursed crime.

Slavery commenced its dreadful work in kidnapping unoffending men in a foreign and distant land, and in piracy on the seas. The plunderers were not the followers of Mahomet, nor the devotees of Hindooism, nor benighted pagans, nor idolaters, but people called Christians, and thus the ruthless traders in the souls and bodies of men fastened upon Christianity a crime and stain at the sight of which it shudders and shrieks.

It is guilty of the most heinous iniquities ever perpetrated upon helpless women and innocent children. Go to the shores of the land of my forefathers, poor bleeding Africa, which, although she has been bereaved, and robbed for centuries, is nevertheless beloved by all her worthy descendants wherever dispersed. Behold a single scene that there meets your eyes. Turn not away neither from shame, pity, nor indifference, but look and see the beginning of this cherished and petted institution. Behold a hundred youthful mothers seated on the ground, dropping their tears upon the hot sands, and filling the air with their lamentations.

Why do they weep? Ah, Lord God, thou knowest! Their babes have been torn from their bosoms and cast upon the plains to die of hunger, or to be devoured by hyenas or jackals. The little innocents would die on the "Middle Passage," or suffocate between the decks of the floating slave-pen, freighted and packed with unparalleled human woe, and the slavers in mercy have cast them out to perish on their native shores. Such is the beginning, and no less wicked is the end of that system which Scribes and Pharisees in the Church and the State pronounce to be just, humane, benevolent and Christian. If such are the deeds of mercy wrought by angels, then tell me what works of iniquity there remain for devils to do?

* * * * *

It is the highly concentrated essence of all conceivable wickedness. Theft, robbery, pollution, unbridled passion, incest, cruelty, cold-blooded murder, blasphemy, and defiance of the laws of God. It teaches children to disregard parental authority. It tears down the marriage altar, and tramples its sacred ashes under its feet. It creates and nourishes polygamy. It feeds and pampers its hateful handmaid, prejudice.

It has divided our national councils. It has engendered deadly strife between brethren. It has wasted the treasure of the Commonwealth, and the lives of thousands of brave men, and driven troops of helpless women and children into yawning tombs. It has caused the bloodiest civil war recorded in the book of time. It has shorn this nation of its locks of strength that was rising as a young lion in the Western world. It has offered us as a sacrifice to the jealousy and cupidity of tyrants, despots, and adventurers of foreign countries. It has opened a door through which a usurper, a perjured, but a powerful prince, might stealthily enter and build an empire on the golden borders of our southwestern frontier, and which is but a stepping-stone to further and unlimited conquests on this continent. It has desolated the fairest portions of our land, "until the wolf long since driven back by the march of civilization returns after the lapse of a hundred years and howls amidst its ruins."

It seals up the Bible, and mutilates its sacred truths, and flies into the face of the Almighty, and impiously asks, "Who art thou that I should obey thee?" Such are the outlines of this fearful national sin; and yet the condition to which it reduces man, it is affirmed, is the best that can possibly be devised for him.

When inconsistencies similar in character, and no more glaring, passed beneath the eye of the Son of God, no wonder he broke forth in language of vehement denunciation. Ye Scribes, Pharisees, and hypocrites! Ye blind guides! Ye compass sea and land to make one proselyte, and when he is made ye make him twofold more the child of hell than yourselves. Ye are like unto whited sepulchres, which indeed appear beautiful without, but within are full of dead men's bones, and all uncleanness!

Let us here take up the golden rule, and adopt the self-application mode of reasoning to those who hold these erroneous views. Come, gird up thy loins and answer like a man, if thou canst. Is slavery, as it is seen in its origin, continuance, and end the best possible condition for thee? Oh, no! Wilt thou bear that burden on thy shoulders, which thou wouldest lay upon thy fellow-man? No. Wilt thou bear a part of it, or remove a little of its weight with one of thy fingers? The sharp and indignant answer is no, no! Then how, and when, and where, shall we apply to thee the golden rule, which says, "Therefore all things that ye would that others should do to you, do ye even so unto them, for this is the law and the prophets."

Let us have the testimony of the wise and great of ancient and modern times:

"Sages who wrote and warriors who bled."

Plato declared that "Slavery is a system of complete injustice."

Socrates wrote that "Slavery is a system of outrage and robbery."

Cyrus said, "To fight in order not to be a slave is noble."

If Cyrus had lived in our land a few years ago he would have been arrested for using incendiary language, and for inciting servile insurrection, and the royal fanatic would have been hanged on a gallows higher than Haman. But every man is fanatical when his soul is warmed by the generous fires of liberty. Is it then truly noble to fight in order not to be a slave? The Chief

Magistrate of the nation, and our rulers, and all truly patriotic men think so; and so think legions of black men, who for a season were scorned and rejected, but who came quickly and cheerfully when they were at last invited, bearing a heavy burden of proscriptions upon their shoulders, and having faith in God, and in their generous fellow-countrymen, they went forth to fight a double battle. The foes of their country were before them, while the enemies of freedom and of their race surrounded them.

Augustine, Constantine, Ignatius, Polycarp, Maximus, and the most illustrious lights of the ancient church denounced the sin of slave-holding.

Thomas Jefferson said at a period of his life, when his judgment was matured, and his experience was ripe, "There is preparing, I hope, under the auspices of heaven, a way for a total emancipation."

The sainted Washington said, near the close of his moral career, and when the light of eternity was beaming upon him, "It is among my first wishes to see some plan adopted by which slavery in this country shall be abolished by law. I know of but one way by which this can be done, and that is by legislative action, and so far as my vote can go, it shall not be wanting."

The other day, when the light of Liberty streamed through this marble pile, and the hearts of the noble band of patriotic statesmen leaped for joy, and this our national capitol shook from foundation to dome with the shouts of a ransomed people, then methinks the spirits of Washington, Jefferson, the Jays, the Adamses, and Franklin, and Lafayette, and Giddings, and Lovejoy, and those of all the mighty, and glorious dead, remembered by history, because they were faithful to truth, justice, and liberty, were hovering over the august assembly. Though unseen by mortal eyes, doubtless they joined the angelic choir, and said, Amen.

Pope Leo X. testifies, "That not only does the Christian religion, but nature herself, cry out against a state of slavery."

Patrick Henry said, "We should transmit to posterity our abhorrence of slavery." So also thought the Thirty-Eighth Congress.

Lafayette proclaimed these words: "Slavery is a dark spot on the face of the nation." God be praised, that stain will soon be wiped out.

Jonathan Edwards declared "that to hold a man in slavery is to be every day guilty of robbery, or of man stealing."

Rev. Dr. William Ellery Channing, in a Letter on the Annexation of Texas in 1837, writes as follows: "The evil of slavery speaks for itself. To state is to condemn the institution. The choice which every freeman makes of death for his child and for every thing he loves in preference to slavery shows what it is. * * * "Every principle of our government and religion condemns slavery.

The spirit of our age condemns it. The decree of the civilized world has gone out against it."

* * * * *

Moses, the greatest of all lawgivers and legislators, said, while his face was yet radiant with the light of Sinai: "Whoso stealeth a man, and selleth him, or if he be found in his hand, he shall surely be put to death." The destroying angel has gone forth through this land to execute the fearful penalties of God's broken law.

The representatives of the nation have bowed with reverence to the Divine edict, and laid the axe at the root of the tree, and thus saved succeeding generations from the guilt of oppression, and from the wrath of God.

Statesmen, jurists, and philosophers, most renowned for learning, and most profound in every department of science and literature, have testified against slavery; while oratory has brought its costliest, golden treasures, and laid them on the altar of God and of freedom, it has aimed its fiercest lightning and loudest thunder at the strongholds of tyranny, injustice, and despotism.

From the days of Balak to those of Isaiah and Jeremiah, up to the times of Paul, and through every age of the Christian Church, the sons of thunder have denounced the abominable thing. The heroes who stood in the shining ranks of the hosts of the friends of human progress, from Cicero to Chatham, and Burke, Sharp, Wilberforce, and Thomas Clarkson, and Curran, assaulted the citadel of despotism. The orators and statesmen of our own land, whether they belong to the past, or to the present age, will live and shine in the annals of history, in proportion as they have dedicated their genius and talents to the defence of Justice and man's God-given rights.

All the poets who live in sacred and profane history have charmed the world with their most enchanting strains, when they have tuned their lyres to the praise of Liberty. When the muses can no longer decorate her altars with their garlands, then they hang their harps upon the willows and weep.

From Moses to Terence and Homer, from thence to Milton and Cowper, Thomson and Thomas Campbell, and on to the days of our own bards, our Bryants, Longfellows, Whittiers, Morrises, and Bokers, all have presented their best gifts to the interests and rights of man.

Every good principle, and every great and noble power, have been made the subjects of the inspired verse, and the songs of poets. But who of them has attempted to immortalize slavery? You will search in vain the annals of the world to find an instance. Should any attempt the sacrilegious work, his genius would fall to the earth as if smitten by the lightning of heaven. Should he lift his hand to write a line in its praise, or defence, the ink would freeze on the point of his pen.

Could we array in one line, representatives of all the families of men, beginning with those lowest in the scale of being, and should we put to them the question, Is it right and desirable that you should be reduced to the condition of slaves, to be registered with chattels, to have your persons, and your lives, and the products of your labor, subjected to the will and the interests of others? Is it right and just that the persons of your wives and children should be at the disposal of others, and be yielded to them for the purpose of pampering their lusts and greed of gain? Is it right to lay heavy burdens on other men's shoulders which you would not remove with one of your fingers? From the rude savage and barbarian the negative response would come, increasing in power and significance as it rolled up the line. And when those should reply, whose minds and hearts are illuminated with the highest civilization and with the spirit of Christianity, the answer deep-toned and prolonged would thunder forth, no, no!

With all the moral attributes of God on our side, cheered as we are by the voices of universal human nature,—in view of the best interests of the present and future generations—animated with the noble desire to furnish the nations of the earth with a worthy example, let the verdict of death which has been brought in against slavery, by the Thirty-Eighth Congress, be affirmed and executed by the people. Let the gigantic monster perish. Yes, perish now, and perish forever!

It is often asked when and where will the demands of the reformers of this and coming ages end? It is a fair question, and I will answer.

When all unjust and heavy burdens shall be removed from every man in the land. When all invidious and proscriptive distinctions shall be blotted out from our laws, whether they be constitutional, statute, or municipal laws. When emancipation shall be followed by enfranchisement, and all men holding allegiance to the government shall enjoy every right of American citizenship. When our brave and gallant soldiers shall have justice done unto them. When the men who endure the sufferings and perils of the battle-field in the defence of their country, and in order to keep our rulers in their places, shall enjoy the well-earned privilege of voting for them. When in the army and navy, and in every legitimate and honorable occupation, promotion shall smile upon merit without the slightest regard to the complexion of a man's face. When there shall be no more class-legislation, and no more trouble concerning the black man and his rights, than there is in regard to other American citizens. When, in every respect, he shall be equal before the law, and shall be left to make his own way in the social walks of life.

We ask, and only ask, that when our poor frail barks are launched on life's ocean—

> "Bound on a voyage of awful length
> And dangers little known,"

that, in common with others, we may be furnished with rudder, helm, and sails, and charts, and compass. Give us good pilots to conduct us to the open seas; lift no false lights along the dangerous coasts, and if it shall please God to send us propitious winds, or fearful gales, we shall survive or perish as our energies or neglect shall determine. We ask no special favors, but we plead for justice. While we scorn unmanly dependence; in the name of God, the universal Father, we demand the right to live, and labor, and to enjoy the fruits of our toil. The good work which God has assigned for the ages to come, will be finished, when our national literature shall be so purified as to reflect a faithful and a just light upon the character and social habits of our race, and the brush, and pencil, and chisel, and lyre of art, shall refuse to lend their aid to scoff at the afflictions of the poor, or to caricature, or ridicule a long-suffering people. When caste and prejudice in Christian churches shall be utterly destroyed, and shall be regarded as totally unworthy of Christians, and at variance with the principles of the gospel. When the blessings of the Christian religion, and of sound, religious education, shall be freely offered to all, then, and not till then, shall the effectual labors of God's people and God's instruments cease.

If slavery has been destroyed merely from *necessity*, let every class be enfranchised at the dictation of *justice*. Then we shall have a Constitution that shall be reverenced by all: rulers who shall be honored, and revered, and a Union that shall be sincerely loved by a brave and patriotic people, and which can never be severed.

Great sacrifices have been made by the people; yet, greater still are demanded ere atonement can be made for our national sins. Eternal justice holds heavy mortgages against us, and will require the payment of the last farthing. We have involved ourselves in the sin of unrighteous gain, stimulated by luxury, and pride, and the love of power and oppression; and prosperity and peace can be purchased only by blood, and with tears of repentance. We have paid some of the fearful installments, but there are other heavy obligations to be met.

The great day of the nation's judgment has come, and who shall be able to stand? Even we, whose ancestors have suffered the afflictions which are inseparable from a condition of slavery, for the period of two centuries and a half, now pity our land and weep with those who weep.

Upon the total and complete destruction of this accursed sin depends the safety and perpetuity of our Republic and its excellent institutions.

Let slavery die. It has had a long and fair trial. God himself has pleaded against it. The enlightened nations of the earth have condemned it. Its death warrant is signed by God and man. Do not commute its sentence. Give it no respite, but let it be ignominiously executed.

Honorable Senators and Representatives! Illustrious rulers of this great nation! I cannot refrain this day from invoking upon you, in God's name, the blessings of millions who were ready to perish, but to whom a new and better life has been opened by your humanity, justice, and patriotism. You have said, "Let the Constitution of the country be so amended that slavery and involuntary servitude shall no longer exist in the United States, except in punishment for crime." Surely, an act so sublime could not escape Divine notice; and doubtless the deed has been recorded in the archives of heaven. Volumes may be appropriated to your praise and renown in the history of the world. Genius and art may perpetuate the glorious act on canvass and in marble, but certain and more lasting monuments in commemoration of your decision are already erected in the hearts and memories of a grateful people.

The nation has begun its exodus from worse than Egyptian bondage; and I beseech you that you say to the people, "that they go forward." With the assurance of God's favor in all things done in obedience to his righteous will, and guided by day and by night by the pillars of cloud and fire, let us not pause until we have reached the other and safe side of the stormy and crimson sea. Let freemen and patriots mete out complete and equal justice to all men, and thus prove to mankind the superiority of our Democratic, Republican Government.

Favored men, and honored of God as his instruments, speedily finish the work which he has given you to do. Emancipate, enfranchise, educate, and give the blessings of the gospel to every American citizen.

Then before us a path of prosperity will open, and upon us will descend the mercies and favors of God. Then shall the people of other countries, who are standing tip-toe on the shores of every ocean, earnestly looking to see the end of this amazing conflict, behold a Republic that is sufficiently strong to outlive the ruin and desolations of civil war, having the magnanimity to do justice to the poorest and weakest of her citizens. Thus shall we give to the world the form of a model Republic, founded on the principles of justice, and humanity, and Christianity, in which the burdens of war and the blessings of peace are equally borne and enjoyed by all.

CRISPUS ATTUCKS[14]

BY GEORGE L. RUFFIN

GEORGE L. RUFFIN *(1834-1885) the first Negro judge to be appointed in Massachusetts, graduated in Law from Harvard, 1869. He served in the legislature of Massachusetts two terms, and in the Boston Council two terms.*

The fifth of March, 1770, had been a cold day, and a slight fall of snow had covered the ground, but at nine o'clock at night it was clear and cold, not a cloud to be seen in the sky, and the moon was shining brightly. A British guard was patrolling the streets with clanking swords and overbearing swagger. A sentry was stationed in Dock Square. A party of young men, four in number, came out of a house in Cornhill. One of the soldiers was whirling his sword about his head, striking fire with it; the sentry challenged one of the four young men; there was no good blood between them, and it took but little to start a disturbance. An apprentice boy cried out to one of the guards, "You haven't paid my master for dressing your hair!" A soldier said, "Where are the d—— d Yankee boogers, I'll kill them!" A boy's head was split, there was more quarrelling between the young men and the guard, great noise and confusion; a vast concourse of excited people soon collected; cries of "Kill them!" "Drive them out!" "They have no business here!" were heard; some citizens were knocked down, as also were some soldiers. Generally speaking, the soldiers got the worst of it; they were reinforced, but steadily the infuriated citizens drove them back until they were forced to take refuge in the Custom-House, upon the steps of which they were pelted with snowballs and pieces of ice.

By this time the whole town was aroused; exaggerated accounts of the event in Dock Square flew like wild-fire all over the settlement; the people turned out *en masse* in the streets and, to add to the general din, the bells of the town were rung. The regiment which held the town at that time was the 29th. Captain Preston seemed to have been in command. He was sent for, went to the Custom-House, learned what had occurred, and at once put troops in motion. On they came up King Street, now State Street, with fixed bayonets, clearing everything before them as they came. They had nearly reached the head of King Street, when they met with opposition. A body of citizens had been formed nearby, and came pushing violently through the street then called Cornhill, around into King Street. They were armed only with clubs, sticks, and pieces of ice, but on they came. Nothing daunted, they went up to the points of the soldiers' bayonets. The long pent-up feeling of resentment against a foreign soldiery was finding a vent. This was the time and the opportunity to teach tyrants that freemen can at least strike back, though for the time they strike in vain.

At the head of this body of citizens was a stalwart colored man, Crispus Attucks. He was the leading spirit of their body, and their spokesman. They pressed the British sorely on all sides, making the best use of their rude arms, crying, "They dare not strike!" "Let us drive them out!" The soldiers stood firm; the reach of their long bayonets protected them from any serious injury for a while.

From time to time Attucks' voice could be heard urging his companions on. Said he, "The way to get rid of these soldiers is to attack the main guard; strike at the root! This is the nest!" At that time some one gave the order to fire. Captain Preston said he did not; at any rate the order was given. The soldiers fired. It was a death dealing volley. Of the citizens three lay dead, two mortally wounded, and a number more or less injured. Crispus Attucks, James Caldwell, and Samuel Gray were killed outright. Attucks fell, his face to the foe, with two bullets in his breast.

That night closed an eventful day. The first martyr-blood had reddened the streets of Boston, and the commencement of the downfall of British rule in America had set in. Said Daniel Webster, "From that moment we may date the severance of the British Empire. The patriotic fires kindled in the breasts of those earnest and true men, upon whose necks the British yoke never sat easily, never were quenched after that massacre, until the invader had been driven from the land and independence had been achieved. The sight of the blood of their comrades in King Street quickened their impulses, and hastened the day for a more general outbreak, which we now call the Revolutionary War." This was no mob, as some have been disposed to call it. They had not the low and groveling spirit which usually incites mobs. This was resistance to tyranny; this was striking for homes and firesides; this was the noblest work which a patriot can ever perform. As well call Lexington a mob and Bunker Hill a mob. I prefer to call this skirmish in King Street on the 5th of March, 1770, as Anson Burlingame called it, "The dawn of the Revolution."

About that time the American people set out to found a government to be dedicated to Freedom, which was to remain an asylum to the oppressed of all lands forever. The central idea of this government was to be Liberty, and a declaration was made by them to the world that all men are created free and equal, and have the right to life, liberty, and the pursuit of happiness. This was the government to be established in the land which had been fought for and won in the sacrifice of the blood of both black and white men. Did they do it? Did they intend to do it? Did they believe in and intend to carry out this magnificent declaration of principles—a declaration which startled the crowned heads of Europe and sent a thrill of delight to the hearts of the lovers of liberty through Christendom? No, they did not do it, neither did they intend to do it! This manifesto of July 4, 1776, was a fraud and a deception; it was the boldest falsification known to history; it was a sham and a lie. Instead of establishing freedom, they built, fostered and perpetuated slavery; instead of equality, they gave us inequality; instead of life, liberty, and the pursuit of happiness, they gave us death, bondage, and misery; instead of rearing on these shores a beautiful temple to Liberty, they made a foul den for slavery; and this country, which should have been the garden-spot of the world, covered with a prosperous and happy population of freemen, was, under the guidance of traitors to Liberty, made the prison-house of slaves, and betrayed in the house of her friends. The Goddess of Liberty, for nearly one hundred years after the establishment of our Government, sat in chains.

Attucks was in feelings, sympathies, and in all other respects, essentially an American, and so were the other colored patriots of the Revolution, and why shouldn't they be? They were born and bred here, and knew no other country; as was true of their fathers. They had been here as long as the Puritans. They came here the same year, 1620; in fact, had been here a little longer, for while Plymouth Rock was only reached in December of that year, the blacks were at Jamestown in the early spring. In every difficulty with the mother country, the colored men took sides with the colonists, and on every battle-field, when danger was to be met, they were found shoulder to shoulder with the rest of the Republicans, sharing the burden of war. At Lexington, where the farmers hastily seized their muskets and gathered on the plain, and at the bridge, to resist with the sacrifice of their lives the approach of the British forces, Prince Estabrook, "Negro man" as the *Salem Gazette* of that day called him, rallied with his neighbors and comrades in arms, and fell on the field, a wounded man, fighting the foe. He, like Attucks, was both of and with the people. Their cause was his cause, their home was his home, their fight was his fight. At Bunker Hill, a few months later, we know there was a goodly number of colored men; history has saved to us the names of some of them; how many there were whose names were not recorded, of course, we cannot now tell. Andover sent Tites Coburn, Alexander Ames, and Barzilai Low; Plymouth sent Cato Howe, and Peter Salem immortalized his name by leveling the piece in that battle which laid low Major Pitcairn. It is fair to presume that other towns, like Andover, sent in the ranks of their volunteers colored Americans. In the town of Raynham, within forty miles of Boston, there is now a settlement of colored people who have been there for three or four generations, the founder of which, Toby Gilmore, was an old Revolutionary veteran who had served his country faithfully. Stoughton Corner contributed Quack Matrick to the ranks of the Revolutionary soldiers; Lancaster sent Job Lewis, East Bridgewater Prince Richards. So did many other towns and States in this Commonwealth. Rhode

Island raised a regiment which did signal service at Red Bank in completely routing the Hessian force under Colonel Donop, but it was not in distinctively colored regiments or companies that colored men chiefly fought in the Revolution; it was in the ranks of any and all regiments, and by the side of their white companions in arms they were mainly to be found.

Attucks was born not a great way from Boston, at Farmingham, where his brothers and sisters lived for a long time. At some time during his life he was a slave; whether he was a slave at the time of the occurrence of the events I am now relating is not so clear. One of the witnesses at the trial of the soldiers testified that Attucks "belonged to New Providence, and was here on his way to North Carolina." I am inclined to think that at this time, in 1770, he was in the possession of his liberty, having got it in the same manner that very many slaves since obtained their freedom, by giving "leg-bail." Nearly twenty years before he had run away from his master, as appears from an advertisement in the *Boston Gazette* of November 20, 1750. From this advertisement it would appear that at the time of the engagement in King Street, Attucks was about 47 years of age, a powerful man, and an ugly foe to encounter. Twenty years of freedom, and moving from one part of the country to the other as far away as North Carolina, must have enlarged his views and given him the spirit of a free man. That he partook of the spirit which animated those of his countrymen who would throw off the British yoke is shown by the language used by him on this memorable occasion. "Let us drive out the rebels; they have no business here!" said he, and they re-echoed them. These words are full of meaning; they tell the story of the Revolution.

One hundred and six years have passed away. King Street and Royal Exchange Lane have lost their names. Cornhill has lost its identity. The King's collectors no longer gather at the Custom-House, and epauletted British officers no longer lounge away winter evenings in the reading-room of Concert Hall; that once stately pile is no more. One hundred and six years ago, George the Third was king, and these colonies were British dependencies. Since that time marvelous changes have been made in the world's history. Probably never before have so many and so great changes taken place in the same space of time. Slavery then existed in Massachusetts, as it did in the other colonies. It grew to huge proportions, and dominated all other interests in the land, and for years brought shame and disgrace upon us.

But our country now stands redeemed, disenthralled. The promises of 1776 are now realized. The immortal heroes of that age did not die in vain. We have now, thanks to the Author of All Good, a free country, a Republic of imperial proportions, a domain as extensive and a government as powerful as that of the nations of antiquity, or of the present time, and better than all over all this broad land there does not walk a slave. In this centennial anniversary of the nation's existence it is quite in order to suggest, and I do suggest that a monument be erected to the memory of the first martyr of the Revolution—Crispus Attucks.

ORATION ON THE OCCASION OF THE UNVEILING OF FREEDMEN'S MONUMENT[15]

BY FREDERICK DOUGLASS

Friends and Fellow Citizens:

I warmly congratulate you upon the highly interesting object which has caused you to assemble in such numbers and spirit as you have to-day. This occasion is, in some respects, remarkable. Wise and thoughtful men of our race, who shall come after us and study the lesson of our history in the United States; who shall survey the long and dreary spaces over which we have traveled; who shall count the links in the great chain of events by which we have reached our present position, will make a note of this occasion; they will think of it and speak of it with a sense of manly pride and complacency.

I congratulate you, also, upon the very favorable circumstances in which we meet to-day. They are high, inspiring, and uncommon. They lend grace, glory, and significance to the object for which we have met. Nowhere else in this great country, with its uncounted towns and cities, unlimited wealth, and immeasurable territory extending from sea to sea, could conditions be found more favorable to the success of this occasion than at this place.

We stand to-day at the national center to perform something like a national act—an act which is to go into history; and we are here where every pulsation of the national heart can be heard, felt, and reciprocated. A thousand wires, fed with thought and winged with lightning, put us in instantaneous communication with the loyal and true men over this country.

Few facts could better illustrate the vast and wonderful change which has taken place in our condition as a people than the fact of our assembling here for the purpose we have to-day. Harmless, beautiful, proper, and praiseworthy as this demonstration is, I cannot forget that no such demonstration would have been tolerated here twenty years ago. The spirit of slavery and barbarism, which still lingers to blight and destroy in some dark and distant parts of our country, would have made our assembling here the signal and excuse for opening upon us the flood-gates of wrath and violence. That we are here in peace to-day is a compliment and a credit to American civilization, and a prophecy of still greater enlightenment and progress in the future. I refer to the past, not in malice, but simply to place more distinctly in front the gratifying and glorious change which has come both to our white fellow citizens and ourselves, and to congratulate all upon the contrast between now and then; the new dispensation of freedom with its thousand blessings to both races, and the old dispensation of slavery with its ten thousand evils to both races—white and black. In view, then, of the past, the present, and the future, with the long and dark history of our bondage behind us, and with liberty, progress, and enlightenment before us, I again congratulate you upon this auspicious day and hour.

Friends and fellow citizens, the story of our presence here is soon and easily told. We are here in the District of Columbia, here in the City of Washington, the most luminous point of American territory, a city recently transformed and made beautiful in its body and in its spirit; we are here, in the place where the ablest and best men of the country are sent to devise the policy, enact the laws, and shape the destiny of the Republic; we are here, with the stately pillars and majestic dome of the Capitol of the nation looking down upon us; we are here, with the broad earth freshly adorned with the foliage and flowers of spring for our church, and all races, colors, and conditions of men for our congregation—in a word, we are here to express, as best we may, by appropriate forms and ceremonies, our grateful sense of the vast, high, and pre-eminent services rendered to ourselves, to our race, to our country, and to the whole world by Abraham Lincoln.

The sentiment that brings us here to-day is one of the noblest that can stir and thrill the human heart. It has crowned and made glorious the high places of all civilized nations with the grandest and most enduring works of art, designed to illustrate the characters and perpetuate the memories of great public men. It is the sentiment, which from year to year adorns with fragrant and beautiful flowers the graves of our loyal, brave, and patriotic soldiers who fell in defense of the Union and Liberty. It is the sentiment of gratitude and appreciation, which often, in the presence of many who hear me, has filled yonder heights of Arlington with the eloquence of eulogy and the sublime enthusiasm of poetry and song; a sentiment which can never die while the Republic lives.

For the first time in the history of our people, and in the history of the whole American people, we join in this high worship, and march conspicuously in the line of this time-honored custom. First things are always interesting, and this is one of our first things. It is the first time that, in this form and manner, we have sought to do honor to an American great man, however deserving and illustrious. I commend the fact to notice; let it be told in every part of the Republic; let men of all parties and opinions hear it; let those who despise us, not less than those who respect us, know that now and here, in the spirit of liberty, loyalty, and gratitude, let it be known everywhere, and by everybody who takes an interest in human progress and in the amelioration of the condition of mankind, that, in the presence and with the approval of the members of the American House of Representatives, reflecting the general sentiment of the country; that in the presence of that august body, the American Senate, representing the highest intelligence and the calmest judgment in the country; in the presence of the Supreme Court and Chief Justice of the United States, to whose decisions we all patriotically bow; in the presence and under the steady eye of the honored and trusted President of the United States, with the members of his wise and patriotic Cabinet, we, the colored people, newly emancipated and rejoicing in our blood-bought freedom, near the close of the first century in the life of this Republic, have now and here unveiled, set apart, and dedicated a monument of enduring granite and bronze, in every line, feature, and figure of which the men of this generation may read, and those of after-coming generations may read, something of the exalted character and great works of Abraham Lincoln, the first martyr President of the United States.

Fellow citizens, in what we have said and done today, and in what we may say and do hereafter, we disclaim everything like arrogance and assumption. We claim for ourselves no superior devotion to the character, history, and memory of the illustrious name whose monument we have here dedicated to-day. We fully comprehend the relations of Abraham Lincoln, both to ourselves and to the white people of the United States. Truth is proper and beautiful at all times and in all places, and it is never more proper and beautiful in any case than when speaking of a great public man whose example is likely to be commended for honor and imitation long after his departure to the solemn shades—the silent continents of eternity. It must be admitted, truth compels me to admit, even here in the presence of the monument we have erected to his memory, Abraham Lincoln was not, in the fullest sense of the word, either our man or our model. In his interests, in his associations, in his habits of thought, and in his prejudices, he was a white man.

He was pre-eminently the white man's President, entirely devoted to the welfare of the white man. He was ready and willing at any time during the first years of his administration to deny, postpone, and sacrifice the rights of humanity in the colored people to promote the welfare of the white people of this country. In all his education and feeling he was an American of the Americans. He came into the Presidential chair upon one principle alone, namely, opposition to the extension of slavery. His arguments in furtherance of this policy had their motive and mainspring in his patriotic devotion to the interests of his own race. To protect, defend, and perpetuate slavery in the States where it existed Abraham Lincoln was not less ready than any other President to draw the sword of the nation. He was ready to execute all the supposed constitutional guarantees of the United States Constitution in favor of the slave system anywhere inside of the slave States. He was willing to pursue, re-capture, and send back the fugitive slave to his master, and to suppress a slave rising for liberty, though his guilty master were already in arms against the Government. The race to which we belong was not the special object of his consideration. Knowing this, I concede to you, my white fellow citizens, a pre-eminence in this worship at once full and supreme. First, midst, and last, you and yours were the objects of his deepest affection and his most earnest solicitude. You are the children of Abraham Lincoln. We are at best, only his step-children; children by adoption, children by force of circumstances and necessity. To you it especially belongs to sound his praises, to preserve and perpetuate his memory, to multiply his statues, to hang his pictures high upon your walls, and commend his example, for to you he was a great and glorious friend and benefactor. Instead of supplanting you at this altar, we would exhort you to build high his monuments; let them be of the most costly material, of the most cunning workmanship; let their forms be symmetrical, beautiful, and perfect; let their bases be upon solid rocks, and their summits lean against the unchanging blue, overhanging sky, and let them endure forever! But while, in the abundance of your wealth, and in the fullness of your just and patriotic devotion, you do all this, we entreat you to despise not the humble offering we this day unveil to view; for while Abraham Lincoln saved for you a country, he delivered us from a bondage, according to Jefferson, one hour of which was worse than ages of the oppression your fathers rose in rebellion to oppose.

Fellow citizens, ours is no new-born zeal and devotion—merely a thing of the moment. The name of Abraham Lincoln was near and dear to our hearts in the darkest and most perilous hours of the Republic. We were no more ashamed of him when shrouded in clouds of darkness, of doubt and defeat, than when we saw him crowned with victory, honor, and glory. Our faith in him was often taxed and strained to the uttermost, but it never failed. When he tarried long in the mountains; when he strangely told us that we were the cause of the war; when he still more strangely told us to leave the land in which we were born; when he refused to employ our arms in defense of the Union; when, after accepting our services as colored soldiers, he refused to retaliate our murder and torture as colored prisoners; when he told us he would save the Union, if he could, with slavery; when he revoked the Proclamation of Emancipation of General Fremont; when he refused to remove the popular Commander of the Army of the Potomac, in the days of its inaction and defeat, who was more zealous in his efforts to protect slavery than to suppress rebellion; when we saw all this and more, we were at times grieved, stunned, and greatly bewildered, but our hearts believed, while they ached and bled. Nor was this, at that time, a blind and unreasoning superstition. Despite the mist and haze that surround him; despite the tumult, the hurry, and confusion of the hour, we were able to take a comprehensive view of Abraham Lincoln, and to make reasonable allowance for the circumstances of his position. We saw him, measured him, and estimated him; not by stray utterances to injudicious and tedious delegations, who often tried his patience; not by isolated facts, torn from their connection; not by partial and imperfect glimpses caught at inopportune moments; but by a broad survey, in the light of the stern logic of great events, and in view of that divinity which "shapes our ends, rough hew them as we will," we came to the conclusion that the hour and the man of our redemption had somehow met in the person of Abraham Lincoln. It mattered little to us what language he might employ on special occasions; it mattered little to us when we fully knew him, whether he was swift or slow in his movements; it was enough for us that Abraham Lincoln was at the head of a great movement, and was in living and earnest sympathy with that movement, which, in the nature of things, must go on until slavery should be utterly and forever abolished in the United States.

When, therefore, it shall be asked what we have to do with the memory of Abraham Lincoln, or what Abraham Lincoln had to do with us, the answer is ready, full, and complete. Though he loved Cæsar less than Rome, though the Union was more to him than our freedom or our future, under his wise and beneficent rule, and by measures approved and vigorously pressed by him, we saw that the handwriting of ages, in the form of prejudice and proscription, was rapidly fading away from the face of our whole country; under his rule, and in due time, about as soon, after all, as the country could tolerate the strange spectacle, we saw our brave sons and brothers laying off the rags of bondage, and being clothed all over in the blue uniforms of the soldiers of the United States; under his rule, we saw two hundred thousand of our dark and dusky people responding to the call of Abraham Lincoln, and with muskets on their shoulders, and eagles on their buttons, timing their high footsteps to liberty and union under the national flag; under his rule, we saw the independence of the black Republic of Haiti, the special object of slave-holding aversion and horror, fully recognized, and her minister, a colored gentleman, duly received here in the City of Washington; under his rule, we saw the internal slave-trade, which so long disgraced the nation, abolished, and slavery abolished in the District of Columbia; under his rule, we saw, for the first time, the law enforced against the foreign slave-trade, and the first slave-trader hanged like any other pirate or murderer; under his rule, assisted by the greatest captain of our age, and his inspiration, we saw the Confederate States, based upon the idea that our race must be slaves, and slaves forever, battered to pieces and scattered to the four winds; under his rule, and in the fullness of time, we saw Abraham Lincoln, after giving the slave-holders three months' grace in which to save their hateful slave system, penning the immortal paper, which, though special in its language, was general in its principles and effect, making slavery forever impossible in the United States. Though we waited long, we saw all this and more.

Can any colored man, or any white man friendly to the freedom of all men, ever forget the night which followed the first day of January, 1863, when the world was to see if Abraham Lincoln would prove to be as good as his word? I shall never forget that memorable night, when in a distant city, I waited and watched at a public meeting, with three thousand others not less anxious than myself, for the word of deliverance which we have heard read to-day. Nor shall I ever forget the outburst of joy and thanksgiving that rent the air when the lightning brought to us the Emancipation Proclamation. In that happy hour we forgot all delay, and forgot all tardiness, forgot that the President had bribed the rebels to lay down their arms by a promise to withhold the bolt that should smite the slave-system with destruction; and we were thenceforward willing to allow the President all the latitude of time, phraseology, and every honorable device that statesmanship might require for the achievement of a great and beneficent measure of liberty and progress.

Fellow citizens, there is little necessity on this occasion to speak at length and critically of this great and good man, and of his high mission in the world. That ground has been fully occupied and completely covered both here and elsewhere. The whole field of fact and fancy has been gleaned and garnered. Any man can say things that are true of Abraham Lincoln, but no man can say anything that is new of Abraham Lincoln. His personal traits and public acts are better known to the American people than are those of any other man of his age. He was a mystery to no man who saw and heard him. Though high in position, the humblest could approach him and feel at home in his presence. Though deep, he was transparent; though strong, he was gentle; though decided and pronounced in his convictions, he was tolerant towards those who differed from him, and patient under reproaches. Even those who only knew him through his public utterances obtained a tolerably clear idea of his character and personality. The image of the man went out with his words, and those who read them knew him.

I have said that President Lincoln was a white man and shared the prejudices common to his countrymen towards the colored race. Looking back to his times and to the condition of his country, we are compelled to admit that this unfriendly feeling on his part may safely be set down as one element of his wonderful success in organizing the loyal American people for the tremendous conflict before them, and bringing them safely through that conflict. His great mission was to accomplish two things: first, to save his country from dismemberment and ruin; and secondly, to free his country from the great crime of slavery. To do one or the other, or both, he must have the earnest sympathy and the powerful co-operation of his loyal fellow countrymen. Without this primary and essential condition to success his efforts must have been vain and utterly fruitless. Had he put the abolition of slavery before the salvation of the Union, he would have inevitably driven from him a powerful class of American people and rendered resistance to rebellion impossible. Viewed from the genuine abolition ground, Mr. Lincoln seemed tardy, cold, dull, and indifferent; but measuring him by the sentiment of his country, a sentiment he was bound as a statesman to consult, he was swift, zealous, radical, and determined.

Though Mr. Lincoln shared the prejudices of his white countrymen against the Negro, it is hardly necessary to say that in his heart of hearts he loathed and hated slavery.[16] The man who could say "Fondly do we hope, fervently do we pray, that this mighty scourge of war shall soon pass away, yet if God wills it continue till all the wealth piled by two hundred years of bondage shall have been wasted, and each drop of blood drawn by the lash shall have been paid for by one drawn by the sword, the judgments of the Lord are true and righteous altogether," gives all needed proof of his feeling on the subject of slavery. He was willing, while the South was loyal, that it should have its pound of flesh, because he thought it was so nominated in the bond; but farther than this, no earthly power could make him go.

Fellow citizens, whatever else in the world may be partial, unjust, and uncertain, time—time—is impartial, just, and certain in its action. In the realm of mind, as well as in the realm of matter, it is a great worker, and often works wonders. The honest and comprehensive statesman, clearly discerning the needs of his country, and earnestly endeavoring to do his whole duty, though covered and blistered with reproaches, may safely leave his course to the silent judgment of time. Few great public men have ever been the victims of fiercer denunciation than Abraham Lincoln was during his administration. He was often wounded in the house of his friends. Reproaches came thick and fast from within and from without, and from opposite quarters. He was assailed by abolitionists; he was assailed by slave-holders; he was assailed by the men who were for peace at any price; he was assailed by those who were for a more vigorous prosecution of the way; he was assailed for not making the war an abolition war; and he was most bitterly assailed for making the war an abolition war.

But now behold the change; the judgment of the present hour is, that taking him for all in all, measuring the tremendous magnitude of the work before him, considering the necessary means to ends, and surveying the end from the beginning, infinite wisdom has seldom sent any man into the world better fitted for his mission than Abraham Lincoln. His birth, his training, and his natural endowments, both mental and physical, were strongly in his favor. Born and reared among the lowly, a stranger to wealth and luxury, compelled to grapple single-handed with the flintiest hardships of life, from tender youth to sturdy manhood, he grew strong in the manly and heroic qualities demanded by the great mission to which he was called by the votes of his countrymen. The hard condition of his early life, which would have depressed and broken down weaker men, only gave greater life, vigor, and buoyancy to the heroic spirit of Abraham Lincoln. He was ready for any kind and quality of work. What other young men dreaded in the shape of toil, he took hold of with the utmost cheerfulness.

"A spade, a rake, a hoe,
A pick-axe, or a bill,
A hook to reap, a scythe to mow
A flail, or what you will."

All day long he could split heavy rails in the woods, and half the night long he could study his English Grammar by the uncertain flare and glare of the light made by a pine-knot. He was at home on the land with his axe, with his maul, with gluts, and his wedges; and he was equally at home on water, with his oars, with his poles, with his planks, and with his boat-hooks. And whether in his flat-boat on the Mississippi River, or on the fireside of his frontier cabin, he was a man of work. A son of toil himself, he was linked in brotherly sympathy with the sons of toil in every loyal part of the Republic. This very fact gave him tremendous power with the American people, and materially contributed not only to selecting him to the Presidency, but in sustaining his administration of the Government.

Upon his inauguration as President of the United States, an office, even where assumed under the most favorable conditions, fitted to tax and strain the largest abilities, Abraham Lincoln was met by a tremendous crisis. He was called upon, not merely to administer the government, but to decide in the face of terrible odds, the fate of the Republic.

A formidable rebellion rose in his path before him; the Union was practically dissolved; his country was torn and rent asunder at the center. Hostile armies were already organized against the Republic, armed with the munitions of war which the Republic had provided for its own defense. The tremendous question for him to decide was whether his country should survive the crisis and flourish, or be dismembered and perish. His predecessor in office had already decided the question in favor of national dismemberment, by denying to it the right of self-defense and self-preservation—a right which belongs to the meanest insect.

Happily for the country, happily for you and me, the judgment of James Buchanan, the patrician, was not the judgment of Abraham Lincoln, the plebeian. He brought his strong common sense, sharpened in the school of adversity, to bear upon the question. He did not hesitate, he did not doubt, he did not falter but at once resolved, at whatever peril, at whatever cost, the Union of the States should be preserved. A patriot himself, his faith was strong and unwavering in the patriotism of his countrymen. Timid men said, before Mr. Lincoln's inauguration, that we had seen the last President of the United States. A voice in influential quarters said, "Let the Union slide."

Some said that a Union maintained by the sword was worthless. Others said that a rebellion of 8,000,000, cannot be suppressed; but in the midst of all this tumult and timidity, and against all this, Abraham Lincoln was clear in his duty, and had an oath in heaven. He calmly and bravely heard the voice of doubt and fear all around him; but he had an oath in heaven, and there was not power enough on earth to make this honest boatman, backwoodsman, and broad-handed splitter of rails evade or violate that sacred oath. He had not been schooled in the ethics of slavery; his plain life had favored his love of truth. He had not been taught that treason and perjury were the proofs of honor and honesty. His moral training was against his saying one thing when he meant another. The trust which Abraham Lincoln had in himself and in the people was surprising and grand, but it was also enlightened and well-founded. He knew the American people better than they knew themselves, and his truth was based upon this knowledge.

Fellow citizens, the fourteenth day of April, 1865, of which this is the eleventh anniversary, is now, and will ever remain a memorable day in the annals of this Republic. It was on the evening of this day, while a fierce and sanguinary rebellion was in the last stages of its desolating power; while its armies were broken and scattered before the invincible armies of Grant and Sherman; while a great nation, torn and rent by war, was already beginning to raise to the skies loud anthems of joy at the dawn of peace, it was startled, amazed, and overwhelmed by the crowning crime of slavery—the assassination of Abraham Lincoln. It was a new crime, a pure act of malice. No purpose of the rebellion was to be served by it. It was the simple gratification of a hell-black spirit of revenge. But it has done good, after all. It has filled the country with a deeper abhorrence of slavery and a deep love for the great liberator.

Had Abraham Lincoln died from any of the numerous ills to which flesh is heir; had he reached that good old age of which his vigorous constitution and his temperate habits gave promise; had he been permitted to see the end of his great work; had the solemn curtain of death come down but gradually—we should still have been smitten with a heavy grief, and treasured his name lovingly. But dying, as he did die, by the red hand of violence, killed, assassinated, taken off without warning, not because of personal hate,—for no man who knew Abraham Lincoln could hate him—but because of his fidelity to union and liberty, he is doubly dear to us, and his memory will be precious forever.

Fellow citizens, I end, as I began, with congratulations. We have done a good work for our race to-day. In doing honor to the memory of our friend and liberator, we have been doing highest honors to ourselves and those who come after us; we have been fastening ourselves to a name and fame imperishable and immortal; we have also been defending ourselves from a blighting scandal. When now it shall be said that the colored man is soulless, that he has no appreciation of benefits or benefactors; when the foul reproach of ingratitude is hurled at us, and it is attempted to scourge us beyond the range of human brotherhood, we may calmly point to the monument we have this day erected to the memory of Abraham Lincoln.

ADDRESS DURING THE PRESIDENTIAL CAMPAIGN OF 1880[17]

BY PINKNEY BENTON STEWART PINCHBACK

PINKNEY BENTON STEWART PINCHBACK *is one of the most interesting and picturesque figures in the race. A staunch fighter in the Reconstruction period in Louisiana, a delegate to many national Republican Conventions; Ex-Lieutenant-Governor of Louisiana.*

Mr. President and Fellow Citizens:

The founders of the Republican party were aggressive men. They believed in the Declaration of Independence and the great truths it contains; and their purpose was to make these truths living realities. Possessing the courage of their convictions and regarding slavery as the arch enemy of the Republic—the greatest obstruction to its maintenance, advancement and prosperity,—they proclaimed an eternal war against it and, marshalling their forces under the banner of freedom and equality before the law for all men, boldly and defiantly met the enemy at every point and fairly routed it all along the line. Those men believed in and relied upon the conscience of the people. To touch and arouse public conscience and to convince it of the justice of their cause, they felt was all that was necessary to enlist the people on their side. Ridiculed, threatened, ostracised, and assaulted, they could not be turned from their purpose, and their achievements constitute the grandeur and glory of the Republican party. There were no apologists for wrong-doers among those men, and there ought to be none in the Republican party to-day. The South was the great disturbing element then as it is now; and the causes which rendered it so are, in a large measure, the same. The people were divided into three classes—slave-holders, slaves, and poor whites, or "poor white trash" as the latter were called by the colored people because of their utter insignificance in that community. Its peculiar condition established in the large land and slave-owning portion of the people a sort of privileged class who claimed and exercised the right not only to rule the South, but the nation; and for many years that class controlled both. Gorged with wealth and drunk with power, considering themselves born to command and govern, being undisputed rulers, almost by inheritance in their States, the Southern politicians naturally became aggressive, dictatorial, and determined to ruin the country and sever the Union rather than consent to relinquish power, even though called upon to do so by constituted methods. Hence it was that, when the people of the great North and Northwest concluded to assert their rights and choose a man from among themselves for President, they rebelled and forced upon the country so far as they were concerned, the most causeless and unnatural war recorded in history.

I shall not dwell upon the history of the war or attempt to detail its horrors and sum up its cost. I leave that task to others. If the wounds made by it have been healed, which I do not concede, far be it from my purpose to re-open them. My sole reason for referring to the war at all is to remind the Northern people of some of the agencies employed in its successful prosecution. When it commenced, the principal labor element of the South—the source of its production and wealth—was the colored race. Four millions and a half of these unfortunate people were there, slaves and property of the men who refused to submit to the will of the people lawfully expressed through the ballot-box. They were the bone and sinew of the Confederacy, tilling its fields and producing sustenance for its armies, while many of the best men of the North were compelled to abandon Northern fields to shoulder a musket in defense of the Union. As a war measure and to deprive the South of such a great advantage, your President, the immortal Lincoln, issued a proclamation in September, 1862, in which he gave public notice that it was his purpose to declare the emancipation of the slaves in the States wherein insurrection existed on January 1, 1863, unless the offenders therein lay down their arms. That notice, thank God, was disregarded, and the proclamation of January 1, 1863, proclaiming universal emancipation followed. Had the requirements of the first proclamation been observed by the people to whom it was addressed who can doubt what would have been the fate of the colored people in the South? It is reasonable to assume, inasmuch as the war was waged to perpetuate the Union and not to destroy slavery—that they would have remained in hopeless bondage. On more than one occasion President Lincoln officially declared that he would save the Union with slavery if he could, and not until it became manifest that slavery was the mainstay of the Confederacy, and the prosecution of the war to a successful close would be difficult without its destruction, did he dare touch it. I do not think that President Lincoln's hesitancy to act upon the question arose from sympathy with the accursed institution, for I believe every pulsation of his heart was honest and pure and that he was an ardent and devoted lover of universal liberty; but he doubted whether his own people would approve of his interference with it. Assured by the manner in which the people of the North received his first proclamation that they appreciated the necessity of destroying this great aid of the enemy, he went forward bravely declaring that, "possibly for every drop of blood drawn by the lash one might have to be drawn by the sword, but if so, as was said over eighteen hundred years ago, the judgments of the Lord are just and righteous altogether," and abolished human slavery from the land forever.

That this great act was a Godsend and an immeasurable blessing to the colored race, I admit, but I declare in the same breath that it was dictated and performed more in the interest of the white people of the North and to aid them in conquering the rebellion than from love of or a disposition to help the Negro. The enfranchisement of the colored race also sprang from the necessities of the nation. At the close of the war the Southern States had to be rehabilitated with civil governments and re-admitted into the Union. The men who had plunged the country into war and had tried to destroy the Government were about to resume their civil and political rights, and, through the election of Representatives and Senators in Congress, regain influence and power in national councils. Apprehending danger from the enormous power they would possess if reinstated in absolute control of eleven States, some means had to be devised to prevent this. A political element, loyal to the Union and the flag, must be created; and again the ever faithful colored people were brought into requisition, and without their asking for it, the elective franchise was conferred upon them. There was no question about the loyalty of these people, and the supposition that they would be a valuable political force and form the basis of a loyal political party in the South was both natural and just, and the wisdom of their enfranchisement was demonstrated by the establishment of Republican governments in several of the States, and the sending of mixed delegations of Republican and Democratic members of Congress therefrom so long as the laws conferring citizenship upon the colored man were enforced.

If the South is to remain politically Democratic as it is to-day, it is not the fault of the colored people. Their fealty to the North and the Republican party is without parallel in the world's history. In Louisiana alone more than five thousand lives attest it. While in nearly every other Southern State fully as many lie in premature graves, martyrs to the cause. Considering themselves abandoned and left to the choice of extermination or the relinquishment of the exercise of their political rights, they have, in large districts in the South, wisely preferred the latter. Kept in a constant condition of suspense and dread by the peculiar methods of conducting canvasses and elections in that section, who can blame them? It is my firm conviction that no other people under God's sun, similarly situated, would have done half so well. The fault is attributable to the vicious practise, which obtains largely even here in the civilized North, of apologizing for and condoning crimes committed for political purposes. Men love power everywhere and Southern Democrats are no exception. On the contrary, deeming themselves "born to command," as I have already remarked, and knowing that there is no power to restrain or punish them for crimes committed upon the poor and defenseless colored citizens, of course they have pushed them to the wall. The inequality between the two races in all that constitutes protective forces was such as to render that result inevitable as soon as Federal protection was withdrawn, and I do not hesitate to affirm that unless some means are devised to enforce respect for the rights of the colored citizens of the South, their enfranchisement will prove a curse instead of a benefit to the country. Emancipated to cripple the South and enfranchised to strengthen the North, the colored race was freed and its people made citizens in the interest of the Republic. Its fundamental law declares them citizens, and the Fifteenth Amendment expressly states that: "The right of citizens of the United States to vote shall not be denied or abridged by the United States or by any State on account of race, color, or previous condition of servitude." The faith and honor of the Nation are pledged to the rigid enforcement of the law in this, as in every other respect, and the interests of the 40,000,000 white people in the Republic demand it. If the law, both constitutional and statutory, affecting the rights and privileges of the colored citizens can be defiantly ignored and disobeyed in eleven States of the Union in a matter of such grave import as this—a matter involving the very essence of republican government, *i. e.*, the right of the majority to rule—who can tell where it will end and how long it will be before elections in all of the States will be armed conflicts, to be decided by the greatest prowess and dexterity in the use of the bowie knife, pistol, shot-gun and rifle?

White men of the North, I tell you this practise of controlling elections in the South by force and fraud is contagious! It spreads with alarming rapidity and unless eradicated, will overtake and overwhelm you as it has your friends in the South. It showed its horrid head in Maine, and came very near wresting that State from a lawful majority. Employed in the South first to drive Republicans from a few counties, it has grown from "autumnal outbreaks" into an almost perpetual hurricane and, gathering force as it goes, has violently seized State after State, mastered the entire South, and is even now thundering at the gates of the national Capital. Whether it shall capture it too, and spread its blighting influence all over the land, is the question *you* must answer at the poles in this election.

It was the intention of the great men who founded this Republic that it should be "A government of the people, for the people, and by the people"; that its citizens, from the highest to the lowest, should enjoy perfect equality before the law. To realize this idea the rule of the majority, to be ascertained through the processes provided by law, was wisely adopted, and the laws providing for and regulating elections are respected and obeyed in the Northern, Eastern, and Western States. The Democracy of the South alone seems privileged to set at defiance the organic as well as every statutory enactment, national and State, designed to secure this essential principle of free government. Those men must be taught that such an exceptional and unhealthy condition of things will not be tolerated; that the rights of citizens of every nationality are sacred in the eyes of the law, and their right to vote for whom they please and have their ballots honestly counted shall not be denied or abridged with impunity; that the faith of the Nation is pledged to the defense and maintenance of these obligations, and it will keep its pledge at whatever cost may be found necessary.

THE BLACK WOMAN OF THE SOUTH: HER NEGLECTS AND HER NEEDS[18]

BY ALEXANDER CRUMMELL, D. D., LL. D.

ALEXANDER CRUMMELL, D.D., *an eminent Negro Episcopal clergyman; a graduate of Oxford University, England; professor in a Liberian College; rector of St. Luke's in Washington and founder of the Negro Academy.*

It is an age clamorous everywhere for the dignities, the grand prerogatives, and the glory of woman. There is not a country in Europe where she has not risen somewhat above the degradation of centuries, and pleaded successfully for a new position and a higher vocation. As the result of this new reformation we see her, in our day, seated in the lecture-rooms of ancient universities, rivaling her brothers in the fields of literature, the grand creators of ethereal art, the participants in noble civil franchises, the moving spirit in grand reformations, and the guide, agent, or assistant in all the noblest movements for the civilization and regeneration of man.

In these several lines of progress the American woman has run on in advance of her sisters in every other quarter of the globe. The advantage, she has received, the rights and prerogatives she has secured for herself, are unequaled by any other class of women in the world. It will not be thought amiss, then, that I come here to-day to present to your consideration the one grand exception to this general superiority of women, viz., *The black woman of the South.*

* * * * *

The rural or plantation population of the South was made up almost entirely of people of pure Negro blood. And this brings out also the other disastrous fact, namely, that this large black population has been living from the time of their introduction into America, a period of more than two hundred years, in a state of unlettered rudeness. The Negro all this time has been an intellectual starveling. This has been more especially the condition of the black woman of the South. Now and then a black man has risen above the debased condition of his people. Various causes would contribute to the advantage of the *men*: the relation of servants to superior masters; attendance at courts with them; their presence at political meetings; listening to table-talk behind their chairs; traveling as valets; the privilege of books and reading in great houses, and with indulgent masters—all these served to lift up a black *man* here and there to something like superiority. But no such fortune fell to the lot of the plantation woman. The black woman of the South was left perpetually in a state of hereditary darkness and rudeness.

* * * * *

In her girlhood all the delicate tenderness of her sex was rudely outraged. In the field, in the rude cabin, in the press-room, in the factory, she was thrown into the companionship of coarse and ignorant men. No chance was given her for delicate reserve or tender modesty. From her girlhood she was the doomed victim of the grossest passions. All the virtues of her sex were utterly ignored. If the instinct of chastity asserted itself, then she had to fight like a tigress for the ownership and possession of her own person; and, ofttimes, had to suffer pains and lacerations for her virtuous self-assertion. When she reached maturity all the tender instincts of her womanhood were ruthlessly violated. At the age of marriage—always prematurely anticipated under slavery—she was mated, as the stock of the plantation were mated, *not* to be the companion of a loved and chosen husband, but to be the breeder of human cattle, for the field or the auction-block. With that mate she went out, morning after morning to toil, as a common field-hand. As it was *his*, so likewise was it her lot to wield the heavy hoe, or to follow the plow, or to gather in the crops. She was a "hewer of wood and a drawer of water." She was a common field-hand. She had to keep her place in the gang from morn till eve, under the burden of a heavy task, or under the stimulus or the fear of a cruel lash. She was a picker of cotton. She labored at the sugar-mill and in the tobacco-factory. When, through weariness or sickness, she has fallen behind her allotted task, there came, as punishment, the fearful stripes upon her shrinking, lacerated flesh.

Her home life was of the most degrading nature. She lived in the rudest huts, and partook of the coarsest food, and dressed in the scantiest garb, and slept, in multitudinous cabins, upon the hardest boards.

Thus she continued a beast of burden down to the period of those maternal anxieties which, in ordinary civilized life, give repose, quiet, and care to expectant mothers. But, under the slave system, few such relaxations were allowed. And so it came to pass that little children were ushered into this world under conditions which many cattle-raisers would not suffer for their flocks or herds. Thus she became the mother of children. But even then there was for her no suretyship of motherhood, or training, or control. Her own offspring were *not* her own. She and husband and children were all the property of others. All these sacred ties were constantly snapped and cruelly sundered. *This* year she had one husband; and next year, through some auction sale, she might be separated from him and mated to another. There was no sanctity of family, no binding tie of marriage, none of the fine felicities and the endearing affections of home. None of these things was the lot of

Southern black women. Instead thereof, a gross barbarism which tended to blunt the tender sensibilities, to obliterate feminine delicacy and womanly shame, came down as her heritage from generation to generation; and it seems a miracle of providence and grace that, notwithstanding these terrible circumstances, so much struggling virtue lingered amid these rude cabins, that so much womanly worth and sweetness abided in their bosoms, as slave-holders themselves have borne witness to.

But some of you will ask: "Why bring up these sad memories of the past? Why distress us with these dead and departed cruelties?" Alas, my friends, these are not dead things. Remember that

"The evil that men do lives after them."

The evil of gross and monstrous abominations, the evil of great organic institutions crop out long after the departure of the institutions themselves. If you go to Europe you will find not only the roots, but likewise many of the deadly fruits of the old Feudal system still surviving in several of its old states and kingdoms. So, too, with slavery. The eighteen years of freedom have not obliterated all its deadly marks from either the souls or bodies of the black woman. The conditions of life, indeed, have been modified since emancipation; but it still maintains that the black woman is the Pariah woman of this land! We have, indeed, degraded women, immigrants, from foreign lands. In their own countries some of them were so low in the social scale that they were yoked with the cattle to plow the fields. They were rude, unlettered, coarse, and benighted. But when they reach *this* land there comes an end to their degraded condition.

"They touch our country and their shackles fall."

As soon as they become grafted into the stock of American life they partake at once of all its large gifts and its noble resources.

Not so with the black woman of the South. Freed, legally she has been; but the act of emancipation had no talismanic influence to reach to and alter and transform her degrading social life.

When that proclamation was issued she might have heard the whispered words in her every hut, "Open, Sesame;" but, so far as her humble domicile and her degraded person were concerned, there was no invisible but gracious Genii who, on the instant, could transmute the rudeness of her hut into instant elegance, and change the crude surroundings of her home into neatness, taste, and beauty.

The truth is, "Emancipation Day" found her a prostrate and degraded being; and, although it has brought numerous advantages to her sons, it has produced but the simplest changes in her social and domestic condition. She is still the crude, rude, ignorant mother. Remote from cities, the dweller still in the old plantation hut, neighboring to the sulky, disaffected master class, who still think her freedom was a personal robbery of themselves, none of the "fair humanities" have visited her humble home. The light of knowledge has not fallen upon her eyes. The fine domesticities which give the charm to family life, and which, by the refinement and delicacy of womanhood, preserve the civilization of nations, have not come to *her*. She has still the rude, coarse labor of men. With her rude husband she still shares the hard service of a field-hand. Her house, which shelters, perhaps, some six or eight children, embraces but two rooms. Her furniture is of the rudest kind. The clothing of the household is scant and of the coarsest material, has ofttimes the garniture of rags; and for herself and offspring is marked, not seldom, by the absence of both hats and shoes. She has rarely been taught to sew, and the field labor of slavery times has kept her ignorant of the habitudes of neatness, and the requirements of order. Indeed, coarse food, coarse clothes, coarse living, coarse manners, coarse companions, coarse surroundings, coarse neighbors, both black and white, yea, every thing coarse, down to the coarse, ignorant, senseless religion, which excites her sensibilities and starts her passions, go to make up the life of the masses of black women in the hamlets and villages of the rural South.

This is the state of black womanhood. Take the girlhood of this same region, and it presents the same aspect, save that in large districts the white man has not forgotten the olden times of slavery and with indeed the deepest sentimental abhorrence of "amalgamation," still thinks that the black girl is to be perpetually the victim of his lust! In the larger towns and in cities our girls in common schools and academies are receiving superior culture. Of the 15,000 colored school teachers in the South, more than half are colored young women, educated since emancipation. But even these girls, as well as their more ignorant sisters in rude huts, are followed and tempted and insulted by the ruffianly element of Southern society, who think that black *men* have no rights which white men should regard, and black *women* no virtue which white men should respect!

And now look at the *vastness* of this degradation. If I had been speaking of the population of a city, or a town, or even a village, the tale would be a sad and melancholy one. But I have brought before you the condition of millions of women. According to the census of 1880 there were, in the Southern States, 3,327,678 females of all ages of the African race. Of these there were 674,365 girls between twelve and twenty, 1,522,696 between twenty and eighty. "These figures," remarks an observing friend of mine, "are startling!"

And when you think that the masses of these women live in the rural districts; that they grow up in rudeness and ignorance; that their former masters are using few means to break up their hereditary degradation, you can easily take in the pitiful condition of this population, and forecast the inevitable future to multitudes of females unless a mighty special effort is made for the improvement of the black womanhood of the South.

I know the practical nature of the American mind, I know how the question of values intrudes itself into even the domain of philanthropy; and, hence, I shall not be astonished if the query suggests itself, whether special interest in the black woman will bring any special advantage to the American nation.

Let me dwell for a few moments upon this phase of the subject. Possibly the view I am about suggesting has never before been presented to the American mind. But, Negro as I am, I shall make no apology for venturing the claim that the Negress is one of the most interesting of all the classes of women on the globe. I am speaking of her, not as a perverted and degraded creature, but in her natural state, with her native instincts and peculiarities.

Let me repeat just here the words of a wise, observing, tender-hearted philanthropist, whose name and worth and words have attained celebrity. It is fully forty years ago since the celebrated Dr. Channing said: "We are holding in bondage one of the best races of the human family. The Negro is among the mildest, gentlest of men. He is singularly susceptible of improvement from abroad.... His nature is affectionate, easily touched, and hence he is more open to religious improvement than the white man.... The African carries with him much more than *we* the genius of a meek, long-suffering, loving virtue."

I should feel ashamed to allow these words to fall from my lips if it were not necessary to the lustration of the character of my black sisters of the South. I do not stand here to-day to plead for the black *man*. He is a man; and if he is weak he must go the wall. He is a man; he must fight his own way, and if he is strong in mind and body, he can take care of himself. But for the mothers, sisters, and daughters of my race I have a right to speak. And when I think of their sad condition down South; think, too, that since the day of emancipation hardly any one has lifted up a voice in their behalf, I feel it a duty and a privilege to set forth their praises and to extol their excellencies. For, humble and benighted as she is, the black woman of the South is one of the queens of womanhood. If there is any other woman on this earth who in native aboriginal qualities is her superior, I know not where she is to be found; for, I do say, that in tenderness of feeling, in genuine native modesty, in large disinterestedness, in sweetness of disposition and deep humility, in unselfish devotedness, and in warm, motherly assiduities, the Negro woman is unsurpassed by any other woman on this earth.

The testimony to this effect is almost universal—our enemies themselves being witnesses. You know how widely and how continuously, for generations, the Negro has been traduced, ridiculed, derided. Some of you may remember the journals and the hostile criticisms of Coleridge and Trollope and Burton, West Indian and African travelers. Very many of you may remember the philosophical disquisitions of the ethnological school of 1847, the contemptuous dissertations of Hunt and Gliddon. But it is worthy of notice in all these cases that the sneer, the contempt, the bitter gibe, have been invariably leveled against the black *man*—never against the black woman! On the contrary, *she* has almost everywhere been extolled and eulogized. The black man was called a stupid, thick-lipped, flat-nosed, long-heeled, empty-headed animal; the link between the baboon and the human being, only fit to be a slave! But everywhere, even in the domains of slavery, how tenderly has the Negress been spoken of! She has been the nurse of childhood. To her all the cares and heart-griefs of youth have been intrusted. Thousands and tens of thousands in the West Indies and in our Southern States have risen up and told the tale of her tenderness, of her gentleness, patience, and affection. No other woman in the world has ever had such tributes to a high moral nature, sweet, gentle love, and unchanged devotedness. And by the memory of my own mother and dearest sisters I can declare it to be true!

Hear the tribute of Michelet: "The Negress, of all others, is the most loving, the most generating; and this, not only because of her youthful blood, but we must also admit, for the richness of her heart. She is loving among the loving, good among the good. (Ask the travelers whom she has so often saved.) Goodness is creative; it is fruitfulness; it is the very benediction of a holy act. The fact that woman is so fruitful I attribute to her treasures of tenderness, to that ocean of goodness which permeates her heart.... Africa is a woman. Her races are feminine.... In many of the black tribes of Central Africa the women rule, and they are as intelligent as they are amiable and kind."

The reference in Michelet to the generosity of the African woman to travelers brings to mind the incident in Mungo Park's travels, where the African women fed, nourished, and saved him. The men had driven him away. They would not even allow him to feed with the cattle; and so, faint, weary, and despairing, he went to a remote hut and lay down on the earth to die. One woman, touched with compassion, came to him, brought him food and milk, and at once he revived. Then he tells us of the solace and the assiduities of these gentle creatures for his comfort. I give you his own words: "The rites of hospitality thus performed toward a stranger in distress, my worthy benefactress, pointing to the mat, and telling me that I might sleep there without apprehension, called to the female part of her family which had stood gazing on me all the while in fixed astonishment, to resume the task of spinning cotton, in which they continued to employ themselves a great part of the night. They lightened their labors by songs, one of which was composed extempore, for I was myself the subject of it. It was sung by one of the young women, the rest joining in a sort of chime. The air was sweet and plaintive, and the words, literally translated, were these: 'The winds roared and the rains fell; the poor white man, faint and weary, came and sat under our tree. He has no mother to bring him milk, no wife to grind his corn. Let us pity the white man, no mother has he,'" etc.

Perhaps I may be pardoned the intrusion, just here, on my own personal experience. During a residence of nigh twenty years in West Africa, I saw the beauty and felt the charm of the native female character. I saw the native woman in her *heathen* state, and was delighted to see, in numerous tribes, that extraordinary sweetness, gentleness, docility, modesty, and especially those maternal solicitudes which make every African boy both gallant and defender of his mother.

I saw her in her *civilized* state, in Sierra Leone; saw precisely the same characteristics, but heightened, dignified, refined, and sanctified by the training of the schools, the refinements of civilization, and the graces of Christian sentiment and feeling. Of all the memories of foreign travel there are none more delightful than those of the families and the female friends of Freetown.

A French traveler speaks with great admiration of the black ladies of Hayti. "In the towns," he says, "I met all the charms of civilized life. The graces of the ladies of Port-au-Prince will never be effaced from my recollections."

It was, without doubt, the instant discernment of these fine and tender qualities which prompted the touching Sonnet of Wordsworth, written in 1802, on the occasion of the cruel exile of Negroes from France by the French Government:

"Driven from the soil of France, a female came
From Calais with us, brilliant in array,
A Negro woman like a lady gay,
Yet downcast as a woman fearing blame;
Meek, destitute, as seemed, of hope or aim
She sat, from notice turning not away,
But on all proffered intercourse did lay
A weight of languid speech—or at the same

Was silent, motionless in eyes and face.
Meanwhile those eyes retained their tropic fire
Which burning independent of the mind,
Joined with the luster of her rich attire
To mock the outcast—O ye heavens, be kind!
And feel, thou earth, for this afflicted race!"

But I must remember that I am to speak not only of the neglects of the black woman, but also of her needs. And the consideration of her needs suggests the remedy which should be used for the uplifting of this woman from a state of brutality and degradation.

* * * * *

Ladies and gentlemen, since the day of emancipation millions of dollars have been given by the generous Christian people of the North for the intellectual training of the black race in this land. Colleges and universities have been built in the South, and hundreds of youth have been gathered within their walls. The work of your own Church in this regard has been magnificent and unrivaled, and the results which have been attained have been grand and elevating to the entire Negro race in America. The complement to all this generous and ennobling effort is the elevation of the black woman. Up to this day and time your noble philanthropy has touched, for the most part, the male population of the South, given them superiority, and stimulated them to higher aspirations. But a true civilization can only then be attained when the life of woman is reached, her whole being permeated by noble ideas, her fine taste enriched by culture, her tendencies to the beautiful gratified and developed, her singular and delicate nature lifted up to its full capacity; and then, when all these qualities are fully matured, cultivated and sanctified, all their sacred influences shall circle around ten thousand firesides, and the cabins of the humblest freedmen shall become the homes of Christian refinement and of domestic elegance through the influence and the charm of the uplifted and cultivated black woman of the South!

AN OPEN LETTER TO THE EDUCATIONAL LEAGUE OF GEORGIA[19]

BY JOSEPHINE ST. PIERRE RUFFIN, of Boston, Mass.

Founder of the National Association of Negro Women

Ladies of the Georgia Educational League:

The telegram which you sent to Governor Northern to read to his audience, informing the people of the North of your willingness to undertake the moral training of the colored children of Georgia, merits more than a passing notice. It is the first time, we believe, in the history of the South where a body of representative Southern white women have shown such interest in the moral welfare of the children of their former slaves as to be willing to undertake to make them more worthy the duties and responsibilities of citizenship. True, there have been individual cases where courageous women have felt their moral responsibility, and have nobly met it, but one of the saddest things about the sad condition of affairs in the South has been the utter indifference which Southern women, who were guarded with unheard of fidelity during the war, have manifested to the mental and moral welfare of the children of their faithful slaves, who, in the language of Henry Grady, placed a black mass of loyalty between them and dishonor. This was a rare opportunity for you to have shown your gratitude to your slaves and your interest in their future welfare.

The children would have grown up in utter ignorance had not the North sent thousands of her noblest daughters to the South on this mission of heroic love and mercy; and it is worthy of remark of those fair daughters of the North, that, often eating with Negroes, and in the earlier days sleeping in their humble cabins, and always surrounded by thousands of them, there is not one recorded instance where one has been the victim of violence or insult. If because of the bitterness of your feelings, of your deep poverty at the close of the war, conditions were such that you could not do this work yourselves, you might have give a Christian's welcome to the women who came a thousand miles to do the work, that, in all gratitude and obligation belonged to you,—but instead, these women were often persecuted, always they have been ruthlessly ostracised, even until this day; often they were lonely, often longed for a word of sympathy, often craved association with their own race, but for thirty years they have been treated by the Christian white women of the South,—simply because they were doing your work,—the work committed to you by your Saviour, when he said, "Inasmuch as you did it to one of the least of these my brethren, you did it unto me,"—with a contempt that would serve to justify a suspicion that instead of being the most cultured women, the purest, bravest missionaries in America, they were outcasts and lepers.

But at last a change has come. And so you have "decided to take up the work of moral and industrial training of the Negroes," as you "have been doing this work among the whites with splendid results." This is one of the most hopeful stars that have shot through the darkness of the Southern sky. What untold blessings might not the educated Christian women of the South prove to the Negro groping blindly in the darkness of the swamps and bogs of prejudice for a highway out of servitude, oppression, ignorance, and immorality!

* * * * *

The leading women of Georgia should not ask Northern charity to do what they certainly must have the means for making a beginning of themselves. If your heart is really in this work—and we do not question it—the very best way for you to atone for your negligence in the past is to make a start yourselves. Surely if the conditions are as serious as you represent them to be, your husbands, who are men of large means, who are able to run great expositions and big peace celebrations, will be willing to provide you with the means to protect your virtue and that of your daughters by the moral training you propose to give in the kindergartens.

There is much you might do without the contribution of a dollar from any pocket, Northern or Southern. On every plantation there are scores, if not hundreds, of little colored children who could be gathered about you on a Sabbath afternoon and given many helpful inspiring lessons in morals and good conduct.

* * * * *

It is a good augury of better days, let us hope, when the intelligent, broad-minded women of Georgia, spurning the incendiary advice of that human firebrand who would lynch a thousand Negroes a month, are willing to join in this great altruistic movement of the age and endeavor to lift up the degraded and ignorant, rather than to exterminate them. Your proposition implies that they may be uplifted and further, imports a tacit confession that if you had done your duty to them at the close of the war, which both gratitude and prudence should have prompted you to do, you would not now be confronted with a condition which you feel it necessary to check, in obedience to the great first law of nature—self-protection. If you enter upon this work you will doubtless be criticised by a class of your own people who think you are lowering your own dignity, but the South has suffered too much already from that kind of false pride to let it longer keep her recreant to the spirit of the age.

If, when you have entered upon it, you need the co-operation, either by advice or other assistance, of the colored women of the North, we beg to assure you that they will not be lacking,—until then, the earnest hope goes out that you will bravely face and sternly conquer your former prejudices and quickly undertake this missionary work which belongs to you.

IN THE WAKE OF THE COMING AGES[20]

BY J. MADISON VANCE, of New Orleans, La.

In these trying times of peace with tears of blood; these times of crimes so horrible and fiendish that Christianity bows in supplication for surcease of sorrow, and the advance of civilization seems in vain; in these times when the Negro is compared to the brute, and his mentality limited to the ordinary; in these times when the holy robes of the Church are used to decry, villify and malign the race; in these times when the subsidized press of the country loudly proclaims the Negro's incapacity for government; in these times I turn with pardonable pride to the Grand United Order of Odd Fellows, an organization the affairs of which are administered entirely by colored men, an organization that typifies the possibilities of the race; the organization whose very existence gives the lie to the damnable aspersions cast upon us by the enemies of humanity.

This grand organization is but a collection of individuals, and as individuals we must shape our destiny. The time is past for pleading; these are days of action. The higher we rise, the sharper will become the prejudice of color. The laboring white is jealous of the competition of the blacks. The problem is to be worked out *in the South*, and largely by ourselves. With all the disadvantages and proscriptive doctrines that encroach upon us in that Southland, I honestly believe that this land with all its natural beauties and advantages, this land below the mountains; this land of passion and pleasure, of fever and fret, this land famed in history, song, and story as the "land of Dixie," is the Negro's coming Arcadia. From its lowlands and marshes will yet come forth the peerless leader, who will not only point out the way, but will climb the battlements of tolerance and race prejudice, backed by the march of civilization, and, with his face to the enemy, fight the battle of common humanity.

The romance of "Emancipation" is fading out. The old slave is rapidly passing. The mythology of his period is extinct. The Republic has declared against the "Force Bill." The "Prætorian Guard" is mustered out, and the sentiment of the times is against paternalism. "Every tub must stand on its own bottom," and the eloquence of the orator cannot arrest the trend of the times. A problem is half solved when facts are apprehended; it is more than half solved when the facts are comprehended, and practical sense succeeds sentiment.

The Negro confronts destiny. He must be the architect of his own fortune. He must demonstrate capacity and independence, because mendicancy is always destructive. The living present calls us away from the ashes of the dead and buried past. Our hopes are brighter and our ambitions higher. Let us stand on our own racial pride, and prove our claim for equality by showing the fruits of thrift, talent, and frugality. The brotherhood of genius will not refuse the need of merit, and within the sweep of our constant observations great artists, musicians, poets, and orators are more than hinted possibilities. We would be criminals to despair. The Negro is here, and here to stay, and traveling rapidly in "the wake of coming ages." We know not how far the goal may still be distant, but at least we think we see it and our most fervent hope is to approach it more and more nearly—

"Till each man find his own in all men's good,
And all men work in noble brotherhood,
Breaking their mailed fleets and armed towers,
And ruling by obeying nature's powers,
And gathering all the fruits of earth and crowned with her flowers."

As the shadows come creeping over the dial of time, the nineteenth century faces the setting sun; a century replete with the grandest inventions of modern times, and with a fullness of scientific investigation beyond the possible conception of man one hundred years ago. This century has emancipated woman, and like the "Dreamers on the brow of Parnassus," she is not forgetful of the toilers on other altitudes within the horizon's rim. She is not blind to the signal lights, which in their blaze proclaim new knowledge, new power for man, new triumphs, new glory for the human spirit in its march on chaos and the dark. Any message of love would be incomplete without her gentle voice. Her love is her life, white-winged and eternal. Her welcome is spontaneous, fervid, whole-souled, generous. Her influence is felt everywhere, throughout the ramifications of our "Order." The wholesome power of her persuasive counsel is ofttimes needed, and the tender mercies of her tireless devotion have smoothed away the grim visage of discontent, brought solace to the fevered brain, and made peaceful that dreary journey from life to death.

* * * * *

We look out upon our vast army of followers, and glory in our stalwart band. * * * * * Out of the darkness of the night, imposing in our numbers, stand we forth, splendid and terrible, in "The Wake of the Coming Ages." And when we look at all the magnificent fabric we call civilization, its incalculable material, its wealth, its amazing mechanical resources, its wonderful scientific discoveries, its many-sided literature, its sleepless and ubiquitous journalism, its lovely art, its abounding charities, its awful fears and sublime hopes, we get a magnificent conception of the possibilities of life, as this latest of the centuries draws its purple robe about its majestic form and stands up to die as the old Roman Cæsar stood, in all the magnificence of its riches, and the plenitude of its power.

But after all, the measure of its value is the character of it humanity.

AN ADDRESS DELIVERED AT THE OPENING OF THE COTTON STATES AND INTERNATIONAL EXPOSITION[21]

By Booker T. Washington, A. M. LL.D.

of Tuskegee Institute

Mr. President and Gentlemen of the Board of Directors, and Citizens:

One-third of the population of the South is of the Negro race. No enterprise seeking the material, civil, or moral welfare of this section can disregard this element of our population and reach the highest success. I but convey to you, Mr. President and Directors, the sentiment of the masses of my race when I say that in no way have the value and manhood of the American Negro been more fittingly and generously recognized than by the managers of this magnificent Exposition at every stage of its progress. It is a recognition that will do more to cement the friendship of the two races than any occurrence since the dawn of our freedom.

Not only this, but the opportunity here afforded will awaken among us a new era of industrial progress. Ignorant and inexperienced, it is not strange that in the first years of our new life we began at the top instead of at the bottom; that a seat in Congress or the State Legislature was more sought than real estate or industrial skill; that the political convention or stump-speaking had more attractions than starting a dairy-farm or truck-garden.

A ship lost at sea for many days suddenly sighted a friendly vessel. From the mast of the unfortunate vessel was seen a signal: "Water, water; we die of thirst!" The answer from the friendly vessel at once came back: "Cast down your bucket where you are." A second time the signal, "Water, water; send us water!" ran up from the distressed vessel, and was answered: "Cast down your bucket where you are." And a third and fourth signal for water was answered: "Cast down your bucket where you are." The captain of the distressed vessel, at last heeding the injunction, cast down his bucket, and it came up full of fresh, sparkling water from the mouth of the Amazon River. To those of my race who depend on bettering their condition in a foreign land, or who underestimate the importance of cultivating friendly relations with the Southern white man, who is their next-door neighbor, I would say: "Cast down your bucket where you are"—cast it down in making friends in every manly way of the people of all races by whom we are surrounded.

Cast it down in agriculture, mechanics, in commerce, in domestic service, and in the professions. And in this connection it is well to bear in mind that whatever other sins the South may be called to bear, when it comes to business, pure and simple, it is in the South that the Negro is given a man's chance in the commercial world, and in nothing is this Exposition more eloquent than in emphasizing this chance. Our greatest danger is, that in the great leap from slavery to freedom we may overlook the fact that the masses of us are to live by the productions of our hands, and fail to keep in mind that we shall prosper in proportion as we learn to dignify and glorify common labor and put brains and skill into the common occupations of life; shall prosper in proportion as we learn to draw the line between the superficial and the substantial, the ornamental gewgaws of life and the useful. No race can prosper till it learns that there is as much dignity in tilling a field as in writing a poem. It is at the bottom of life we must begin, and not at the top. Nor should we permit our grievances to overshadow our opportunities.

To those of the white race who look to the incoming of those of foreign birth and strange tongue and habits for the prosperity of the South, were I permitted I would repeat what I say to my own race, "Cast down your bucket where you are." Cast it down among the 8,000,000 Negroes whose habits you know, whose fidelity and love you have tested in days when to have proved treacherous meant the ruin of your firesides. Cast down your bucket among these people who have, without strikes and labor wars, tilled your fields, cleared your forests, builded your railroads and cities, and brought forth treasures from the bowels of the earth and helped make possible this magnificent representation of the progress of the South. Casting down your bucket among my people, helping and encouraging them as you are doing on these grounds, and to education of head, hand, and heart, you will find that they will buy your surplus land, make blossom the waste places in your fields, and run your factories. While doing this, you can be sure in the future, as in the past, that you and your families will be surrounded by the most patient, faithful, law-abiding, and unresentful people that the world has seen. As we have proved our loyalty to you in the past, in nursing your children, watching by the sick-beds of your mothers and fathers, and often following them with tear-dimmed eyes to their graves, so in the future, in our humble way, we shall stand by you with a devotion that no foreigner can approach, ready to lay down our lives, if need be, in defense of yours, interlacing our industrial, commercial, civil, and religious life with yours in a way that shall make the interests of both races one. In all things that are purely social we can be as separate as the fingers, yet one as the hand in all things essential to mutual progress.

There is no defense or security for any of us except in the highest intelligence and development of all. If anywhere there are efforts tending to curtail the fullest growth of the Negro, let these efforts be turned into stimulating, encouraging, and making him the most useful and intelligent citizen. Efforts or means so invested will pay a thousand per cent. interest.

These efforts will be twice blessed—"blessing him that gives and him that takes."

There is no escape through law of man or God from the inevitable:

"The laws of changeless justice bind
Oppressor with oppressed;
And close as sin and suffering joined
We march to fate abreast."

Nearly sixteen millions of hands will aid you in pulling the load upwards, or they will pull against you the load downwards. We shall constitute one-third and more of the ignorance and crime of the South, or one-third its intelligence and progress; we shall contribute one-third to the business and industrial prosperity of the South, or we shall prove a veritable body of death, stagnating, depressing, retarding every effort to advance the body politic.

Gentlemen of the Exposition, as we present to you our humble effort at an exhibition of our progress, you must not expect overmuch. Starting thirty years ago with ownership here and there in a few quilts and pumpkins and chickens, remember the path, that has led from these to the invention and production of agricultural implements, buggies, steam-engines, newspapers, books, statuary, carving, paintings, the management of drug stores and banks, has not been trodden without contact with thorns and thistles. While we take pride in what we exhibit as a result of our independent efforts, we do not for a moment forget that our part in this exhibition would fall far short of your expectations but for the constant help that has come to our educational life, not only from the Southern States, but especially from Northern philanthropists, who have made their gifts a constant stream of blessing and encouragement.

The wisest among my race understand that the agitation of questions of social equality is the extremest folly, and that progress in the enjoyment of all the privileges that will come to us must be the result of severe and constant struggle rather than of artificial forcing. No race that has anything to contribute to the markets of the world is long in any degree ostracized. It is important and right that all privileges of the law be ours, but it is vastly more important that we be prepared for the exercises of these privileges. The opportunity to earn a dollar in a factory just now is worth infinitely more than the opportunity to spend a dollar in an opera-house.

In conclusion, may I repeat that nothing in thirty years has given us more hope and encouragement, and drawn us so near to you of the white race, as this opportunity offered by the Exposition; and here bending, as it were, over the altar that represents the results of the struggles of your race and mine, both starting practically empty-handed three decades ago, I pledge that in your effort to work out the great and intricate problem which God has laid at the doors of the South you shall have at all times the patient, sympathetic help of my race; only let this be constantly in the mind that, while from representations in these buildings of the product of field, of forest, of mine, of factory, letters, and art, much good will come, yet far above and beyond material benefits will be that higher good, that let us pray God will come, in a blotting out of sectional differences and racial animosities and suspicions, in a determination to administer absolute justice, in a willing obedience among all classes to the mandates of law. This, this, coupled with our material prosperity, will bring into our beloved Southland a new heaven and a new earth.

THE NEGRO AS A SOLDIER[22]

BY CHRISTIAN A. FLEETWOOD

CHRISTIAN A. FLEETWOOD, *Sergeant-Major, United States Volunteer Infantry, 1863-1866. Received a Medal of Honor from Congress for meritorious action in saving the colors at Chapin Farm, September 29, 1864, where he seized them after two color-bearers had been shot down, and bore them throughout the fight. Also has a General B. F. Butler Medal for bravery and courage before Richmond.*

For 1600 years prior to the war between Great Britain and the Colonies, the pages of history bear no record of the Negro as a soldier. Tracing his separate history in the Revolutionary War is a task of much difficulty, for the reason that while individual instances of valor and patriotism abound, there were so few separate bodies of Negro troops that no separate record appears to have been made. The simple fact is that the fathers as a rule enlisted men both for the Army and Navy, just as now it is only continued by the Navy; that is to say, they were assigned wherever needed, without regard to race or color. Varner's Rhode Island Battalion appears to have been the only large aggregation of Negroes in this war, though Connecticut, New York, and New Hampshire each furnished one separate company in addition to individuals scattered through their other organizations, so that ere the close of the war, there were very few brigades, regiments, or companies in which the Negro was not in evidence.

The free Negro appears to have gone in from the beginning without attracting or calling out special comment. Later, as men grew scarcer and necessity more pressing, slaves were taken in also, and then the trouble began. Those who held slaves did not care to lose them in this way. Others who had not did not think it just the thing in a war for avowed freedom to place an actual slave in the ranks to fight. Some did not want the Negro, bonded or free, to take part as a soldier in the struggle. So that in May, 1775, the Massachusetts Committee of Safety voted that thereafter only free men should be enlisted. In July, General Gates issued an order prohibiting further enlistments of Negroes, but saying nothing of those already in the service.

In October a council of war presided over by General Washington, comprising three major-generals and six brigadier-generals, voted unanimously against the enlistment of slaves, and by a decided majority against further enlistments of Negroes. Ten days later in a conference held at Cambridge, Mass., participated in by General Washington, Benjamin

Franklin, Benjamin Harrison, Thomas Lynch, and the deputy governors of Connecticut and Rhode Island, a similar action was taken.

On the 7th November, 1775, Earl Dundore, commanding the force of His Majesty the King, issued a proclamation offering freedom and equal pay to all slaves who would join his armies as soldiers. It did not take the colonists long to find out their mistake, although General Washington, in accordance with the expressed will of his officers and of the Committee of Safety, did on the 17th of November, 1775, issue a proclamation forbidding the further enlistment of Negroes. Less than two months later, that is to say on the 30th of December, 1775, he issued a second proclamation again authorizing the enlistment of free Negroes. He advised Congress of his action, and stated that he would recall it if so directed. But he was not. The splendid service rendered by the Negro and the great and pressing need of men were such, that although the opposition continued from some sections, it was not thereafter strong enough to obtain recognition. So the Negroes went and came, much as other men.

In all the events of the war, from Bunker Hill to Yorktown, they bore an honorable part. The history of the doings of the armies is their history, as in everything they took part and did their share. Their total enlistment was about 3,000 men,—a very fair percentage for the population of that period. I might instance the killing of Major Pitcairn, at Bunker Hill, by Peter Salem, and of Major Montgomery, at Fort Griswold, by Jordan Freeman. The part they took in the capture of Major-General Prescott at Newport; their gallant defense of Colonel Greene, their beloved commander, when he was surprised and murdered at Croton River, May 13, 1781, when it was only after the last of his faithful guards had been shot and cut down that he was reached; or the battle of Rhode Island, when a battalion of 400 Negroes withstood three separate and distinct charges from 1,500 Hessians under Count Donop, and beat them back with such tremendous loss that Count Donop at once applied for an exchange, fearing that his men would kill him, if he went into battle with them again, for having exposed them to such slaughter; and many other instances that are of record. The letter following, written December 5, 1775, explains itself:

"TO THE HONORABLE GENERAL COURT OF THE MASSACHUSETTS BAY:

"The subscribers beg leave to report to your Honorable House (which we do in justice to the character of so brave a man) that under our own observation we declare that a Negro man named Salem Poor, of Colonel Frye's Regiment, Captain Ames' Company, in the late battle at Charleston, behaved like an experienced officer as well as an excellent soldier. To set forth particulars of his conduct would be tedious. We would only beg to say, in the person of this Negro centers a brave and gallant soldier. The reward due to so great and distinguished a character we submit to Congress."

This is a splendid and well-attested tribute to a gallant and worthy Negro. There were many such, but, beyond receiving and reading, no action was taken thereon by Congress. There is no lack of incidents, and the temptation to quote many of them is great, but the time allotted me is too brief for extended mention, and I must bring this branch of my subject to a close. It is in evidence that while so many Negroes were offering their lives a willing sacrifice for the country, in some sections the officers of the Continental forces received their bounty and pay in Negroes, "grown" and "small," instead of "dollars" and "cents." Fighting for *liberty* and taking pay in *slaves*!

When the war was over the free men returned to meet their same difficulties; the slaves were caught when possible and re-enslaved by their former masters. In Boston a few years later we find a party of black patriots of the Revolution mobbed on Boston Common while celebrating the anniversary of the abolition of the slave-trade.

The captain of a vessel trading along the coast tells of a Negro who had fought in the war and been distinguished for bravery and soldierly conduct. He was reclaimed and re-enslaved by his master after the war, and served him faithfully until old age rendered him useless. The master then brought the poor old slave to this captain and asked him to take him along on his trip and try to sell him. The captain hated to sell a man who had fought for his country, but finally agreed, took the poor old man to Mobile, and sold him for $100 to a man who put him to attending a chicken-coop. His former master continued to draw the old slave's pension as a soldier in the Revolution, until he died.

The War of 1812 was mainly fought upon the water, and in the American Navy at that time the Negro stood in the ratio of about one to six. We find record of complaint by Commodore Perry at the beginning because of the large number of Negroes sent him, but later the highest tribute to their bravery and efficiency. Captain Shaler, of the armed brig *General Thompson*, writing of an engagement between his vessel and a British frigate, says:

"The name of one of my poor fellows who was killed ought to be registered in the book of fame, and remembered as long as bravery is a virtue. He was a black man, by name John Johnson. A twenty-four pound shot struck him in the hip, and took away all the lower part of his body. In this state the poor brave fellow lay on the deck, and several times exclaimed to his shipmates: 'Fire away, my boys; nor haul a color down!' Another black man, by the name of John Davis, who was struck in much the same manner, repeatedly requested to be thrown overboard, saying that he was only in the way of the others."

I know of nothing finer in history than these incidents of valor and patriotism.

As before, the Negro was not universally welcomed to the ranks of the American Army; but later, continued reverses and a lack of enthusiasm in enlistments made it necessary to seek his aid, and from Mobile, Ala., on September 21, 1814, General Jackson issued a stirring call to the free colored people of Louisiana for aid.

In a remarkably short period, two battalions were raised, under Majors LaCaste and Savary, which did splendid service in the battle of New Orleans. New York enrolled two battalions, and sent them to Sacketts Harbor. Pennsylvania enrolled 2400, and sent them to Gray's Ferry at the capture of Washington, to prepare for the invading column. Another battalion also was raised, armed, equipped, and ready to start to the front, when peace was declared.

In one of the actions of this war, a charging column of the American Army was repulsed and thrown into great disorder. A Negro private named Jeffreys, seeing the disaster, sprang upon a horse, and by heroic effort rallied the troops, led them back upon a second charge, and completely routed the enemy. He was rewarded by General Jackson with the honorary title of Major. Under the laws he could not commission him.

When the war was over, this gallant man returned to his home in Nashville, Tenn., where he lived for years afterward, highly respected by its citizens of all races.

At the age of seventy years, this black hero was obliged, *in self-defense*, to strike a white ruffian, who had assaulted him. Under the laws of the State he was arrested and given nine and thirty lashes on his bare back. It broke his heart, and Major Jeffreys died.

It seems a little singular that in the tremendous struggle between the States in 1861-1865, the South should have been the first to take steps toward the enlistment of Negroes. Yet such is the fact. Two weeks after the fall of Fort Sumter, the *Charleston Mercury* records the passing through Augusta of several companies of the the 3rd and 4th Georgia Regiment, and of sixteen well-drilled companies *and one Negro company* from Nashville, Tenn.

The Memphis Avalanche and *The Memphis Appeal* of May 9, 10, and 11, 1861, gave notice of the appointment by the "Committee of Safety" of a committee of three persons "to organize a volunteer company composed of our patriotic freemen of color of the city of Memphis, for the service of our common defense."

A telegram from New Orleans dated November 23, 1861, notes the review by Governor Moore of over 28,000 troops, and that one regiment comprised "*1,400 colored men*." The *New Orleans Picayune*, referring to a review held February 9, 1862, says: "We must also pay a deserved compliment to the companies of free colored men, all very well drilled and comfortably equipped."

It is a little odd, too, that in the evacuation of New Orleans a little later, in April, 1862, all of the troops succeeded in getting away except the Negroes. They "got left."

It is not in our line to speculate upon what would have been the result of the war had the South kept up this policy, enlisted the freemen, and emancipated the enlisting slaves and their families. The immense addition to their fighting force, the quick recognition of them by Great Britain, to which slavery was the greatest bar, and the fact that the heart of the Negro was with the South but for slavery, and the case stands clear. But the primary successes of the South closed its eyes to its only chance of salvation, while at the same time the eyes of the North were opened.

In 1865, the South saw, and endeavored to remedy, its error. On March 9, 1865, the Confederate Congress passed a bill, recommended by General Lee, authorizing the enlistment of 200,000 Negroes; but it was then too late.

The North came slowly and reluctantly to recognize the Negro as a factor for good in the war. "This is a white man's war," met the Negroes at every step of their first efforts to gain admission to the armies of the Union.

To General David Hunter, more than to any other one man, is due the credit for the successful entry upon the stage of the Negro as a soldier in this war.

In the spring of 1862, he raised and equipped a regiment of Negroes in South Carolina, and when the fact because known in Washington and throughout the country, such a storm was raised about the ears of the Administration that they gracefully stood aside and left the brave general to fight his enemies in the front and rear as best he might. He was quite capable to do both, as it proved.

* * * * *

The beginning of 1863 saw the opening of the doors to the Negro in every direction. General Lorenzo Thomas went in person to the valley of the Mississippi to supervise it there. Massachusetts was authorized to fill its quota with Negroes. The States of Maryland, Missouri, Delaware, and Tennessee were thrown open by order of the War Department, and all slaves enlisting therefrom declared free. Ohio, Connecticut, Pennsylvania, and New York joined the band and sent the stalwart black boy in blue to the front singing, "Give us a flag, all free, without a slave." For two years the fierce and determined opposition had kept them out, but now the bars were down and they came pouring in. Some one said, "he cared not who made the laws of a people if he could make their songs." A better exemplification of this would be difficult to find than is the song written by "Miles O'Reilly" (Colonel Halpine), of the old 10th Army Corps. I cannot resist the temptation to quote it here. With General Hunter's letter and this song to quote from, the episode was closed:

"Some say it is a burning shame to make the Naygurs fight,
An' that the trade o' being kilt belongs but to the white;
But as for me, upon me sowl, so liberal are we here,
I'll let Sambo be murthered, in place of meself, on every day of the year.
On every day of the year, boys, and every hour in the day,
The right to be kilt I'll divide wid him, and divil a word I'll say.

In battles' wild commotion I shouldn't at all object
If Sambo's body should stop a ball that was coming for me direct,
An' the prod of a Southern bayonet; so liberal are we here,
I'll resign and let Sambo take it, on every day in the year,
On every day in the year, boys, an' wid none of your nasty pride,
All right in Southern baynet prod, wid Sambo I'll divide.

The men who object to Sambo should take his place and fight,
An' it is betther to have a Naygur's hue, than a liver that's weak an' white,
Though Sambo's black as the ace of spades, his finger a thryger can pull,
An' his eye runs straight on the barrel-sight from under its thatch of wool.
So hear me all, boys, darlin', don't think I'm tipping you chaff,—
The right to be kilt, I'll divide with him, an' give him the largest half."

It took three years of war to place the enlisted Negro upon the same ground as the enlisted white man as to pay and emoluments; *perhaps* six years of war might have given him shoulder-straps, but the war ended without authorization of law for that step. At first they were received, under an act of Congress that allowed each one, without regard to rank, ten dollars per month, three dollars thereof to be retained for clothing and equipments. I think it was in May, 1864, when the act was passed equalizing the pay, but not opening the doors to promotion.

Under an act of the Confederate Congress, making it a crime punishable with death for any white person to train Negroes or mulattoes to arms, or aid them in any military enterprise, and devoting the Negro caught under arms to the tender mercies of the "present or future laws of the State" in which caught, a large number of *promotions* were made by the way of a rope and a tree along the first year of the Negro's service. (I can even recall one instance as late as April, 1865, though it had been long before then generally discontinued.)

What the Negro did, how he did it, and where, it would take volumes to properly record, I can however give but briefest mention to a few of the many evidences of his fitness for the duties of the war, and his aid to the cause of the Union.

The first fighting done by organized Negro troops appears to have been done by Company A, 1st South Carolina Negro Regiment, at St. Helena Island, November 3 to 10, 1862, while participating in an expedition along the coast of Georgia and Florida under Lieutenant-Colonel O. T. Beard, of the 48th New York Infantry, who says in his report:

"The colored men fought with astonishing coolness and bravery. I found them all I could desire,—more than I had hoped. They behaved gloriously, and deserve all praise."

The testimony thus inaugurated runs like a cord of gold through the web and woof of the history of the Negro as a soldier from that date to their final charge, the last made at Clover Hill, Va., April 9, 1865.

Necessarily the first actions in which the Negro bore a part commanded most attention. Friends and enemies were looking eagerly to see how they would acquit themselves, and so it comes to pass that the names of Fort Wagner, Olustee, Millikens Bend, Port Hudson, and Fort Pillow are as familiar as Bull Run, Antietam, Shiloh and Gettysburg, and while those first experiences were mostly severe reverses, they were by that very fact splendid exemplifiers of the truth that the Negroes could be relied upon to fight under the most adverse circumstances, against any odds, and could not be discouraged.

Let us glance for a moment at Port Hudson, La., in May, 1863, assaulted by General Banks with a force of which the 1st and 2nd Regiments, Louisiana Native Guards, formed a part. When starting upon their desperate mission, Colonel Stafford of the 1st Regiment, in turning over the regimental colors to the color-guard, made a brief and patriotic address, closing with the words:

"Color-guard: Protect, defend, die for, but do not surrender, these colors." The gallant flag-sergeant, Plancianos, taking them replied: "Colonel: I will bring back these colors to you in honor, or report to God the reason why."

Six times with desperate valor they charged over ground where success was hopeless, a deep bayou between them and the works of the enemy at the point of attack rendering it impossible to reach them, yet strange to say, six times they were ordered forward and six times they went to useless death, until swept back by the blazing breath of shot and shell before which nothing living could stand. Here fell the gallant Captain Cailloux, black as the ace of spades. Refusing to leave the field though his arm had been shattered by a bullet, he returned to the charge until killed by a shell.

A soldier limping painfully to the front was halted and asked where he was going. He replied, "I am shot bad in de leg, and dey want me to go to de hospital, but I guess I can give 'em a little more yet."

The colors came back, but crimsoned with the blood of the gallant Plancianos, who reported to God from that bloody field.

Shall we glance from this to Millikens Bend, La., in January, 1863, garrisoned by the 9th and 11th Louisiana and the 1st Mississippi, all Negroes, and about 160 of the 23rd Iowa (white), about 1100 fighting men in all? Attacked by a force of six Confederate regiments, crushed out of their works by sheer weight of numbers, borne down toward the levee, fighting every step of the way, hand to hand—clubbed musket, bayonets, and swords,—from three A. M. to twelve noon, they fought desperately until a Union gun-boat came to the rescue and shelled the desperate foe back to the woods, with a total loss to the defenders of 437 men,—two-fifths of their strength.

Shall we turn with sadness to Fort Wagner, S. C., in July, 1863, when the 54th Massachusetts won its deathless fame, and its grand young commander, Colonel Robert Gould Shaw, passed into the temple of immortality? After a march of all day, under a burning sun, and all night through a tempest of wind and rain, drenched, exhausted, hungry, they wheeled into line, without a murmur for that awful charge, that dance of death, the struggle against hopeless odds, and the shattered remnants were hurled back as from the mouth of hell, leaving the dead bodies of their young commander and his noble followers to be buried in a common grave. Its total loss was about one-third of its strength.

Here it was that the gallant flag-sergeant, Carney, though grievously wounded, bore back his flag to safety, and fell fainting and exhausted with loss of blood, saying, "Boys, the old flag never touched the ground!" Or another glance, at ill-starred Olustee, where the gallant 8th United States Colored Troops lost 87 killed of its effective fighting force, the largest loss in any one colored regiment in any one action of the war. And so on, by Fort Pillow, which let us pass in merciful silence, and to Honey Hill, S. C., perhaps the last desperate fight in the far south, in which the 32nd, 35th, and 102nd United States Colored Troops and the 54th and 55th Massachusetts Infantry won fresh and fadeless laurels for splendid fighting against hopeless odds and insurmountable difficulties, and then to Nashville, Tenn., with its recorded loss of 84 killed in the effectives of the 13th United States Colored Troops.

These were all brilliant actions, and they covered the actors with, and reflected upon the race, a blaze of glory. But it was in the armies of the James and of the Potomac that the true metal of the Negro as a soldier rang out its clearest notes amid the tremendous diapasons that rolled back and forth between the embattled hosts. Here was war indeed, upon its grandest scale and in all its infinite variety: The tireless march under burning sun, chilling frosts, and driven tempests; the lonely vigil of the picket under starless skies, the rush and roar of countless "hosts to battle driven" in the mad charge and the victorious shout that pursued the fleeing foe; the grim determination that held its line of defenses with set teeth, blood-shot eye, and strained muscle, beating back charge after charge of the foe; the patient labor in trench and mine, on hill and in valley, swamp and jungle, with disease adding its horrors to the decimation of shot and shell.

Here the Negro stood in the full glare of the greatest search-light, part and parcel of the grandest armies ever mustered upon this continent, competing side by side with the best and bravest of the Union Army against the flower of the Confederacy, the best and bravest of Lee's army, and losing nothing in the contrast. Never again while time lasts will the doubt arise as in 1861, "Will the Negro fight?" As a problem, it has been solved; as a question, it has been answered; and as a fact, it is as established as the eternal hills. It was the Negroes who rang up the curtain upon the last act of the bloody tragedy at Petersburg, Va., June 15, 1864, and they who rang it down at Clover Hill, Va., April 9, 1865. They were one of the strong fingers upon the mighty hand that grasped the giant's throat at Petersburg and never flexed until the breath went out at Appomattox. In this period it would take page on page to recount their deeds of valor and their glorious victories.

See them on the 15th of June, 1864, carrying the out-post at Baylor's field in early morning, and all that long, hot, summer day advancing, a few yards at a time, then lying down to escape the fire from the works, but still gradually creeping nearer and nearer, until, just as the sun went down, they swept like a tornado over the works and started upon a race for the city, close at the heels of the flying foe, until mistakenly ordered back. Of this day's experience General Badeau writes: "No worse strain on the nerves of troops is possible, for it is harder to remain quiet under cannon fire, even though comparatively harmless, than to advance against a storm of musketry." General W. F. "Baldy" Smith, speaking of their conduct, says: "No nobler effort has been put forth to-day, and no greater success achieved than that of the colored troops."

* * * * *

Or, again, at the terrible mine explosion of July 30, 1864, on the Petersburg line, and at the fearful slaughter of September 29, 1864, at New Market Heights and Fort Harrison. On this last date in the Fourth United States Colored Troops, out of a color-guard of twelve men, but one came off the field on his own feet. The gallant flag-sergeant, Hilton, the last to fall, cried out as he went down, "Boys, save the colors"; and they were saved.

* * * * *

Some ten or more years later, in Congress, in the midst of a speech advocating the giving of civil rights to the Negro, General Butler said, referring to this incident:

"There, in a space not wider than the clerk's desk, and three hundred yards long, lay the dead bodies of 543 of my colored comrades, slain in the defense of their country, who had laid down their lives to uphold its flag and its honor, as a willing sacrifice. And as I rode along, guiding my horse this way and that, lest he should profane with his hoofs what seemed to me the sacred dead, and as I looked at their bronzed faces upturned in the shining sun, as if in mute appeal against the wrongs of the country for which they had given their lives, and whose flag had been to them a flag of stripes, in which no star of glory had ever shone for them—feeling I had wronged them in the past, and believing what was the future duty of my country to them,—I swore to myself a solemn oath: 'May my right hand forget its cunning, and my tongue cleave to the roof of my mouth, if ever I fail to defend the rights of the men who have given their blood for me and my country this day and for their race forever.' And, God helping me, I will keep that oath."

* * * * *

History further repeats itself in the fact that in every war so far known to this country, the first blood, and, in some cases, the last also, has been shed by the faithful Negro, and this in spite of all the years of bondage and oppression, and of wrongs unspeakable. Under the sun there has nothing been known in the history of any people more marvellous than these facts!

Oh, to the living few,
Comrades, be just, be true.
Hail them as heroes tried,
Fight with them side by side;
Never in field or tent,
Scorn the Black Regiment.

It is but a little thing to ask, they could ask no less: *be just*; but, oh, the shame of it for those who need be asked!

There is no need for panegyric, for sounding phrases or rounded periods. The simple story is eloquent with all that is necessary to make the heart swell with pride. In the hour allotted me to fill, it is possible only to indicate in skeleton the worth of the Negro as a soldier. If this brief sketch should awaken even a few to interest in his achievements, and one be found willing and fitted to write the history that is their due, that writer shall achieve immortality.

AN ADDRESS AT THE UNVEILING OF THE ROBERT GOULD SHAW MONUMENT[23]

BY BOOKER T. WASHINGTON, A. M., LL.D.

Mr. Chairman and Fellow Citizens:

In this presence, and on this sacred and memorable day, in the deeds and death of our hero, we recall the old, old story, ever old yet ever new, that when it was the will of the Father to lift humanity out of wretchedness and bondage, the precious task was delegated to Him who, among ten thousand, was altogether lovely, and was willing to make himself of no reputation that he might save and lift up others.

If that heart could throb and if those lips could speak, what would be the sentiment and words that Robert Gould Shaw would have us feel and speak at this hour? He would not have us dwell long on the mistakes, the injustice, the criticisms of the days

"Of storm and cloud, of doubt and fears,
Across the eternal sky must lower;
Before the glorious noon appears,"

he would have us bind up with his own undying fame and memory and retain by the side of his monument, the name of John A. Andrews, who, with prophetic vision and strong arm, helped to make the existence of the 54th Regiment possible; and that of George L. Stearns, who, with hidden generosity and a great sweet heart, helped to turn the darkest hour into day, and in doing so, freely gave service, fortune, and life itself to the cause which this day commemorates. Nor would he have us forget those brother officers, living and dead, who by their baptism in blood and fire, in defense of union and freedom, gave us an example of the highest and purest patriotism.

To you who fought so valiantly in the ranks, the scarred and scattered remnant of the 54th Regiment, who, with empty sleeve and wanting leg, have honored this occasion with your presence, to you, your commander is not dead. Though Boston erected no monument and history recorded no story, in you and the loyal race which you represent Robert Gould Shaw would have a monument which time could not wear away.

But an occasion like this is too great, too sacred for mere individual eulogy. The individual is the instrument, national virtue the end. That which was 300 years being woven into the warp and woof of our democratic institutions could not be effaced by a single battle, as magnificent as was that battle; that which for three centuries had bound master and slave, yea, North and South, to a body of death, could not be blotted out by four years of war, could not be atoned for by shot and sword, nor by blood and tears.

Not many days ago in the heart of the South, in a large gathering of the people of my race, there were heard from many lips praises and thanksgiving to God for His goodness in setting them free from physical slavery. In the midst of that assembly there arose a Southern white man the former owner of many slaves, gray of hair and with hands which trembled, and from his quivering lips, there came the words; "My friends, you forget in your rejoicing that, in setting you free, God was also good to me and my race in setting us free." But there is a higher and deeper sense in which both races must be free than that represented by the bill of sale. The black man who cannot let love and sympathy go out to the white man is but half free. The white man who would close the shop or factory against a black man seeking an opportunity to earn an honest living is but half free. The white man who retards his own development by opposing a black man is but half free. The full measure of the fruit of Fort Wagner and all that this monument stands for will not be realized until every man covered with a black skin shall, by patience and natural effort, grow to that height in industry, property, intelligence, and moral responsibility, where no man in all our land will be tempted to degrade himself by withholding from his black brother any opportunity which he himself would possess.

Until that time comes this monument will stand for effort, not victory complete. What these heroic souls of the 54th Regiment began, we must complete. It must be completed not in malice, not in narrowness; nor artificial progress, nor in efforts at mere temporary political gain, nor in abuse of another section or race. Standing as I do to-day in the home of Garrison and Phillips and Sumner, my heart goes out to those who wore gray as well as to those clothed in blue; to those who returned defeated, to destitute homes, to face blasted hopes and a shattered political and industrial system. To them there can be no prouder reward for defeat than by a supreme effort to place the Negro on that footing where he will add material, intellectual, and civil strength to every department of State.

This work must be completed in public school, industrial school, and college. The most of it must be completed in the effort of the Negro himself, in his effort to withstand temptation, to economize, to exercise thrift, to disregard the superficial for the real—the shadow for the substance, to be great and yet small, in his effort to be patient in the laying of a firm foundation, so to grow in skill and knowledge that he shall place his services in demand by reason of his intrinsic and superior worth. This is the key that unlocks every door of opportunity, and all others fail. In this battle of peace the rich and poor, the black and white, may have a part.

What lesson has this occasion for the future? What of hope, what of encouragement, what of caution? "Watchman, tell us of the night; what the signs of promise are." If through me, an humble representative, nearly ten millions of my people might be permitted to send a message to Massachusetts, to the survivors of the 54th Regiment, to the committee whose untiring energy has made this memorial possible, to the family who gave their only boy that we might have life more abundantly, that message would be, "Tell them that the sacrifice was not in vain, that up from the depth of ignorance and poverty, we are coming, and if we come through oppression out of the struggle, we are gaining strength. By the way of the school, the well-cultivated field, the skilled hand, the Christian home, we are coming up; that we propose to invite all who will to step up and occupy this position with us. Tell them that we are learning that standing-ground for the race, as for the individual, must be laid in intelligence, industry, thrift, and property, not as an end, but as a means to the highest privileges; that we are learning that neither the conqueror's bullet nor fiat of law could make an ignorant voter an intelligent voter, could make a dependent man an independent man, could give one citizen respect for another, a bank account, a foot of land, or an enlightened fireside. Tell them that, as grateful as we are to artist and patriotism for placing the figures of Shaw and his comrades in physical form of beauty and magnificence, that after all, the real monument, the greater monument, is being slowly but safely builded among the lowly in the South, in the struggles and sacrifices of a race to justify all that has been done and suffered for it."

One of the wishes that lay nearest Colonel Shaw's heart was, that his black troops might be permitted to fight by the side of white soldiers. Have we not lived to see that wish realized, and will it not be further realized in the future? Not at Wagner, not with rifle and bayonet, but on the field of peace, in the battle of industry, in the struggle for good government, in the lifting up of the lowest to the fullest opportunities. In this we shall fight by the side of white men, North and South. And if this be true, as under God's guidance it will, that old flag, that emblem of progress and security, which brave Sergeant Carney never permitted to fall on the ground, will still be borne aloft by Southern soldier and Northern soldier, and, in a more potent and higher sense, we shall all realize that

"The slave's chain and the master's alike are broken;
The one curse of the race held both in tether;
They are rising, all are rising—
The black and the white together."

THE LIMITLESS POSSIBILITIES OF THE NEGRO RACE[24]

By CHARLES W. ANDERSON, of New York

Mr. Chairman, Ladies and Gentlemen:

I sometimes feel that we, as a race, do not fully appreciate the importance of industrial education. I feel that the day is near at hand when the physical apparatus of civil education will play a larger part in the progress of the world than it has hitherto done. In other words, I firmly believe that the industrial victories are in the future and not in the past. We have done much and wrought many miracles, but the miracles are but evidences of possible powers rather than the high-tide marks of development. In my mind the possibilities of physical and scientific achievement are limitless, and beyond the compass of human conception. Look at iron alone. See what has been done with it in the last fifty years. See what you are able to do with it here in Tennessee. From it are made things dainty and things dangerous, carriages and cannon, spatula and spade, sword and pen, wheel, axle and rail, as well as screw, file, and saw. It is bound around the hull of ships and lifted into tower and steeple. It is drawn into wire, coiled into springs, woven into gauze, twisted into rope, and sharpened into needles. It is stretched into a web, finer by comparison than the gossamer of the morning along the bed of the ocean, and made to tick out the yesterday of Europe on the to-day of America. All of this variety of use has been made out of the stubbornness of metals by the sovereign touch of industrial and scientific education. There is inexhaustible promise in this development. It has brought, and is still bringing, the two great races closer together. These iron veins and arteries which interlock our cities and confederate our States do much to familiarize each race with the hopes and aspirations of the other, and to weave their histories into one harmonious contexture, as telegraphic messages fly instantaneously across them, and screaming trains rush back and forth like shuttles upon a mighty loom. When our fullest expectations shall have been fulfilled, both races will have the freest opportunity for the development of their varied capabilities, and, through mutual bonds of interest and affection and mutual bonds of sympathy and purpose, will rise the unmatched harmonies of a united people to the imperial accompaniment of two mighty oceans.

It is a peculiar fact that immediately after the abolition of human slavery the country started upon an unparalleled career of prosperity. The West, then almost unexplored, began to develop, and has continued to do so until now it is studded with proud cities, teeming with throbbing life, growing like the grass of the prairies in spring-time, advancing like the steam-engine, baffling distance like the telegraph, and spreading the pulsations of their mighty hearts to the uttermost parts of the world. There they stand with their echoing marts of trade, their stately spires of worship and their magnificent institutions of learning, as free as the encircling air, as independent as the soaring eagle, and more powerful than the Roman Empire when in the plenitude of her power. All of this has been accomplished since the energies of men were unfettered. Thus it may be said that both races started almost simultaneously on their careers to fulfill the destiny of this great country among the countries of the world. And as we started together substantially, we must end together. We started with most unequal equipment, to be sure, and under conditions as far apart as the sky from this pavilion, but we have marched to the same music and in the same direction ever since, with varying fortunes and unequal steps, but with no steps backward, until to-day we are able to recognize in each other and be recognized by all mankind as equals in our attachment to the land, the laws, the institutions, and the flag of our common country.

The responsibility now rests upon you to improve each minute of your lives in fitting yourselves for a wiser, better and worthier discharge of the obligations of American citizenship. You may be constrained to ask, "What shall we do?" or, with Archimedes of old, exclaim "Give me where to stand and I will move the world." Let me advise you to stand where you are. That's the place. Act well your part, and you shall have accomplished all that is expected of you. My friends, a country like ours is not governed by law, or courts of justice, or judges, however wise or puissant. It is governed by public sentiment. Once poison it, and courts are impotent and judges powerless. Therefore we are responsible, each and all of us, according to our talents and influence, for the public sentiment of the day. If it is healthy and just, it is we who have made it so; if it is unhealthy and unjust, it is we who have made it or permitted it to become so. And what is this all-powerful, but imperceptible, entity, this potent influence which controls presidents, cabinets, congresses, courts, judges, juries, the press and—I regret to say it—the pulpit? What is public sentiment or public opinion? It is the multiplied, accumulated opinion of all the people. Every word spoken or written by man or woman goes to make up this great stream of public opinion, just as every drop of dew or water goes to make up that mighty river which divides this imperial continent and turns the spindles of the ten thousand factories which hug its shores. Hence we are all responsible for our contribution to the public opinion of the day, whether our contribution be a raindrop or a Niagara. We are responsible for what we say and what we leave unsaid, for what we do and what we leave undone, for what we write and what is unwritten. We are responsible for the errors we have committed and for those we have taken no part in overthrowing. So, whether we realize it or not, we are consciously or unconsciously, intentionally or unintentionally, directly or indirectly, according to our opportunities and our influence, responsible for the public sentiment which secures or deprives every citizen of his rights and of the opportunity for the highest intellectual and industrial development.

I know that it is sometimes said that we have done very little. Be that as it may. Thirty years is but a brief time compared with the centuries in which Norman, Saxon, and Dane have been fusing into the English race. And yet, we have something to remember when great names are counted, something to show when great deeds are told. At the same time I would not have you sit supinely down and wait for the millennium. Far from it. It is said that all things come to him who waits. That is in part true, but it is only fifty per cent. of the whole truth. All things come to him who waits, if he hustles while he waits.

You will need not only education and character, but you also need level-headedness and accuracy of judgment. Acquire intellectuality, but acquire practicality at the same time. Do not join that large and constantly increasing class in this country to whom nothing is desirable but the impossible. Do not indulge in the pastime of throwing stones at the stars. Learn to be practical, and, whatever you attempt in life, remember to think out a plan and a policy before you begin the work. When you are called upon to go out and do battle, stop and reflect, and see if there is a reasonable probability of your whipping anybody. If the probability is not apparent, I would advise you to decline the glove and reserve your lance for a more "convenient season." Martyrdom is very attractive, especially attractive to vigorous young men, but it "butters no parsnips." Therefore, cultivate prudence as well as valor, and study men as well as books; for you will needs be prepared to meet the living issues of the present; and if you are wise, you will anticipate the possible exigencies of the future. To do this you will want both courage and discretion. Learn the proper value of organization and union, and never cease to remember that an army divided is an army defeated. You will neither be able to help yourself nor hurt the enemy by firing paper bullets. You must organize.

To make steam effective you must bind it up in an engine; to make water serviceable, you must harness it in a mill; to make electricity manageable, you must mask it in a battery; and to make men useful in reformatory or remedial work, you must recruit them into an organization.

And to those present who have not enjoyed the advantages of an education, let me direct a few remarks. You must not believe that you cannot assist in the work of building character for the race. Every man or woman who plays his or her part according to the best lights, who bears a respected name, or bears the proud title of a "good citizen," who is industrious, temperate, upright, law-abiding, and devoted to whatever is lovely and of good report, is unconsciously pleading the cause of the race before the great tribunal of the civilized world.

To all such we can only render the tribute which history accords to those who fight as privates in the battles of human progress, with all the more devotion and fidelity because their names will never be known. Whenever a man earns the respect of the community in which he resides, some part of that respect, some breath of that fragrance is reflected upon the race of which he is a member.

As a race, we have done much, but we must not forget how much more there is still to do. We have already demonstrated the possession of powers, but we must now bring forth the fruits of sustained racial achievement. To some extent we have been given opportunity, but we must not cease to remember that no race can be given relative rank—it must win equality of rating for itself. Hence, we must not only acquire education, but character as well. It is not only necessary that we should speak well, but it is more necessary that we should speak the truth. We must not only acquire that culture which is the golden key that unlocks all doors and unbars all gates, but we must cultivate that straightforwardness of purpose and unconquerable determination which enables a people to face conditions "without fear and without reproach."

And so the last suggestion comes which the hour presents. In the work of race advancement, we need the service and assistance of all true men and women. We must have the co-operation of all sections and all conditions. The cotton-fields of Alabama, the sugar-plantations of Louisiana, and the coal-mines of Tennessee; the great lakes of the North which winter roofs with ice, and from which drips refreshing coolness through the hot summer months, from the fisheries and the factories, from wheat-fields and pine forests, from meadows billowed with golden grain and orchards bending beneath their burdens of golden fruit, this advance movement must receive support. The humble laborer following his plow afield must do his part; the blacksmith at his forge, the lawyer at the bar, the fisherman on the banks, the man of science putting nature to the question, all, without distinction and without exception, must contribute, according to his station and his opportunity, to the hastening of the day when the Negro shall take his place by the side of the other great race of men and form that grand spectacle which Tennyson had in mind when he spoke of "the parliament of man, the federation of the world."

THE PARTY OF FREEDOM AND THE FREEDMEN—A RECIPROCAL DUTY[25]

BY WILLIAM SANDERS SCARBOROUGH, D.D., LL.D

WILLIAM SANDERS SCARBOROUGH, M. A., PH. D., LL.D., *President of Wilberforce University, Ohio. Author of "First Lessons in Greek," the first and only Greek book written by a Negro, largely used as text-book in both white and Negro schools. Author of a large number of classical interpretations, and philological pamphlets.*

Slavery has been well called the "perfected curse of the ages." Every civilization, ancient and modern, has experienced its blighting, withering effect, and it has cost thrones to learn the lesson that

"The laws of changeless justice blind
Oppressor and oppressed";

that

"Close as sin and suffering joined,"

these two

"March to Fate—abreast."

Since the world began, freedom has been at war with all that savored of servitude. The sentiment of liberty is innate in every human breast. Freedom of speech and of action—the right of every man to be his own master—has ever been the inestimable privilege sought, the boon most craved. For this guerdon men have fought; for this they have even gladly died.

It was the unquenchable desire for liberty that brought the Pilgrim Fathers to Plymouth Rock. They knew that all that is highest and noblest in the human soul is fostered to its greatest development only under the blazing sunlight of freedom. And it was the same flame burning in the heart of the young nation planted on these Western shores that led to the ratification of the sentiment placed by the hand of Thomas Jefferson in the corner-stone of our American independence: "We hold these truths to be self-evident—that all men are created free and equal, that they are endowed by their Creator with certain inalienable rights; that among them are life, liberty, and the pursuit of happiness." Here was heralded to the nation prophetic freedom for all mankind and for all generations.

However, the years of bondage for Africa's sons and daughters in this fair land stretched on over a half century more before the issue was raised. But at last the grasping arms of the gigantic octopus, that was feeding at the nation's heart, reached out too far, and the combat with the monster was begun. Then that laurelled champion and leader of freedom's cause, Charles S. Sumner, laid his hand upon that Declaration of Independence and declared that the nation was "dedicated to liberty and the rights of human nature."

I count it the glory of that gifted humanitarian that he gave his magnificent talents and energies to the organization of a party that could add to its *amor patriæ* the larger, broader, nobler love of freedom for all mankind; and I count it the glory of that party that it stood for

"the voice of a people—uprisen, awake";

that it was "born to make men free."

No matter what name has been inscribed on its banner during its existence of a full half century, the cause that the party of freedom espoused has given its standard-bearer a right to claim that it, and it alone, is the legitimate heir to power in this land where the forefathers sought the liberty the Old World denied. Who dares dispute the claim? Who dares challenge the assertion? Time and events have sanctioned it; age has but strengthened it. And to-day, holding as tenaciously the same principles of truth and justice, the party that, among the parties of this Republic, alone stands as the synonym of freedom is the Republican party.

None dare gainsay it. And, among the growing multitudes in this broad land of ours, none know this better than ten millions of Afro-Americans who but for its strong arm of power might still be suffering from "Man's inhumanity to man."

Forget it? The mightiest draughts from Lethe's stream could not blot from the remembrance of the race the deed of that Republican leader enthroned upon the seat of government, the deed of the immortal Lincoln, whose birth we commemorate here to-night, the deed of that second Abraham who, true to his name as the "father of the faithful," struck the chains from the Negro's limbs and bade him stand forever free.

But did the great work stop there? No; the fast following amendments to the Constitution show that the party of freedom never paused; and the bond forged during the long years of struggle and riveted by emancipation was indissolubly welded when that party crowned the freedman with the glorious rights and privileges of citizenship. Ah, what lamentations loud and long filled the land! What dire predictions smote the nation's ear! What a multitude of evils imagination turned loose like a horde of Furies! What a war of opinion raged 'twixt friends and foes of the race that drew the first full breath of freedom! More than three decades have passed. Have these dismal prophecies been fulfilled? No race under the sun has been so patient under calumny, under oppression, under mob violence; no race has ever shown itself so free from resentment.

But it has been said the Negro was not worth the struggle. Not worth the struggle when, at every call to arms in the nation's history, the black man has nobly responded, whether slave or freeman? Not worth the struggle when, in the Revolution, on Lake Erie with Perry, at Port Hudson, at Millikens Bend, in that fearful crater at Petersburg, he shed his blood freely in the nation's behalf? Not worth the struggle, when he won his way from spade to epaulet in the defense of the nation's honor? *The freedmen fathers were neither cowards nor traitors. Nor do the sons disgrace their sires.*

Who saved the Rough Riders from annihilation at Las Guasimas? Who stormed with unparalleled bravery the heights at El Caney and swept gallantly foremost in that magnificent charge up San Juan hill? Comrades, leaders, onlookers—all with one voice have made reply: "The Negro soldier." Aye; the race has proved its worth, and the whole country, irrespective of party or section, owes it a debt, not only for its heroic service on the battle-field in times of national peril, which was its duty, but for its splendid self-control generally, under the most harassing situations, under most inexcusable assaults.

No; the faith of the party of freedom in the Negro has not been unfounded. In all these years the race has been steadily gaining wealth, education, refinement, places of responsibility and power. It might have done far more for the lasting good of all concerned, had it learned that in all things the

"... Heights are not gained by a single bound,
But we built the ladder by which we rise,...
And we mount to its summit round by round."

But the prophecies of the past are far behind us. The world has passed its verdict on what has been. Mistakes must yield us profit as the problems of the future confront us. We are to look forward with hope. And in preparation for that future,

"The riddling Sphynx puts dim things from our minds,
And sets us to the questions at our doors."

As the Republican party and the Negro face the coming years, one question is of equal moment to both. What shall be the mutual relations in the future? Shall the party of freedom declare at an end its duty toward the party it made men and citizens? On the other hand, shall the Negro say: "Indebtedness ceased with our fathers; we are free to make alliance where we will"?

In view of the blood shed so freely for Republican principles by the Negro as slave and freeman; in view of the loyalty, the courage, the patriotism, the strength, and the needs of the race; in view of this country's prospective broadened domain and the millions of dusky wards to be added to the nation o'er which the American eagle hovers to-day; and in view of the principles that inhere in Republicanism, the party of freedom should find but one answer: "It is and shall be our duty to view you ever as men and citizens, to see that no chain of our forging manacles you to lower planes, that no bar is thrown by us across your pathway up the hill of progress, to help maintain your rights, to throw the weight of our influence for fair treatment, for the side of law and order and justice. The Republican party must not forget for a moment the truth of the argument that Demosthenes once made against Philip with such striking force,—"*All power is unstable that is founded on injustice.*" This party cannot afford to be less than just. The Negro should not ask for more.

This duty laid upon itself on the one hand, it becomes incumbent upon the Negro to reciprocate, and the reciprocation calls for his support of the party. This should be a support, wise and open-eyed, born of appreciation and intelligence. It should be a support, steadfast and loyal, based upon faith in the party's motives and the knowledge that it has stood and still stands for all that the Negro holds most dear. It should be a support that frees itself from selfish leaders and ranting demagogues, that puts aside all mere personal gain, and seeks the good of the race as a whole that it, too, may be lifted up. And lastly, it should be a support that looks for no reward but that which comes because of true worth and ability.

Reciprocity becomes a mutual duty, for there are mutual needs. The Negro's strength is not to be ignored by the party; but the race cannot stand alone. It needs alliance with friendly power; and there is no friend like the tried friend, no party for the freedman like the party that stands upon the high, broad platform of freedom and human rights, irrespective of race, or color, or previous condition.

But having said this, I would be false to the race and my own convictions did I not pause to give the warning that, after all, neither parties nor politics alone can save the Negro. He needs to make a new start in his civil and political career. He must pay less attention to politics and more to business, to industry, to education, to the building up of a strong and sturdy manhood everywhere—to the assimilation generally of all that goes to demand the world's respect and consideration. He must lop off, as so many *incubi*, the professional Negro office-seeker, the professional Negro office-holder, and the Negro politician who aspires to lead the race, for the revenue that is in it. The best men, the wisest, the most unselfish, and above all, the men of the most profound integrity and uprightness, must take the helm or retrogression will be the inevitable result. Politics followed as an end has been the curse of the race. Under it problems have multiplied, and under it the masses have remained longer than they should in the lower stages of development. Only in the hands of men of noble mold, and used only as a *means* to an end, can politics accomplish the highest good for all the race.

The Negro can keep all this in view and yet yield loyal support to the party that set him free.

Let the party of freedom and the freedmen recognize and observe these duties as reciprocal, and a force may be created, having its basis on undying principles, that will pave the way for the ultimate success of the highest aspirations of each—a force that will stretch southward and westward bearing, wherever Old Glory floats, the promise to the oppressed: Freedom, equality, prosperity. And though men may apostatize, this mutual righteous cause shall live to sway for unnumbered years the fortunes of this grand Republic, for the God who reared the continents above the seas and peopled them with nations, who gave these nations freedom of conscience and will, and who has watched their rise and fall from the dawn of creation, still guides the destinies of races and of parties, and standeth

"... within the shadow,
Keeping watch above his own."

THE TEACHINGS OF HISTORY CONSIDERED IN RELATION TO RACE PROBLEMS IN AMERICA[26]

BY NATHAN F. MOSSELL, A. M., M. D.

Surgeon-in-Chief, Frederick Douglass Hospital, Philadelphia, Pa.

Those who are familiar with history will testify that the blacks were a fundamental element in the civilized races of antiquity, as also of the primitive races of southern Europe. In fact, all history is pregnant with traces of the Negro element. The world will ever look with wonder and amazement upon the marks of ancient culture in the valley of the Nile, and we may continue to look as far back as records and inscriptions lend us light, only to find the black man, above all others, leading in the ancient arts and sciences.

History places the earliest civilization in Egypt. The ruling tribes among the people were called the Hamites, the "sunburnt race," according to Dr. Winchell. Says Professor J. Boughton: "The wanderings of these people since prehistoric history began has not been confined to the American continent. In Paleolithic times the black man roamed all over the fairer portions of the Old World; Europe, as well as Asia and Africa, acknowledged his sway. No white man had, so far, appeared to dispute his authority in the vine-clad valleys of France or Germany, or upon the classic hills of Greece or Rome. The black man preceded all others, and carried Paleolithic culture to its very height."

The history of all the lands has been but the history of succeeding races; more often, however, by fusion of different racial types and by the mingling of various tribes and peoples, have been evolved new races, superior to any of the original types. Greece and Rome, the study of history will tell you, had their race and social problems. Inter-marriage at last settled the question. The ethnology of Spain tells the same story. There is not a nation on the globe of pure ethnic character. From the ethnic standpoint, the blood of the black race is everywhere apparent. Ask the Frenchman, the Italian, the Spaniard, whence comes his dark skin and hair; it surely does not come from the Aryan blonde. Ethnology alone can give the answer. In considering the future of our racial problems, it is fitting that we shall recall these facts of history to know the Negro's past place in the world's annals.

* * * * *

American slavery, the most accursed institution the world has ever known, did more to degrade the master than the slave, a truth most often overlooked. It is here I take strong exception to the literal interpretation of the injunction,

"Whosoever will smite thee on the right cheek, turn to him the other also," and "If any man take away thy coat, let him have thy cloak also." Not so; but, on the contrary, we should resist evil with our energy. The tyrant who smites you on one cheek is only made more of a brute by permitting him to continue in the practise by smiting you on the other. It is our moral duty, therefore, to resist him, and not more for our own sake than for his. The brutalizing influence of slavery upon the master class is the curse of the Southern States to-day, and has much more to do with the difficulties of solving the race problems than does the ignorance of the blacks. The Government is not guiltless in this matter of interpretation of the scriptural injunction. In the matter of State rights, Southern election laws, and mob violence, our Government has turned the other cheek also. What has been the result? Why the tyrants continue to become more and more brutal, until they are not only running black men out, but they have recently, at the muzzle of the shot gun, forced their own kith and kin, men to the manor born, to leave the States. I have no hesitancy in proclaiming that this brutality is a legacy left us by slavery, against which we have to contend, making itself felt in the organized mob and in disregard of constituted authority.

In these days of imperialism and territorial expansion, when there is, likewise, much discussion on the subject of inferior races, it is fitting that we should place ourselves aright upon the question of suffrage and rights of franchise. William Lloyd Garrison, Jr., says: "Whosoever laments the scope of suffrage, and talks of disfranchising men on account of ignorance or poverty, has as little comprehension of the meaning of self-government as a blind man has of the colors of the rainbow. I declare my belief that we are suffering, not from a too extended ballot, but from one too limited and unrepresentative. We enunciate a principle of government, and then deny it in practise. If experience has established anything, it is that the interest of one class is never safe in the hands of another. There is no class so poor or ignorant in a republic that it does not know its own suffering and needs better than the wealthy or educated classes. By the rule of justice, it has the same right precisely to give it legal expression. That expression is bound to come, and it is wiser to have it come through the ballot-box than through mobs and violence, born of a feeling of despair and misery." Those States in the South which are passing laws restricting suffrage, to promote the selfish ends of a class, are sowing to the wind and will surely reap the whirlwind. In a republican government, supposed to be ruled by the popular vote, a people's liberty has practically been taken when the right to vote is denied them. In such States, personal liberty, the right to testify in courts of law, the right to hold, buy, and sell real estate, and, in fact, all other rights, become mere privileges, held at the option of others. People are no longer free when the rights of franchise have been annulled. Slavery is truly re-enacted in those States which have succeeded in disfranchising the Negro.

I have neither patience nor respect for those among us who are truckling to the prejudice of our enemies by giving credence to the lie that the ballot was placed in the black man's hand too soon. Lowell was right when he said: "The right to vote makes a safety-valve of every voter, and the best way to teach a man to vote is to give him a chance to practise. It is cheaper in the long run to lift men up than to hold them down; the ballot in their hands is less dangerous to society than a sense of wrong in their heads." The so-called Negro domination of the reconstruction period has no record of misrule such as exists in most of the Southern States to-day. It is our privilege (an oppressed people, who know by bitter experience whereof we speak) to give this government timely warnings as to its duties toward the inhabitants of our newly acquired territory.

I have no confidence in the Government's ability to ameliorate the race conflicts of the South through the course recently outlined by the President of this nation in speeches of flattery and encomiums upon the dead and living heroes of the Southern Confederacy. This policy of conciliation was repeatedly attempted before the war, with the results that the slave influence continued to spread further north and west. It was proved then, as it ever shall be, that no nation can succeed by making a compact with the devil. One must tremble for this country's future when they read upon the statute-books of the Southern States these diabolical laws against social purity, against the civil and political rights of our citizens. It is hoped that the coming Congress will rise to a sense of our impending danger, and see to it that the strong arm of the Government is brought forward to protect each and every citizen in his civil and political rights. Until this is done, we are by no means prepared to add nine millions more of a dark race to those with which we now have to deal. There are those already high in the nation's council who predict that the result of our present war[27] will be a *curse* instead of a *blessing*, that the nation's incapacity to deal justly with our recently liberated slaves proves our inability to deal with nine millions more of untutored and so-called inferior people.

* * * * *

The final conclusion of the whole matter may be forecasted thus: The Negro element in this country is permanent and indestructible. So great are the numbers of the Negroes, and so intimate their relations with the white people, that it is safe to say without fear of contradiction that the status of the Negro element will determine in a large degree the future of the white. Let this truth once be learned. Let the thoughtful people of the nation cease trying to deceive themselves. The inevitable teachings of history will not be reversed. The blood of these varied races will finally be mingled until race distinctions will ultimately be obliterated. The docile nature of the Negro race, his intimate domestic and other relations with the whites, make this conclusion inevitable. The two races are complements of each other and cannot be separated.

A DEFENSE OF THE NEGRO RACE[28]

By Hon. George H. White

Member of Congress from North Carolina

Mr. Chairman:

I want to enter a plea for the colored man, the colored woman, the colored boy, and the colored girl of this country. I would not thus digress from the question at issue and detain the House in a discussion of the interests of this particular people at this time but for the constant and the persistent efforts of certain gentlemen upon this floor to mold and rivet public sentiment against us as a people, and to lose no opportunity to hold up the unfortunate few, who commit crimes and depredations and lead lives of infamy and shame, as other races do, as fair specimens of representatives of the entire colored race. And at no time, perhaps, during the 56th Congress were these charges and countercharges, containing, as they do, slanderous statements, more persistently magnified and pressed upon the attention of the nation than during the consideration of the recent reapportionment bill, which is now a law. As stated some days ago on this floor by me, I then sought diligently to obtain an opportunity to answer some of the statements made by gentlemen from different States, but the privilege was denied me; and I therefore must embrace this opportunity to say, out of season, perhaps, that which I was not permitted to say in season.

In the catalogue of members of Congress in this House perhaps none have been more persistent in their determination to bring the black man into disrepute and, with a labored effort, to show that he was unworthy of the right of citizenship than my colleague from North Carolina, Mr. Kitchin. During the first session of this Congress, while the Constitutional amendment was pending in North Carolina, he labored long and hard to show that the white race was at all times and under all circumstances superior to the Negro by inheritance if not otherwise, and the excuse for his party supporting that amendment, which has since been adopted, was that an illiterate Negro was unfit to participate in making the laws of a sovereign State and the administration and execution of them; but an illiterate white man living by his side, with no more or perhaps not as much property, with no more exalted character, no higher thoughts of civilization, no more knowledge of the handicraft of government, had by birth, because he was white, inherited some peculiar qualification, clear, I presume, only in the mind of the gentleman who endeavored to impress it upon others, that entitled him to vote, though he knew nothing whatever of letters. It is true, in my opinion, that men brood over things at times which they would have exist until they delude themselves and actually, sometimes honestly, believe that such things do exist.

I would like to call the gentleman's attention to the fact that the Constitution of the United States forbids the granting of any title of nobility to any citizen thereof, and while it does not in letters forbid the inheritance of this superior caste, I believe in the fertile imagination of the gentleman promulgating it, his position is at least in conflict with the spirit of that organic law of the land. He insists and, I believe, has introduced a resolution in this House for the repeal of the fifteenth amendment to the Constitution.

* * * * *

It would be unfair, however, for me to leave the inference upon the minds of those who hear me that all of the white people of the State of North Carolina hold views with Mr. Kitchin and think as he does. Thank God there are many noble exceptions to the example he sets, that, too, in the Democratic party; men who have never been afraid that one uneducated, poor, depressed Negro could put to flight and chase into degradation two educated, wealthy, thrifty white men. There never has been, nor ever will be, any Negro domination in that State, and no one knows it any better than the Democratic party. It is a convenient howl, however, often resorted to in order to consummate a diabolical purpose by scaring the weak and gullible whites into support of measures and men suitable to the demagogue and the ambitious office-seeker, whose craving for office overshadows and puts to flight all other considerations, fair or unfair.

As I stated on a former occasion, this young statesman has ample time to learn better and more useful knowledge than he has exhibited in many of his speeches upon this floor, and I again plead for him the statute of youth for the wild and spasmodic notions which he has endeavored to rivet upon his colleagues and this country. But I regret that Mr. Kitchin is not alone upon this floor in these peculiar notions advanced. I refer to another young member of Congress, hailing from the State of Alabama, Mr. Underwood.

* * * * *

It is an undisputed fact that the Negro vote in the State of Alabama, as well as most of the other Southern States, has been effectively suppressed, either one way or the other—in some instances by constitutional amendment and State legislation, in others by cold-blooded fraud and intimidation, but whatever the method pursued, it is not denied, but frankly admitted in the speeches in this House, that the black vote has been eliminated to a large extent. Then, when some of us insist that the plain letter of the Constitution of the United States, which all of us have sworn to support, should be carried out, as expressed in the second section of the fourteenth amendment thereof.

That section makes the duty of every member of Congress plain, and yet the gentleman from Alabama [Mr. Underwood] says that the attempt to enforce this section of the organic law is the throwing down of fire-brands, and notifies the world that this attempt to execute the highest law of the land will be retaliated by the South, and the inference is that the Negro will be even more severely punished than the horrors through which he has already come.

Let me make it plain: The divine law, as well as most of the State laws, says, in substance: "He that sheddeth man's blood, by man shall his blood be shed." A highwayman commits murder, and when the officers of the law undertake to arrest, try, and punish him commensurate with the enormity of his crime, he straightens himself up to his full height and defiantly says to them: "Let me alone; I will not be arrested, I will not be tried, I'll have none of the execution of your laws, and in the event you attempt to execute your laws upon me, I will see to it many more men, women, or children are murdered."

Here's the plain letter of the Constitution, the plain, simple, sworn duty of every member of Congress; yet these gentlemen from the South say "Yes, we have violated your Constitution of the nation; we regarded it as a local necessity; and now, if you undertake to punish us as the Constitution prescribes, we will see to it that our former deeds of disloyalty to that instrument, our former acts of disfranchisement and opposition to the highest law of the land will be repeated manifoldly."

Not content with all that has been done to the black man, not because of any deeds that he has done, Mr. Underwood advances the startling information that these people have been thrust upon the whites of the South, forgetting, perhaps, the horrors of the slave-trade, the unspeakable horrors of the transit from the shores of Africa by means of the middle passage to the American clime; the enforced bondage of the blacks and their descendants for two and a half centuries in the United States. Now, for the first time perhaps in the history of our lives, the information comes that these poor, helpless, and in the main inoffensive people were thrust upon our Southern brethren.

* * * * *

If the gentleman to whom I have referred will pardon me, I would like to advance the statement that the musty records of 1868, filed away in the archives of Southern capitols, as to what the Negro was thirty-two years ago, is not a proper standard by which the Negro living on the threshold of the twentieth century should be measured. Since that time we have reduced the illiteracy of the race at least 45 per cent. We have written and published near 500 books. We have nearly 300 newspapers, 3 of which are dailies. We have now in practise over 2,000 lawyers and a corresponding number of doctors. We have accumulated over $12,000,000 worth of school property and about $40,000,000 worth of church property. We have about 140,000 farms and homes, valued at in the neighborhood of $750,000,000, and personal property valued at about $170,000,000. We have raised about $11,000,000 for educational purposes, and the property per capita for every colored man, woman, and child in the United States is estimated at $75.

We are operating successfully several banks, commercial enterprises among our people in the Southland, including 1 silk-mill and 1 cotton-factory. We have 32,000 teachers in the schools of the country; we have built, with the aid of our friends, about 20,000 churches, and support 7 colleges, 17 academies, 50 high schools, 5 law schools, 5 medical schools, and 25 theological seminaries. We have over 600,000 acres of land in the South alone. The cotton produced, mainly by black labor, has increased from 4,669,770 bales in 1860 to 11,235,000 in 1899. All this we have done under the most adverse circumstances. We have done it in the face of lynching, burning at the stake, with the humiliation of "Jim Crow" cars, the disfranchisement of our male citizens, slander and degradation of our women, with the factories closed against us, no Negro permitted to be conductor on the railway-cars, whether run through the streets of our cities or across the prairies of our great country, no Negro permitted to run as engineer on a locomotive, most of the mines closed against us. Labor-unions—carpenters, painters, brick-masons, machinists, hackmen, and those supplying nearly every conceivable avocation for livelihood have banded themselves together to better their condition, but, with few exceptions, the black face has been left out. The Negroes are seldom employed in our mercantile stores. At this we do not wonder. Some day we hope to have them employed in our own stores. With all these odds against us, we are forging our way ahead, slowly, perhaps, but surely. You tie us and then taunt us for a lack of bravery, but one day we will break the bonds. You may use our labor for two and a half centuries and then taunt us for our poverty, but let me remind you we will not always remain poor. You may withhold even the knowledge of how to read God's word and learn the way from earth to glory and then taunt us for our ignorance, but we would remind you that there is plenty of room at the top, and we are climbing.

After enforced debauchery, with the many kindred horrors incident to slavery, it comes with ill grace from the perpetrators of these deeds to hold up the shortcomings of some of our race to ridicule and scorn.

"The new man, the slave who has grown out of the ashes of thirty-five years ago, is inducted into the political and social system, cast into the arena of manhood, where he constitutes a new element and becomes a competitor for all its emoluments. He is put upon trial to test his ability to be counted worthy of freedom, worthy of the elective franchise; and after thirty-five years of struggling against almost insurmountable odds, under conditions but little removed from slavery itself, he asks a fair and just judgment, not of those whose prejudice has endeavored to forestall, to frustrate his every forward movement, rather those who have lent a helping hand, that he might demonstrate the truth of 'the fatherhood of God and the brotherhood of man.'"

* * * * *

Now, Mr. Chairman, before concluding my remarks I want to submit a brief recipe for the solution of the so-called American Negro problem. He asks no special favors, but simply demands that he be given the same chance for existence, for earning a livelihood, for raising himself in the scales of manhood and womanhood that are accorded to kindred nationalities. Treat him as a man; go into his home and learn of his social conditions; learn of his cares, his troubles, and his hopes for the future; gain his confidence; open the doors of industry to him; let the word "Negro," "colored," and "black" be stricken from all the organizations enumerated in the federation of labor.

Help him to overcome his weaknesses, punish the crime-committing class by the courts of the land, measure the standard of the race by its best material, cease to mold prejudicial and unjust public sentiment against him, and my word for it, he will learn to support, hold up the hands of, and join in with that political party, that institution, whether secular or religious, in every community where he lives, which is destined to do the greatest good for the greatest number. Obliterate race hatred, party prejudice, and help us to achieve nobler ends, greater results, and become more satisfactory citizens to our brother in white.

This, Mr. Chairman, is perhaps the Negroes' temporary farewell to the American Congress; but let me say, Ph[oe]nix-like he will rise up some day and come again. These parting words are in behalf of an outraged, heart-broken, bruised, and bleeding, but God-fearing people, faithful, industrious, loyal people—rising people, full of potential force.

Mr. Chairman, in the trial of Lord Bacon, when the court disturbed the counsel for the defendant, Sir Walter Raleigh raised himself up to his full height and, addressing the court, said:

"Sir, I am pleading for the life of a human being."

The only apology that I have to make for the earnestness with which I have spoken is that I am pleading for the life, the liberty, the future happiness, and manhood-suffrage for one-eight of the entire population of the United States.

THE NEGRO'S PART IN THE REDEMPTION OF AFRICA[29]

BY LEVI J. COPPIN,

Bishop A. M. E. Church

The land once lying in darkness, but now fast coming to the light, is claiming the best thought and the best energies of the civilized world.

Africa, on account of a lack of coast indentations, has been the last among the continents to be penetrated by the beneficent influence of commerce; and this largely accounts for that long obscurity, during which it was given the name, the "Dark Continent."

Its situation beneath the line of the Equator has had also something to do with staying the onward march of civilization from without. The world learned first to think only of the enervating influence of a torrid sun upon the inhabitants of the great continent, and this was not inviting to immigration.

Nations have reached their highest and best development, not by isolation, but by taking advantage of whatever of good they found among others. But as the years and centuries have passed, it has dawned upon the world that Africa enjoys the unique distinction of occupying a place in three zones, and hence offering the largest variety of climatic influences that are favorable to life and health.

Abounding in mineral wealth, with millions of acres suitable for agriculture, and with immense forests of valuable wood; with palm oil, ivory, and other desirable products, Africa is now being sought by the world's capital, and is giving rich rewards to combined capital and labor.

But what of her peoples? When as a Christian Church we speak of the redemption of Africa, we do not refer to her material resources chiefly, though these are a means to an end. The one supreme thought with us is, how the millions of her inhabitants may be reached by the light of the gospel and saved. In their isolated condition, the people have for long centuries become the victims of customs and habits not in keeping with the better life which is the result only of Christian civilization. The customs and habits formed and fixed by centuries cannot be thoroughly changed by a few years of effort. The success already attained by missionary enterprise in Africa is not to be measured by the years of effort it has cost, nor by the amount of money expended. Missionary records from other fields will fully justify this statement. In all such work we may expect to have the exemplification of nature's course, "first the blade, then the ear; after that, the full corn in the ear."

One hundred and sixty-six years have passed since the Moravians, as pioneer Protestant missionaries began work on the Gold Coast. From 1736 to 1832, much effort was expended by a number of societies on the West Coast, during which more or less progress was made, accompanied with no little sacrifice, and a large death-roll of missionaries. But, at this time the missionary field is no longer confined to any particular section of Africa. The missionary has followed in the wake of the explorer and planted his stations. In South Africa the work is most hopeful. In West Africa, the foothold is permanent; in Central Africa the work proceeds, and is not likely to stop until every tribe shall read the story of the Cross in his own dialect.

Those missionaries who have studied the native tongues—of which there are many—and translated the Bible in the vernacular of various tribes, have done a work that is of inestimable value. The difficulty of language, is, after all, the greatest obstacle in evangelistic progress in Africa. If there were but one tongue to contend with, the work of the Missionary would be comparatively easy; but there are many tongues. In my own district in South Africa, we have the Bible in three native dialects, namely: the Zulu, Bechauna, and the so-called Kaffir. Besides these, we have the Dutch as well as the English Bible.

So much has been accomplished by missionaries, and at so great a sacrifice, that it seems quite out of place to suggest a criticism or complaint, and yet all the Christian workers should be ready to receive any suggestion that would help them to achieve better results.

In carrying the Gospel to an unenlightened people, there is a strong temptation to emphasize unduly the commercial element that very naturally accompanies it. Civilization and evangelization must go hand in hand, but the greater importance should always be given to the work of evangelization. In our highest civilization are to be found objectionable and hurtful elements, and these are likely to be the first to intrude themselves upon an unsuspecting people.

It is ever to be regretted, that the civilization that opened the way for the missionary, also gave an opportunity for the introduction of evils, among which none have wrought greater harm than the introduction of alcoholic beverages.

To what extent, anyone directly connected with Missionary enterprise has ever been responsible for such a sad result, we do not know; but it does seem evident that the idea of pecuniary gain has not always been kept away from the Missionary field. The acquisition of lands for other than ecclesiastical purposes, and traffic in native products, offer a great temptation to the Missionary, some of whom have availed themselves of these advantages, to the detriment of their legitimate work. It is not always an easy thing for one to become so forgetful of himself in his efforts to bless others as to be in his life, and work a perfect exemplar of the Divine Master, whose Kingdom he seeks to promote, but whose Kingdom is not of this world.

Professor Drummond, in a speech in 1888, among other important statements upon foreign missionary works, made the following: "I was taught to believe that the essential to a missionary was strong faith. I have since learned that it is more essential for him to have strong love. I was taught, out there in the missionary field, that he needed to have great knowledge. I have learned that, more than knowledge even, is required personal character. I have met men in mission fields in different parts of the world who could make zealous addresses, at evangelistic meetings at home, who left for their fields of labor, laden with testimonials from churches and Sunday-schools, but who became utterly demoralized within a year's time, because they had not learned that love is a greater thing than faith. That is a neglected part of a Missionary's education, it seems to me, and yet it is a most essential one. I would say that the thing to be certain of in picking out a man for such a field as Africa, where the strain upon a man's character is tremendous, and the strain upon his spiritual life owing to the isolation, is more tremendous, that we must be sure that we are sending a man of character and heart; morally sound to the core, with a large and brotherly sympathy for the native." These are the words of Professor Drummond, and in my opinion he spoke the exact truth; and in making this quotation, I am glad that it is from such an eminent authority; one who could have no sinister motives for such utterances. He does not arraign the missionaries as a whole but frankly states some thing that he had learned from observation.

The native African, as a rule, is virtuous and honest. The uncivilized tribes, in striving for the mastery among themselves, commit many acts that would not be approved by the rules governing modern warfare: deeds of cruelty, that made the need of the Gospel among them imperative. But, in their individual lives, free from the exciting influence of war they have rules and customs governing their home life that are entirely in keeping with the highest state of Christian civilization. To them, polygamy is not a sinful practise. Without light beyond that which comes from their own fireside, they do not see the necessity of breaking away from a practise that is peculiar to mankind in the earliest stages of social life. But they hold tenaciously to the rule, that all men and all women among them must respect the matrimonial customs by which they are governed. These customs cannot be violated with impunity, and the penalty for such violations is often death. They are disposed to be true to their professions, and faithful in what they believe. When they are persuaded that there is a better life, and induced to embrace it, they bring with them their characteristic sincerity. How great, then, is the need of missionaries who will not, by the deplorable example set by their own unfaithfulness and insincerity, lower the standard of the native.

The spirit which impels one to work in the foreign field generally leaves him without a choice as to post of duty. The first thought to him is: "Lord what wilt Thou have me to do?" And hence the missionary goes forth without questioning the race variety among which his lot should be cast. But in this day of systematic method even in Christian effort, and when missionaries from every race variety are being prepared for the work, I think it would not be out of place to maintain a closer respect for the laws of adaptation and fitness.

* * * * *

The religious field, and especially the great continent of Africa, seems to offer the greatest opportunity for the man of color to do his best work. As we stand in the open door of a new century, God is calling us to new duties and responsibilities. The preparation for this work was through a school of hard experiences, but perhaps the trials were no harder than those which had been borne by others. We waited long for the call to take our place among other agencies for the redemption of the world; and now that it has come, we have no time nor disposition to brood over past experiences. Our business is now with the exacting present, and the portentious future, and we must adjust ourselves to the new situation.

God is calling men of every race and clime to take a part in the world's redemption and face the responsibilities that come with the unfolding years. If we are found ready and willing to take our place, then may we claim the promise of His presence and help: but, if we are found to be unwilling, and unworthy, the call may not come to us again.

"Stretch forth thy hand; Jehovah bids thee come
And claim the promise; thou hast had thy doom,
If forth in sorrow, weeping, thou hast gone,
Rejoicing to thy God thou shalt return.

"Stretch forth thy hand, no longer doubt, arise;
Look! See the 'signo' in the vaulted skies!
Greet the new century with faith sublime,
For God is calling now, this is thy time.

"Stretch forth thy hand to God, the night is past;
The morning cometh, thou art free at last.

No brigands draw thee from thy peaceful home,
But messengers of love to greet thee come.

"Stretch forth thy hand to kindred o'er the sea;
Our cause is one, and brothers still are we.
Bone of our bone, one destiny we claim;
Flesh of our flesh, thy God and ours the same.

"Stretch forth thy hand: "What tho' the heathen rage"
And fiends of darkness all their wrath engage.
The hand of God still writes upon the wall,
"Thy days are numbered; all the proud shall fall."

"Stretch forth thy hand, nor yet in terror flee;
Thick darkness but a swaddling-band shall be
The waves and billows which thy way oppose
Shall in their bosom bury all thy foes.

"Stretch forth thy hand to God, 'tis not for thee
To question aught, nor all his purpose see.
The hand that led thee through the dreary night
Does not thy counsel need when comes the light.

"Stretch forth thy hand; stretch forth thy hand to God;
Nor falter thou, nor stumble at His word.
And if in service thou shalt faithful be,
His promise of salvation thou shalt see."

A PLEA FOR INDUSTRIAL OPPORTUNITY[30]

BY FANNY JACKSON COPPIN

FANNY MIRIAM JACKSON COPPIN, *the first Negro woman in America to graduate from college—Oberlin, 1865. From 1837 to 1902, teacher and principal of the Institute for Colored Youth in Philadelphia.*

The great lesson to be taught by this Fair is the value of co-operative effort to make our cents dollars, and to show us what help there is for ourselves in ourselves. That the colored people of this country have enough money to materially alter their financial condition, was clearly demonstrated by the millions of dollars deposited in the Freedmen's Bank; that they have the good sense, and the unanimity to use this power, are now proved by this industrial exhibition and fair.

It strikes me that much of the recent talk about the exodus has proceeded upon the high-handed assumption that, owing largely to the credit system of the South, the colored people there are forced to the alternative, to "curse God, and die," or else "go West." Not a bit of it. The people of the South, it is true, cannot at this time produce hundreds of dollars, but they have millions of pennies; and millions of pennies make tens of thousands of dollars. By clubbing together and lumping their pennies, a fund might be raised in the cities of the South that the poorer classes might fall back upon while their crops are growing; or else, by the opening of co-operative stores, become their own creditors and so effectually rid themselves of their merciless extortioners. "Oh, they won't do anything; you can't get them united on anything!" is frequently expressed. The best way for a man to prove that he can do a thing is to do it, and that is what we have shown we can do. This Fair, participated in by twenty four States in the Union, and gotten up for a purpose which is of no pecuniary benefit to those concerned in it, effectually silences all slanders about "we won't or we can't do," and teaches its own instructive and greatly needed lessons of self-help,—the best help that any man can have, next to God's.

Those in charge, who have completed the arrangement of the Fair, have studiously avoided preceding it with noisy and demonstrative babblings, which are so often the vapid precursors of promises as empty as those who make them; therefore, in some quarters, our Fair has been overlooked. It is not, we think, a presumptuous interpretation of this great movement, to say, that the voice of God now seems to utter "Speak to the people that they go forward." "Go forward" in what respect? Teach the millions of poor colored laborers of the South how much power they have in themselves, by co-operation of effort, and by a combination of their small means, to change the despairing poverty which now drives them from their homes, and makes them a millstone around the neck of any community, South or West. Secondly, that we shall go forward in asking to enter the same employments which other people enter. Within the past ten years we have made almost no advance in getting our youth into industrial and business occupations. It is just as hard for instance, to get a boy into a printing-office now as it was ten years ago. It is simply astonishing when we consider how many of the common vocations of life colored people are shut out of. Colored men are not admitted to the printers' trade-union, nor, with very rare exceptions are they employed in any city of the United States in a paid capacity as printers or writers; one of the rare exceptions being the employment of H. Price Williams, on the *Sunday Press* of this city. We are not employed as salesmen or pharmacists, or saleswomen, or bank clerks, or merchants' clerks, or tradesmen, or mechanics, or telegraph operators, or to any degree as State or government officials, and I could keep on with the string of "ors" until to-morrow morning, but the patience of an audience has its limit.

Slavery made us poor, and its gloomy, malicious shadow tends to keep us so. I beg to say, kind hearers, that this is not spoken in a spirit of recrimination. We have no quarrel with our fate, and we leave your Christianity to yourselves. Our faith is firmly fixed in that "Eternal Providence," that in its own good time will "justify the ways of God to man." But, believing that to get the right men into the right places is a "consummation most devoutly to be wished," it is a matter of serious concern to us to see our youth with just as decided diversity of talent as any other people, herded together into but three or four occupations.

It is cruel to make a teacher or a preacher of a man who ought to be a printer or a blacksmith, and that is exactly the condition we are now obliged to submit to. The greatest advance that has been made since the War has been effected by political parties, and it is precisely the political positions that we think it least desirable our youth should fill. We have our choice of the professions, it is true, but, as we have not been endowed with an overwhelming abundance of brains, it is not probable that we can contribute to the bar a great lawyer except once in a great while. The same may be said of medicine; nor are we able to tide over the "starving time," between the reception of a diploma and the time that a man's profession becomes a paying one.

Being determined to know whether this industrial and business ostracism lay in ourselves or "in our stars," we have from time to time, knocked, shaken, and kicked, at these closed doors of employment. A cold, metallic voice from within replies, "We do not employ colored people." Ours not to make reply, ours not to question why. Thank heaven, we are not obliged to do and die; having the preference to do or die, we naturally prefer to do.

But we cannot help wondering if some ignorant or faithless steward of God's work and God's money hasn't blundered. It seems necessary that we should make known to the good men and women who are so solicitous about our souls, and our minds, that we haven't quite got rid of our bodies yet, and until we do, we must feed and clothe them; and this attitude of keeping us out of work forces us back upon charity.

That distinguished thinker, Mr. Henry C. Carey, in his valuable works on political economy, has shown by the truthful and forceful logic of history, that the elevation of all peoples to a higher moral and intellectual plane, and to a fuller investiture of their civil rights, has always steadily kept pace with the improvement in their physical condition. Therefore we feel that resolutely and in unmistakable language, yet in the dignity of moderation, we should strive to make known to all men the justice of our claims to the same employments as other's under the same conditions. We do not ask that anyone of our people shall be put into a position because he is a colored person, but we do most emphatically ask that he shall not be kept out of a position because he is a colored person. "An open field and no favors" is all that is requested. The time was when to put a colored girl or boy behind a counter would have been to decrease custom; it would have been a tax upon the employer, and a charity that we were too proud to accept; but public sentiment has changed. I am satisfied that the employment of a colored clerk or a colored saleswoman wouldn't even be a "nine days' wonder." It is easy of accomplishment, and yet it is not. To thoughtless and headstrong people who meet duty with impertinent dictation I do not now address myself; but to those who wish the most gracious of all blessings, a fuller enlightment as to their duty,—to those I beg to say, think of what is suggested in this appeal.

AN APPEAL TO OUR BROTHER IN WHITE[31]

BY W. J. GAINES, D. D.

Bishop of the A.M.E. Church in Georgia

Providence, in wisdom, has decreed that the lot of the Negro should be cast with the white people of America. Condemn as we may the means through which we were brought here, recount as we may the suffering through which, as a race, we passed in the years of slavery, yet the fact remains that today our condition is far in advance of that of the Negroes who have never left their native Africa. We are planted in the midst of the highest civilization mankind has ever known, and are rapidly advancing in knowledge, property, and moral enlightenment. We might, with all reason, thank God even for slavery, if this were the only means through which we could arrive at our present progress and development.

We should indeed count ourselves blest if our white brethren would always extend to us that kindness, justice, and sympathy which our services to them in the past should inspire, and our dependence upon them as the more enlightened and wealthy race should prompt them to bestow.

Why should there be prejudice and dislike on the part of the white man to his colored brother? Is it because he was once a slave, and a slave must forever wear the marks of degradation? Is there no effacement for the stigma of slavery—no erasement for this blot of shame? Will our white brother not remember that it was his hand that forged the links of that chain and that riveted them around the necks of the people who had roved for thousands of years in the unrestrained liberty of the boundless forests in far-away Africa? As well might the seducer blacken the name and reputation of the fair and spotless maiden he has cruelly and wantonly seduced. Go far enough back and it is more than probable that you will find the taint of slavery in your line and its blot upon your escutcheon. The proud Saxon became the slave to the Norman, and yet to-day millions are proud to be called Anglo-Saxons.

Will our white brother refuse us his cordial fellowship because of our ignorance? Ignorance is indeed a great evil and hindrance. The enlightened and refined cannot find fellowship with the ignorant, the benighted, the untutored. If this be the line of demarkation, we can and will remove it. No people ever made more heroic efforts to rise from ignorance to enlightenment. Forty-three per cent. of the Negro race can read and write, and with time we can bring our race up to a high degree of civilization. We are determined, by the help of Providence, and the strength of our own right arms, to educate our people until the reproach of ignorance can no longer be brought against us. When we do, will our white brothers accord that respect which is the due of intelligence and culture?

Does our white brother look with disdain upon us because we are not cleanly and neat? It is true that the masses of our race have not shown that regard for personal cleanliness and nicety of dress, which a wealthy and educated people have the means and the time for. Our people by the exigencies of their lot, have had to toil and toil in menial places, the places where drudgery was demanded and where contact with dust and filth was necessary to the accomplishment of their work. But even this can be remedied, and cleanliness and neatness can be made a part of the Negro's education until he can present, as thousands of his race are now doing, a creditable appearance. Will improvement along these lines help us to gain the esteem and respectful consideration of our white brothers? If so, the time is not far distant when this barrier will be removed. Education will help solve this difficulty as it does all others, and give to our race that touch of refinement which insures physical as well as mental soundness.—*mens sana in corpore sano.*

But is our moral condition the true reason of our ostracism? Are we remanded to the back seats and ever held in social dishonor because we are morally unclean? Would that we could reply by a denial of the allegation and rightly claim that purity which would be at the foundation of all respectable social life. But here we ask the charitable judgment of our white brethren, and point them to the heroic efforts we have made and are making for the moral elevation of our race. Even a superficial glance at the social side of the Negro's life will convince the unprejudiced that progress is being made among the better classes of our people toward virtuous living. Chastity is being urged everywhere in the school house, and the church, and the home, for our women, and honesty and integrity for our men. We can and will lift the shadow of immorality from the great masses of our race, and demonstrate to the whole world what religion and education can do for a people. We are doing it. Among the thoroughly cultured and rightly trained of our women, virtue is as sacred as life, and among our men of similar advantages, honor and integrity are prized as highly as among any people on the globe.

Is our poverty the barrier that divides us from a closer fellowship with our white brethren? Would wealth cure all the evils of our condition, and give us the cordial recognition we ask from them? If so, we can remove even this barrier. Our labor has already created much of the wealth of the South, and it only needs intelligence to turn it into our own coffers and make it the possession of our own people. Among the whites money seems to be the *sesame* that opens the doors to social recognition, and converts the shoddy into a man of influence and rank. Barney Barnato, a London Jew, who began life with a trained donkey, became at length the "South African diamond king," and then all London paid homage to this despised son of a hated race. Would money thus convert our despised people into honorable citizens, give them kindly recognition at the hands of our white neighbors, and take from them the stigma which has so long marked them with dishonor and shame? If so, we can hope to secure even this coveted prize, and claim like Barney Barnato the respect of mankind.

But if it is none of these things that doom us to ostracism and degradation, as a people, I ask finally is it our *color*? Alas, if it be this, we can do nothing to remove the line of separation, unless it be to wait the slow process of amalgamation which despite our efforts, the white people of this country seem bound to consummate. If we knew of any chemical preparation by which we could change the color of our skins and straighten our hair we might hope to bring about the desired consummation at once, but alas, there is no catholicon for this ill, no mystic concoction in all the pharmacies of earth to work this miracle of color. We must fold our hands in despair and submit to our fate with heavy hearts.

To be serious, however, I would plead with our white brothers not to despise us on account of our color. It is the inheritance we received from God, and it could be no mark of shame or dishonor. "Can the leopard change his spots or the Ethiopian his skin?" No disgrace can be attached to physical characteristics which are the result of heredity, and cannot be removed by any volition or effort. How cruel it is to visit upon the colored man contempt and dishonor because of the hue of his skin, or the curling peculiarity of his hair. Let him stand or fall upon his merit. Let him be respected if he is worthy. Let him be despised if he is unworthy.

We appeal to our white brothers to accord us simple justice. If we deserve good treatment give it to us, and do not consider the question of color any more than you would refuse kindness to a man because he is blind.

All we ask is a fair show in the struggle of life. We have nothing but the sentiment of kindness for our white brethren. Take us into your confidence, trust us with responsibility, and above all, show us cordial kindness. Thus will you link our people to you by the chains of love which nothing can break, and we will march hand in hand up the steep pathway of progress.

THE POLITICAL OUTLOOK FOR AFRICA[32]

BY EDWARD WILMOT BLYDEN

EDWARD WILMOT BLYDEN, *one of the greatest scholars of the race; native of St. Thomas, West Indies. Secretary of State of the Republic of Liberia; sent on diplomatic missions to the interior of Africa, and reported proceedings before Royal Geographical Society; Minister Plenipotentiary of the Republic of Liberia at the Court of St. James; Secretary of State for Foreign Affairs; Ambassador to France from Liberia; Fellow of the American Philological Association; Honorary Member Athaneum Club. Presented with medal by the Sultan of Turkey in recognition of his services as Mohammedan Commissioner of Education.*

...Now as to our political relations, the gift of the African does not lie in the direction of political aggrandizement. His sphere is the church, the school, the farm, the workshop. With us, the tools are the proper instruments of the man. This is why our country has been partitioned among the political agencies of the world—the Japhetic powers, for they can best do the work to be done in the interest of the temporal as a basis for the spiritual advancement of humanity. The African and the Jew are the spiritual races, and to them political ascendence among the nations of the earth is not promised. It was M. Renan, the great French agnostic, who said: "The fate of the Jewish people was not to form a separate nationality; it is a race which always cherishes a dream of something that transcends nations."

This truth will stand, though we cannot help sympathizing with the intense and glowing patriotism of Mr. Zangwill as described in the *Daily News* the other day. Then as Africans we must sympathize with and assist the powers that be, as ordained by God, whom He will hold to a strict account for their proceedings. We cannot alter this arrangement, whatever our opinion as to the rudeness and ruggedness of the methods by which the human instruments have arrived at it.

It is a fact. Let us then, to the best of our ability, assist those to whom has been committed rule over our country. Their task is not an easy one. They are giving direction to a state of things that must largely influence the future. As conscientious men, they are often in perplexity. The actual rulers of British West African Colonies are to-day an exceptional class of men. And in keeping with the spirit of the times, and in the critical circumstances in which they labor, they are doing their best under the guidance of a chief in this country of large sympathies and a comprehensive grasp of situations.

THE DUTY AND RESPONSIBILITY OF THE ANGLO-SAXON IDEA OF CITIZENSHIP[33]

BY W. JUSTIN CARTER
of Harrisburg, Pennsylvania

Mr. Chairman, Ladies and Gentlemen:

I am going to speak to you to-night of what your race has contributed and is contributing to this great stream on whose bosom is borne the freighted destiny of the human race, and whose currents wash every shore.

More than two and one half centuries of progress and achievement, on this continent alone, may well vaunt your pride and give you the resolution which belongs to the children themselves of destiny.

Exult copiously, if you will, over the triumphal march of a great material civilization, the marvelous expansion of your territory, your wonderful development of hidden resources, your power and dignity at home or abroad, but invite not, nor condone that spirit of listless satiety, nor sink into that national egotism which lets the dagger steal to the heart of the nation while your reveling conceals the presence of the foe. For, remember, pomp and splendor, wealth, ease, and power's pride and heraldry's boast once echoed

"Through haughty Rome's imperial street."

If American citizenship contains a hope and promise, a wealth, a blessing, and a content, aye! and immortality and just renown, it lives to-day in hearts, and not in stones; it lives in feelings and not in lands; it resides in aspirations and not in coffers, it lives in ideals and not in vaunt and splendor.

It is yours to fulfill its duties; to meet well its responsibilities; it is what your fathers builded out of heart and soul, out of love, compassion, and generous fellowship, and not out of blood and brawn; it is humanity's own; yours be it to study and repeat, if need be, the sacrifices of those who planted its first seeds with the sword, nourished them with their blood and suffering, and with wisdom, blessed by Heaven, consecrated by heroic sacrifices and sanctified by prayer, left it to you and to all of us, more wisely fashioned, more glittering in its prospect and more alluring to our fancy than anything political wisdom ever offered to human hope.

But in order to know and feel what there is of universal interest which we have to do, what there is for humanity's glory and weal we have to preserve; what is the task set to us, as our work in forwarding the current of human life and liberty, we must look to the past, and learn what fundamental, essential truths have grown from its toil and achievement. Many such the American idea of citizenship contains; but of one let us speak.

The American idea of citizenship and its ideal, its aims, possibilities, and destiny, had its origin and enshrinement in that Anglo-Saxon spirit of freedom which has been the peculiar characteristic of a race whose civil and judicial development in the remotest and darkest days of its history distanced all rival clans and, from Alfred to William III, from tribe to Empire, has cherished and sustained a system of civil and religious liberty, which, intolerant of every form of oppression, has made the English language the vernacular of liberty.

In the earliest periods of these peoples' history we find the germinal elements of those great charters of liberty which are to become the chief corner-stone of free government and mighty guarantees of personal liberty.

A philosophical review of the evolution of these early ideas of personal liberty to their full growth into a free constitutional government would make an instructive and interesting study; but I lack the learning and the ability for such disquisitions. I must therefore content myself for the purpose of unfolding the duties and destinies of American citizenship, to review but historically, how from simple communities seeking to free themselves from the rule of individuals or classes, to govern themselves by law, and make that law supreme in every exigency, great charters were established and the reign of law instead of the rule of princes permanently established.

Even in the establishing of their free system of public administration, the Anglo-Saxon aim and purpose was to secure the most absolute guarantees of personal security. The liberty of the individual unit of society secured in the exercise of the largest liberty consistent with the public welfare, and that liberty protected by the just and righteous administration of public laws, was the ideal of the Anglo-Saxon state.

In their religion, philosophy, poetry, oratory, and literature they have always confessed that oppression was venal and wrong. If selfishness, greed, or pride have allured them for a while from that royal path of national rectitude and honor, they have in the final test returned conquering to their true and higher selves. Their inborn hate of oppression, their magnanimous and tolerant spirit of freedom gloriously in the ascendant.

Thus it is that the free institutions of Great Britain and America have grown and towered in strength, and in their onward march startled the world by their progress, and appalled the very lips of prophecy by their bold and daring sweep. They will not stop, for liberty is fearless and the current of freedom is irresistible.

But in the early Anglo-Saxon Commonwealth, the rights, liberties, and privileges of the citizen were not as broad and full as we find them to-day. The spirit of liberty was weak at first, but her demands grew apace with her strength. Neither by the generosity of princes, nor by the wisdom of legislation, were the ordinary English rights of free citizenship enlarged and established. Nor are the first and elemental principles of free government which we find springing up on English soil after the conquests, and whose history in the re-establishment of political liberty we shall trace through countless struggles and repressions, the original of that divine idea of freedom which it has been the mission of the Anglo-Saxon race to give to the world.

It is but a part of that great race spirit which the Conqueror could not conquer; the lingering spirit of freedom which the iron heel of despotic usurpation could not stamp out, the memory of a lost freedom ranking in the hearts of men determined to restore in their island home those ancient rights which no man dared to question in the days of the Saxon, Edward the Confessor.

The condition of the early Saxon as it was raised by the wisdom and benevolence of good King Alfred, and as it remained until the end of the reign of the unfortunate Harold, was that of a freeman, a freeman not merely in the sense of being his own master, but "he was a living unit in the State." He held his lands in his own right. He attended the courts, and entered in their deliberations. He bore arms and, by authority of law, could use them in his own defense. The animating principle of Anglo-Saxon government was local sovereignty. Matters from the smallest to the greatest were vested in the local power.

* * * * *

The establishment, after the granting of the Magna Charta, thus firmly of the liberties of England has been accomplished by bitter and fierce struggles; the obstructive forces were strong, but yielded in the end to the onward sweep of liberty directed by the aggressive spirit of intelligence, manhood, and humanity. At the end of the sixteenth century this much had been gained for freedom. The principles of liberty, which had been constantly acknowledged in written documents or had been established by precedents and examples (some of which were the remains of their ancient liberties) had been embodied as a part of the fundamental law of the land; those local institutions, which a while ago we found among the free Saxons, and even now pregnant with the seeds of liberty,—the jury, the right of holding public meetings, of bearing arms, and finally the Parliament itself had become a part of the common law of England.

Then came the Reformation and its demand for religious freedom. Against the claim of a divinely ordained kingly power, the Cavalier was found ready to revolt. The Puritans writhed under their religious restraint. The Puritan and the Cavalier joined their cause; political liberty invoked the aid of Faith, and Faith hallowed and strengthened the crusade of human liberty. The struggle increased against absolute power, spiritual and political, now concentrated in kingly hands. Giants they were who took up the quarrel of liberty in those dark days of civil strife. Men they were who inherited the blood of the saintly Langton and of his lordly Barons. Five centuries of heroic strife against oppression had sanctified the name of Liberty. They were mad with the hatred of tyranny, and centuries of bitter, heart-rending experience had made them wise and valorous for the fray. Liberty is now about to win on Saxon soil, but not there alone, for those of her yeomanry, who were hardiest for the fight and cherished the broadest liberty, transplanted themselves now upon this new soil of America and laid the foundation of a new Empire, which then and forever should be untrammeled by the conservation of princes and unabashed by the sneers of monarchs. They rejected primogeniture and the other institutions of the Middle Ages, and adopted the anti-feudal custom of equal inheritance. They brought with them the Magna Charta and the Bill of Rights; they threw around themselves the safeguard of Anglo-Saxon liberty purified and burned by those years of oppression. They transplanted Saxon England freed from the dross of Norman rule and feudal aristocracy. Liberty and law are henceforth to work out the destinies of men. And who contemplating the manner of men and whence they derived their faith, their hopes and fears, can quibble about the aims and purposes of the founders of this Republic? The fathers did not borrow their political ideals from the juriscounsuls of Rome; not from the free democracy of Greece; nor did they fuse into their system the feudal aristocratic imperialism of Europe.

To govern themselves by law, and secure therewith the largest liberty with the greatest security of individual rights and property, was their ideal of statecraft, and this idea, inseparable from the principles they laid down, must endure while the fabric lasts.

I have told you that the government the fathers planted was Anglo-Saxon in law; but it was Anglo-Saxon too in religion and spirit. Nothing has been so conquering in its influence as the Anglo-Saxon spirit; it has assimilated wherever it has gone, and like the leaven that leaveneth the whole, homogeneity has followed in its fierce wake of progress with not a whit lost of its great and fearless impulse of law and freedom.

No race has been so domineering, none stronger and with a more exclusive spirit of caste, none with a more contemptuous dislike of inferiority, none more violent in prejudice once formed, or dislikes once engendered; yet doth the spirit and impulse of freedom move majestic "in the chambers of their soul," raising them finally above those hated obliquities, conquering their repugnance, enfeebling and vanishing their hates. Thus one by one grave wrongs inflicted upon weaker races by the cold, calculating hand of greed have been arrested and blotted out in the holy names of right. Thus it is, and has been, that nations, sects, and creeds coming to these shores lose, in the fascination of free institutions and the august majesty of liberty, the distinctive qualities of their old allegiance, and thus it is that over a broad land composed of all nations, sects, and creeds there reigns one grand homogeneity and a single patriotic impulse of faith and destiny. Few there are of Americans who can to-day trace even the faintest spark of their lineage to an English or even a Norman source. Yet the spirit of the Anglo-Saxon is the presiding genius of our destiny. Its spirit is the spirit of our law, and its religion is the evangel of our political faith.

Inheritors of this great circumstance of power and rule, need I remind you that, though you sacrifice your labor and toil, though you may have brought forth this jewel of liberty regulated by law, you cannot keep it unless you share it with the world. The evils which in days past men had to wipe out in tears and blood will arise again and precipitate convulsions in which liberty may expire.

The very spectacle of seeming grandeur and the outward cast of luxury and splendor invite the enemies' quest and fans into blood-red heat his latent ire, while pride, vanity, and hate surround the heart with the humor of death-breeding slime into which the corroding worm is spawned.

I care nothing for the shell; the fleshy parts are no longer food for the living, but the pearl contained in this Anglo-Saxon mollusk has for me an irresistible charm. The pure spirit of its lofty ideals, distilled from his life and struggles, and living in quickening touch with human thought and aspiration, like the exaltation which lingers after some Hosanna chorus; his sublimated actions and deeds, whose swelling flood of cadence throb with the heart-beat of universal man,—these I love with inexpressible devotion; these are worth preserving. All else, cast in the rubbish heap with past delusions.

Mr. Chairman, men are great and small, they roam the vast wilderness of the stars, and soar the very empyrean of thought and action, and they fear and crouch and kneel; and in their quaking fears and driveling doubts seem like puny things crawling on the ground; they are saints and sinners; sometimes emissaries of light and love, and yet again harbingers of ill, and sometimes the very Nemesis of hate; but in the composite elements of their human thinking, throbbing energies of heart and mind, they are as but a single soul, governed by one law, imbued with one spirit, hearkening to one voice, touched by the one sympathy, inspired by one hope, and in trend of aspiration, love and ideal, impelled by the onward flux of one great life-struggle and purpose.

What, then, are you and I but sentient units in one great evolving process of life-activity and thought; and yet so circumvolved in that process that the impulse, which we irradiate from the point of our single particular seat of energy and feeling, thrills through the vast spheres of human purpose and endeavor, and raises the standard of truth or forwards the advance of enlightened order like each rhythmic melody is gathered in the mightier confluence of chime and strain to swell the torrent of a mighty symphony.

The work we have to do is not outside, but deep down in the teeming flow of struggling human souls. Think of them as your other self, and your own souls will interpret the meaning of their complaints, the quality of their striving, and the measure of their justice.

You will then behold the race of men as I have beheld them once when my single soul seemed with sympathy winged and I sat with the lowly outcast and felt his outrage and his shame; I brooded with him over all his wrongs; I felt within my breast the poison shaft of hate, and clinched like him my fist, scowled, and vengeance swore on them who drove my despair and misery to crime by scoff and rancor and unforgiving hate.

I stood amidst a motley throng and felt my brain bereft of noble thought; I lived in a squalid home and despised the pity which the disdainful cast upon my lot; laughed at ribald jests and quaffed the liquid flame, and the dark-hued nectar which concealed the serpent beneath its foam; I held my head aloft to seem with pride imbued; I gibed at fortune's whim and grinned a soulless sneer at my fate to conceal a deep despair.

I roamed with the savage Indians across the arid plains, stood with them in lonely worship of the great *Unknown*, and dropped like him a silent tear for the woodlands gone; the fleet-footed game no longer at his door; his father's dust, scattered by winds over consecrated and hallowed battle-plains.

I stood beside the enchanted Nile and wondered at the mystery of the Sphinx; I felt the lure, the wanderlust of the mysterious arid plains and laid my body down on the desert sand to sleep, a weapon by my side; I arose to greet the rising sun and, with "*Allah*" on my tongue, bowed my head in solemn worship towards Mecca's distant domes.

I wandered through Africa's torrid forest and scorching plains and sat naked before a bamboo hut; I felt the savage's freedom and his ease; I learned the songs of birds, the shriek of beasts, the omens of the moons, and kenned the dread and sacred lore which tradition single tongue had brought from the ages past and gone.

I walked beside the Ganges' sacred shores, worshiped at the shrine of mighty gods and felt the spirit of the mighty *All* vibrate through my being. I chanted the songs whose authors are forgot, and studied strange philosophies of sages passed; I starved and hungered on his arid plains; I felt the whips and scorn of cast; the curse of fated birth and the iron rule of oppression's heartless greed.

I was slave, and by fortune scorned; I felt the whip cut into my quivering flesh and my blood rush hot to the gaping wound; I knew the agony of unrequited toil, and with aching limbs dragged my hopeless body to my hut, to think, but not to sleep.

I learned to dream and hate, and at Nemesis' bloody altar immolated in thought and hope the whole detested tribe of human oppressors and cried *Content.*

And thus I know the bondage which men endure, the realty and the delusion in what they think and feel; and the subtlety and strength of those evil forces which color his disposition and becloud his prospect.

And I stand amidst his turbulent fortunes and above the storm and rage of his contentions and despairs to proclaim the divinity of his soul, and to herald a new awakening under which his quickened energies will yet surge forward in mighty waves of better things.

If the Republic is true to the great principles of liberty and justice which it proclaims; if you have learned the lesson of your own history, and appropriated the experience coined out of your own struggles, then will Anglo-Saxon genius and achievement glow like a mighty flame to light the path of struggling men, and Anglo-Saxon glory light angels to restore the rights of man.

THE ARMY AS A TRAINED FORCE[34]

BY THEOPHILUS G. STEWARD, D. D.

Chaplain 25th United States Infantry

Reverend Bishops, and Brethren of the Ministry, and my Brethren of the Laity:

I thank the honorable Commission from my heart for the distinguished favor they have conferred upon me in inviting me to address this august assembly. Never before, during all my forty years of public life, have I been granted so majestic a privilege; never before have I ventured to assume so grave a responsibility; and, I may add, never before have I felt so keenly my inability to do justice to the occasion.

I am encouraged, however, by the reflection that I am in the house of my friends, where I may hope for an indulgent hearing, and especially upon the subject which I have the high honor to bring before you.

The purport of my address is the conservation of life; the development of physical and moral power as well as of mental alertness; the creation of bravery and the evolution of that higher and broader element—courage; the formation of character sturdy enough to upbear a State, and intelligent enough to direct its government. What I have to say will be toward the production of a robust and chivalric manhood, the only proper shelter for a pure and glorious womanhood. Noble women are the crown of heroic men. None but the brave deserve the fair, and none but the brave can have them.

For the purpose of illustrating and enforcing these great social, physical, and moral truths, I have chosen the Army of our country, or the character and training of the American soldier. In this I do not depart from Biblical practise. How many hearts have been cheered and strengthened by the thrilling pictures painted by St. Paul of the soldiers of his times! How many have in thought beheld his armed hosts and heard his stirring exhortation: "Fight the good fight of faith!"

We owe our existence as a nation to the men in arms who for eight years met the force of Great Britain with counter force, and thus cleared the field for the statesmanship that can make the proverbial two blades of grass grow. The man with the gun opened the way for the man with the hoe. We who are here, and the race we represent, owe our deliverance from chattel slavery to the men in arms who conquered the slaveholders' Rebellion. It is a sad thought, but nevertheless one too true thus far in human history, that liberty, man's greatest earthly boon, can be reached only through a pathway of blood. The Army made good our declaration of independence; and upon the Army and Navy Lincoln relied for the efficacy of his plan of emancipation. Abstract right is fair to look upon, and has furnished the theme for charming essays by such beautiful writers as Ruskin and Emerson; but right, backed up by battalions, is the right that prevails. When the men of blood and iron come, there is no longer time for the song or the essay. It is, "Get in line or be shot." The days of rhetoricals are over. The eloquence of the soldier silences all. Even the laws are dumb when the sword is unsheathed.

Is this horrible doctrine? It is only God overthrowing Pharaoh by means more humane than His fearful plagues, and less destructive than the billows of that relentless sea over which redeemed Israel so exultingly sang. No, brethren; the sword of the Lord and of Gideon has not ceased to be a useful instrument. It is the proper thing for evil doers.

The army is the national sword, and the "powers that be" bear it "not in vain." It is a fearful engine of destruction, pure and simple. Von Moltke says: "The immediate aim of the soldier's life is destruction, and nothing but destruction; and whatever constructions wars result in are remote and non-military."

An Austrian officer says: "Live and let live is no device for an army. Contempt for one's own comrades, for the troops of the enemy, and, above all, fierce contempt for one's own person, are what war demands of every one. Far better is it for an army to be too savage, too cruel, too barbarous, than to possess too much sentimentality and human reasonableness. If the soldier is to be good for anything as a soldier, he must be exactly the opposite of a reasoning and thinking man. The measure of goodness in him is his possible use in war. War, and even peace, require of the soldier absolutely peculiar standards of morality. The recruit brings with him common moral notions of which he must seek immediately to get rid. For him, victory—success—must be everything. The most barbaric tendencies in man come to life again in war, and for war's uses they are incommensurably good."

Perhaps the greatest of American psychologists, Professor William James, adds to these remarks: "Consequently the soldier can not train himself to be too feelingless to all those usual sympathies and respects, whether for persons or for things that make for conservation. Yet," he says, "the fact remains that war is a school of strenuous life and heroism and, being in the line of aboriginal instinct, is the only school that as yet is universally available."

Emerson says: "War educates the senses, calls into action the will, perfects the physical constitution, brings men into such swift and close collision in critical moments that man measures man."

It is not my purpose, however, to glorify war. War to me is horrible beyond description or conception, and it is for war that armies are trained;

yet the training of an army, like the training of even a pugilist, is a work of great moral value.

Notwithstanding the fact that the Army gave us our independence, when the Revolution had succeeded, and the Constitution had been framed, and the country launched on her career, there was a tendency to forget Joseph. So strong was the feeling against a standing army that it was with difficulty that even a nucleus was maintained. The first legislation on this subject gave us but one battalion of artillery and one regiment of infantry, the whole consisting of 46 officers and 840 men. In 1814, because of the war with England, the army ran up to 60,000; but the next year fell to 12,000, and continued even below that number up to 1838, when it again went up to about 12,000. In 1846, during the Mexican War, it reached about 18,000. When the Civil War broke out it was about 12,000. There were in the Army, at the time of the beginning of the Civil War, over 1,000 officers. Two hundred and eighty-six of these left the service of the United States, and subsequently served in the Confederate Army. Of these 286, 187 had been educated at West Point. But so far as I am able to say now, not a single enlisted man followed the example of these officers.

Beside the staff departments, the Army now consists of 15 regiments of cavalry, 30 batteries of field artillery, 126 companies of coast artillery, and 30 regiments of infantry. These different classes are known as the three arms of the service: Cavalry, artillery, and infantry. Our whole Army to-day numbers 67,259 men. We are the greatest nation, with the smallest army. Our Army, however, is capable of rapid expansion; and, with our National Guard, we need not fear any emergency. This Army, though so small, is in one sense a trained athlete, ready to defend the nation's honor and flag. In another sense, it is a vast practical school, in which the military profession is taught. The students are not only the 60,000 who are now serving, but the many thousands also, who come and go. Men enlist for three years, and although many re-enlist, the Army is constantly receiving recruits, and constantly discharging trained soldiers. These discharged soldiers are often found among our best citizens.

The entire corps of over 3,800 officers may be regarded as professors or instructors, whose duty it is to bring the Army up to a state of perfection. To this corps of 3,800 commissioned officers must be added, also, the large number of intelligent non-commissioned officers, who are assistant instructors of the very highest utility. The work of the Army consists of study and practice, instruction and drill. It is an incessant school. There are officers' school, non-commissioned officers' school, school of the soldier, school of the company, school of the battalion, post school,—besides drills and lectures without number. The actual scientific information imparted to the enlisted men is considerable. To specify only in small part: It includes all methods of signaling, up to telegraphy; all methods of preserving and preparing food; all methods of first treatment of wounds; how to estimate distance, to map a country, to care for property and stock, and the most thorough knowledge of weapons and warfare. To become a second lieutenant in the Army, a man must either go through West Point, or have the equivalent of a college education, especially in mathematics, history, and law; and have, besides, an accurate knowledge of what is purely military. And when he is made a second lieutenant and enters upon his career as an officer, his studies begin afresh. He must study to prepare himself for subsequent promotions. Failure in this means dismission. The army officer to-day must be exceedingly thorough and accurate in his knowledge.

General Corbin says: "Never before in the history of the Army have there been so many acceptable candidates for promotion as there are at this time. Never before has the Army been in a higher state of efficiency and in more perfect accord than it is to-day. Until within a short time, an officer graduated at the Military Academy at West Point was looked upon as a man with 'a finished education'; but to-day, and for the last four years, we accept that education merely as the foundation upon which a more advanced education is to be built. This theory is in general practice, and has been so accepted. The service schools at Fort Monroe, Fort Totten, Fort Riley, Fort Leavenworth, and the War College at Washington are, in most respects, high-class post-graduate schools. In addition of this, every post is a school of application, educating officers and men for the duties now required of them."

What, then, is this training of the army for which the officer must possess this most accurate, thorough, and scientific education? He is required to have this education that he may train the soldier up to the highest point of efficiency. The officer must know, and must be able to impress the soldier with the fact that he *does* know. The officer must have the full *science* of everything pertaining to the soldier's work, in order that he may teach the soldier the *art* of it. The nature of the training to which the soldier is subjected may be best understood by considering its end. This, as in all training, is more important than the method. The primary object of the training is to unify the army and make it the efficient instrument for executing the nation's will. By discipline, individual efforts are brought under control of the chief. A company is well disciplined when, in its movement, its collective soul, so to speak, is identified with that of its commander. The officer must have possession of his men, so that when the command is given, an electric current will seem to pass through the company, and the movement will, as it were, execute itself. In a well-drilled and well-disciplined company, the orders do not seem to pass through the intellects of the men. Without reflection, but simply by concentrated attention, the work is done. The wills of the men are not only temporarily dislodged, but in their place is substituted the dominant will of the commander. This is the psychological end sought; and this condition secures instantaneous obedience to orders. It is this which brings about those marvels of execution which occur among disciplined men. Men perform acts in which neither their personal reason nor even their personal will has any part.

A second end of the training is to habituate the men so firmly in the performance of certain movements that no emotion can interfere with their action. Upon the battle-field there is nothing left of the exercises of the times of peace, but that which has become a habit, or in a word, an instinct. The soldier must be so trained that he will go on with his work as long as he has the ability to do so. One has said: "It must be the aim of the new discipline to make the private soldier capable of keeping steadfastly in mind for the whole of the day, or even for several days, and striving with all his might to carry out, what he has been told by a superior who is no longer present, and who, for all he may know, is dead."

A third end sought in military training is to render the soldier strong and agile, so that he can move with rapidity, sustain long marches, and handle his weapon with dexterity.

* * * * *

Every consideration in feeding, clothing, sheltering, both men and animals, has but one object,—efficiency. All questions of moral duty, all ideas of the spiritual or immortal interests, are completely submerged beneath the ever-present thought of material force. Power must be had by men, horses, machinery; power, aggressive power, is the all-pervading and all-controlling thought of the army.

* * * * *

An army is properly an incarnation of the fiend of destruction. Every part of its legitimate work is to destroy. If it constructs bridges and builds roads, erects forts and digs trenches, these are all that it may destroy, or prevent some other incarnation from destroying *it.* Armies lay waste and destroy. Cornfields, orchards, lawns, life, and treasure are all prey for the voracious destroyer.

The motive employed in bringing the soldier to the high state of excellence here described is always that of duty. The word "duty" is very prominent and very full of meaning in the army. Military duty is made a moral obligation founded upon patriotism. This sentiment of duty is the moral force in the army that gives dignity to its obedience. The army develops, strengthens, and educates this *sense of duty*, until it becomes supreme. It is this *sense of duty* which produces endurance to undergo privations, and leads men to be patient under the greatest sacrifices. The physical force which we see in the army depends upon the moral or spiritual which we do not see.

The whole life of the army, its very soul, the breath which animates its every part, is *preparation for war*. To be *ready for war* is the supreme end toward which all its efforts tend. The mechanical parts of the work are so numerous and various that I can barely outline them here. There are those exercises which conduce to health and vigor, known as the setting-up drill. These exercises correct the form of the body and transform the recruit into a soldier. The constant drills all have their effect upon the bearing and gait of the men. The extensive system of calisthenics gives to the body suppleness. All this work is done under direction, so that obedience and discipline are taught at the same time with physical culture. Apart from these exercises are *voluntary athletics*, which are greatly encouraged. It is believed that athletic exercises, by bettering the bodies of the men, better also their minds; that, for the welfare of the army, these exercises rank next to training in shooting. I know you will take pride in the fact that the black soldiers, both of infantry and cavalry, occupy a place in the very front rank in all these manly exercises. They are equal to America's best on the drillground, on the athletic grounds, and on the field of bloody strife.

The practise of cleanliness is enjoined all the time, along with these exercises. The soldier is taught how to make his bed and to put all his effects in order, and is then compelled to do it; and thus there is established within him a love of order. Punctuality, cleanliness, and order are the soldier's three graces. The hygiene of his body, care of his arms and equipments, respect for his uniform, are driven into his inmost soul. Our regiment lived in the midst of cholera, without suffering from the disease. Hence the army is a great object-lesson of what care and training can make of men.

But the army in our Republic is of far greater value in a moral sense than in a physical sense. In these days when authority is departing from the home, the church, and the school, it is well that it can find refuge somewhere in the country. The working of the army rests entirely upon authority. One single will pervades every part of it, although this will is participated in by thousands. Every subordinate is independent within limits; but one general will controls all. Respect for authority is enforced, and thus taught, not in theory alone, but by practice. The corporal is not the same as a private. The man who holds a commission from the President represents the high authority of the Republic; and the true soldier yields him both obedience and respect. Everywhere the soldier is taught obedience to law. After all that I have said, it is scarcely necessary to emphasize the fact that the soldier's obedience becomes voluntary, and that he takes pride in his profession. Hence the army is a body of men, not moving according to their own wills, not a deliberative assembly, but a purely executive body, the incarnation of law and of force. It is silent, but powerful. It does not talk, but acts; army spells action.

The men who are trained in our Army are not likely to become members of the lawless element. They have learned too well the lessons of order and the necessity of subordination. The attitude of the Army upon the vexed race question is better than that of any other secular institution of our country. When the Fifth Army Corps returned from Cuba and went into camp at Montauk Point, broken down as it was by a short but severe campaign, it gave to the country a fine exhibition of the moral effects of military training. There was seen the broadest comradeship. The four black regiments were there, and cordially welcomed by their companions in arms. In the maneuvers at Fort Riley, no infantry regiment on the ground was more popular than the 25th; and in contests the men of the 25th proved their mettle by carrying off nearly every medal and trophy in sight.

"Perhaps the most notable series of events, in the light of the popular notion of Negro inferiority, were the athletic sports. The first of these was the baseball game for the championship of the Department of the Missouri and a silk banner. This contest had gone through the several organizations, and was finally narrowed down to the 10th Cavalry and the 25th Infantry. On October 27th, which was set apart as a field day for athletic sports, the officers of the encampment, many women and civilians, as well as the soldiers of the regular Army present, assembled on the athletic grounds at 10.30 A. M. to witness the game. A most interesting and thoroughly scientific game was played, the 25th winning in the eleventh inning by a score of 4 to 3. The banner would have gone to colored soldiers in either case."

We must not expect too much of the army. It is not a church, not a Sunday-school, not a missionary society. Its code of morals is very short, very narrow, but it enforces what it has. Its commandments are:

1. Thou shalt not fail to obey thy superior officer.

2. Thou shalt not miss any calls sounded out by the trumpeter.

3. Thou shalt not appear at inspection with anything out of order in thy person, clothing, or equipment.

4. Thou shalt not lie.

5. Thou shalt not steal.

6. Thou shalt not leave the post or garrison without permission.

I would say, further, that warfare now requires so much from the man who carries it on, that it is impossible to unite the general and the statesman in one person. The army must be purely executive, carrying out the mandates of the State. The moral and political questions must be resolved by men of other professions. The soldier has all that he can do to attend to the exigencies of the battle.

The Army of our Republic has a great moral mission which it is performing almost unconsciously. It is a most influential witness against lawlessness. By its own perfect order and obedience to discipline it gives the force of a powerful example in favor of loyalty to the Republic and respect for the laws. The best school of loyalty in the land is the army. Every evening in the camp, to see ten thousand men stand in respectful attention to our song to the national banner is a lesson of great moral force. In still another sense our Army is also a great moral force. When men see what a terrific engine of destruction it is, the good people rejoice because they know this engine is in safe hands; and the evil-disposed look on and are enlightened. Fierce anarchists will stop to count ten, at least, before they begin their attack upon the government.

Lastly, the Army, by the very aristocracy of its constitution, contributes much to make effective the doctrines of equality. The black soldier and the white soldier carry the same arms, eat the same rations, serve under the same laws, participate in the same experience, wear the same uniforms, are nursed in the same hospitals, and buried in the same cemeteries. The Roman Catholic Church, by its priestly aristocracy, has always been a bulwark against caste. So, in the same manner, the Army of our Republic, by its aristocracy of commission, has proven itself the most effectual barrier against the inundating waves of race discrimination that the country has as yet produced.

THE SUNDAY-SCHOOL AND CHURCH AS A SOLUTION OF THE NEGRO PROBLEM[35]

BY D. WEBSTER DAVIS, D. D.

of Richmond, Virginia

If I were asked to name the most wonderful and far-reaching achievement of the splendid, all-conquering Anglo-Saxon race, I would ignore the Pass of Thermopylæ, the immortal six hundred at Balaklava, Trafalgar, Waterloo, Quebec, Bunker Hill, Yorktown, and Appomattox; I would forget its marvelous accumulations of wealth; its additions to the literature of the world, and point to the single fact that it has done the most to spread the religion of Jesus Christ, as the greatest thing it has accomplished for the betterment of the human family.

The Jews preserved the idea of a one God, and gave the ethics to religion—the ten commandements, the Lord's Prayer, and the Sermon on the Mount; the Greeks contributed philosophy; the Romans, polity; the Teutons, liberty and breadth of thought; but it remained to the Anglo-Saxon implicitly to obey the divine command: "Go ye into all the world, and preach the Gospel to every creature."

If some man would ask me the one act on the part of my own race that gives to me the greatest hope for the Negro's ultimate elevation to the heights of civilization and culture, I would not revel in ancient lore to prove them the pioneers in civilization, nor would I point to their marvelous progress since Emancipation that has surprised their most sanguine friends, but I would take the single idea of their unquestioned acceptance of the dogmas and tenets of the Christian religion as promulgated by the Anglo-Saxon, as the highest evidence of the future possibilities of the race.

Ours was indeed a wonderful faith that overleaped the barriers of ecclesiastical juggling to justify from Holy Writ the iniquitous traffic in human flesh and blood; forgot the glaring inconsistencies of a religion that prayed, on Sunday, "Our Father which art in heaven," and on Monday sold a brother, who, though cut in ebony, was yet the image of the Divine. The Negro had in very truth,

"That faith that would not shrink,
Tho' pressed by every foe;
That would not tremble on the brink
Of any earthly woe.
That faith that shone more bright and clear

When trials reigned without;
That, when in danger, knew no fear,
In darkness felt no doubt."

If it is indeed true that "by faith are ye saved," not only in this world, but in the world to come, then God will vouchsafe to us a most abundant salvation.

It is my blessed privilege to-night, while you are pleading for the "Winning of a generation," and at this special session for "the relation of the Sunday-school to missions, both home and foreign," to plead for my people, and my prayer is that God may help me to make my plea effective. For the people for whom I plead are bone of my bone and flesh of my flesh. I plead for help for my own bright-eyed boy and girl, and for all the little black boys and girls in my far-off Southern home.

If the great race problem is to be settled (and it is a problem, notwithstanding all that has been said to the contrary), it is to be settled, not in blood and carnage, not by material wealth and accumulation of lands and houses, not in literary culture nor on the college campus, not in industrial education, or in the marts of trade, but by the religion of Him who said, "And I, if I be lifted up, will draw all men unto Me." These things are resultant factors in the problem, but the problem itself lies far deeper than these.

Calhoun is reported to have said, "If I could find a Negro who could master the Greek syntax, I would believe in his possibilities of development." A comparatively few years have passed away, and a Negro not only masters the Greek syntax, but writes a Greek grammar accepted as authority by some of the ablest scholars of the States. But Abbé Gregori of France published, in the fifteenth century, "Literature of the Negro," telling of the achievements of Negro writers, scholars, priests, philosophers, painters, and Roman prelates in Spain, Portugal, France, Italy, Holland, and Turkey, which prompted Blumenbach to declare it would be difficult to meet with such in the French Academy; and yet, literature and learning have not settled the problem. No, the religion of Jesus Christ is the touchstone to settle all the problems of human life. More than nineteen hundred years ago, Christ gave solution when he said, "Ye are brethern," "Love is the fulfilling of the law," and "Whatsoever ye would that men should do to you, do ye even so to them."

Is the Negro in any measure deserving of the help for which I plead? The universal brotherhood, and common instincts of humanity should be enough. I bring more. Othello, in speaking of Desdemona, says, "She loved me for the dangers I had passed, I loved her that she did pity me." If pity and suffering can awaken sympathy, then we boldly claim our right to the fullest measure of consideration. Two hundred and fifty years of slavery, with all its attendant evils, is one of our most potent weapons to enlist sympathy and aid.

I come with no bitterness to North or South. For slavery I acknowledge all the possible good that came to us from it; the contact with superior civilization, the knowledge of the true God, the crude preparation for citizenship, the mastery of some handicraft; yet, slavery had its side of suffering and degradation. North and South rejoice that it is gone forever, and yet, many of its evils cling to us, like the Old Man of the Sea to Sinbad the sailor, and, like Banquo's ghost, they haunt us still.

As I stand here to-night, my mind is carried back to a plantation down in "Old Virginia." It is the first day of January, 1864. Lincoln's immortal proclamation is a year old, and yet I see an aunt of mine, the unacknowledged offspring of her white master, being sent away from the old homestead to be sold. The proud Anglo-Saxon blood in her veins will assert itself as she resists with all the power of her being the attempts of the overseer to ply lash to her fair skin, and for this she must be sold "Way down Souf." I see her now as she comes down from the "Great House," chained to twelve others, to be carried to Lumpkin's jail in Richmond to be put upon the "block." She had been united to a slave of her choice some two years before, and a little innocent babe had been born to them. The husband, my mother with the babe in her arms, and other slaves watch them from the "big gate" as they come down to the road to go to their destination some twenty miles away. As she saw us, great tears welled up in her big black eyes; not a word could she utter as she looked her last sad farewell. She thought of one of the old slave-songs we used to sing in the cabin prayer-meetings at night as we turned up the pots and kettles, and filled them up with water to drown the sound. Being blessed, as is true of most of my race, with a splendid voice, she raised her eyes, and began to sing:

"Brethren, fare you well, brethren, fare you well,
May God Almighty bless you until we meet again."

Singing these touching lines she passed out of sight. More than forty years have passed, and she and her loved ones have never met again, unless they have met in the Morning land, where partings are no more.

For the sufferings we have endured, leaving their traces indelibly stamped upon us, I claim your aid that we may have for our children this blessed Gospel, the panacea for all human ills.

The Negro has elements in his nature that make him peculiarly susceptible to religious training. He stands as a monument to faithfulness to humble duty, one of the highest marks of the Christ-life. He is humble and faithful, but not from cowardice, in evidence of which I recall his achievements at Boston, Bunker Hill, New Orleans, Milikens Bend, Wilson's Landing, and San Juan Hill.

He fought when a slave, some would say, from compulsion, but would he fight for love of the flag of the Union? God gave him a chance to answer the question at San Juan Hill. The story is best understood as told to me by one of the brave 9th Cavalry as he lay wounded at Old Point Comfort, Va.

* * * * *

Up go the splendid Rough Riders amid shot and shell from enemies concealed in fields, trees, ditches, and the block-house on the hill. The galling fire proves too much for them and back they come. A second and third assault proves equally unavailing. They must have help. Help arrives, in the form of a colored regiment. See them as they come, black as the sable plume of midnight, yet irresistible as the terrible cyclone. As is the custom of my race under excitement of any kind, they are singing, not

"My country, 'tis of thee,
Sweet land of Liberty,
Of thee I sing,"

though fighting willingly for the land that gave them birth; not, "The Bonnie blue flag," though they were willing to die for the flag they loved; they sing a song never heard on battle-field before, "There's a hot time in the old town to-night." On they come, trampling on the dead bodies of their comrades; they climb the hill. "To the rear!" is the command. "To the front!" they cry; and leaderless, with officers far in the rear, they plant the flag on San Juan Hill, and prove to the world that Negroes can fight for love of country.

They were faithful to humble duty in the dark days of the South from 1861 to 1865. When Jefferson Davis had called for troops until he had well-nigh decimated the fair Southland, and even boys, in their devotion to the cause they loved dearly, were willing to go to the front, my young master came to my old mistress and asked to be allowed to go. Calling my Uncle Isaac, my old mistress said to him, "Isaac, go along with your young Mars Edmund, take good care of him, and bring him home to me." "I gwy do de bes I kin," was his reply. Off these two went, amid the tears of the whole plantation, and we heard no more of them for some time. One night we were startled to hear the dogs howling down in the pasture-lot, always to the Southern heart a forewarning of death. A few nights thereafter, my mother heard a tapping on the kitchen window, and, on going to the door, saw Uncle

Isaac standing there—alone. "What in the world are you doing here?" was the question of my mother. "Whar's mistis'?" was the interrogative answer. My mother went to call the mistress, who, white as a sheet repeated the question. "Mistis', I done de bes' I could." Going a few paces from the door, while the soft southern moon shone pitilessly through the solemn pines, he brought the dead body of his young master and laid it tenderly at his mother's feet. He had brought his dead "massa" on his back a distance of more than twenty miles from the battle-field, thus faithfully keeping his promise. Such an act of devotion can never be forgotten while memory holds its sacred office. Not one case of nameless crime was ever heard in those days, though the flower of the womanhood of the South was left practically helpless in the hands of black men in Southern plantations.

"But as a faithful watch-dog stands and guards with jealous eye,
He cared for master's wife and child, and at the door would lie,
To shed his blood in their defense, 'gainst traitors, thieves, and knaves,
Altho' those masters went to fight to keep them helpless slaves."

Some have claimed that, instead of putting so much money in churches, the Negro, after the war, should have built mills and factories, and thus would have advanced more rapidly in civilization; but I rejoice that he did build churches, and to-day can say that of the three hundred millions he has accumulated, more than forty millions are in church property in the sixteen Southern States. This shows his fidelity and gratitude to God, and that by intuition he had grasped the fundamental fact that faith and love and morality are greater bulwarks for the perpetuity of a nation than material wealth; that somehow he was in accord with God's holy mandate that "man does not live by bread alone." Guided by a superior wisdom, he first sought the kingdom of heaven, and it does seem that "all these things" are slowly being added to him. Education and wealth, unsanctified by the grace of God, are after all, curses rather than a blessing. We are to rise, not by our strong bodies, our intellectual powers, or material wealth, although these are necessary concomitants, but by the virtue, character, and honesty of our men and women.

We are proud of our 30,000 teachers, 2,000 graduated doctors, 1,000 lawyers, 20,000 ordained ministers, 75,000 business men, 400 patentees, and 250,000 farms all paid for, as evidences of our possibilities, but proudest of the fact that nearly three millions of our almost ten millions of Negroes are professing Christians. It is true that the black man is not always the best kind of a Christian. He is often rather crude in worship, with a rather hazy idea of the connection between religion and morality. A colored man, on making a loud profession of religion, was asked if he were going to pay a certain debt he had contracted, remarked, "'Ligun is 'ligun, an' bisnes' is bisnes', an' I aint gwy mix um," yet I am afraid ours is not the only race that fails to "mix um," and he does not have to go far to find others with advantages far superior to his, who have not reached the delectable mountain. We, like others, are seeking higher ground, and some have almost reached it. Thank God we can point to thousands of Negro Christians whose faith is as strong as that of the prophets of old, and whose lives are as pure and sweet as the morning dew.

Our greatest curse to-day is the rum-shop, kept far too often by men of the developed and forward race to filch from us our hard earnings, and give us shame and misery in return. And a man who would deliberately debauch and hinder a backward race, struggling for the light, would "rob the dead, steal the orphan's bread, pillage the palace of the King of Kings, and clip the angels' pinions while they sing."

Right by the side of this hindrance, especially in the country districts, is our ignorant, and, in too many cases, venial ministry, for ignorance is the greatest curse on earth, save sin. The Sunday-school is destined to be the most potent factor in the removal of this evil. As our children see the light as revealed in the Sunday-school by the teachers of God's word, they will demand an intelligent and moral ministry and will support no other. Let me say to you that there is no agency doing more in that absolutely necessary and fundamental line than this God-sent association.

Wherever your missionaries have gone, there have been magical and positive changes for good, and the elevating power of this work for us can never be told. God bless the thousands of Sunday-school teachers whose names may never be known outside their immediate circles, and yet are doing a work so grand and noble that angels would delight to come down and bear them company.

There is a beautiful story told in Greek mythology that when Ulysses was passing in his ship by the Isle of the Sirens, the beautiful sirens began to play their sweetest music to lure the sailors from their posts of duty. Ulysses and his sailors stuffed wax in their ears, and lashed themselves to the masts that they might not be lured away; but, when Orpheus passed by in the search of the golden fleece and heard the same sweet songs, he simply took out his harp and played sweeter music, and not a sailor desired to leave the vessel. The sirens of sin and crime are doing all in their power to lure us from the highest and best things in life. Wealth, education, political power are, after all, but wax in the ears, the ropes that may or may not hold us to the masts of safety; but that sweeter music of the heart, played on the harp of love by the fingers of faith will hold us stronger than "hoops of steel." Let the great Sunday-school movement continue to play for us this sweeter music, and no sirens can lure us away from truth and right and heaven. The mission that will be of real help to us will be the mission dictated by love, for no race is more susceptible to kindness than ours. It must be undertaken in the spirit of the Master who said, "I call ye not servants, for the servant knoweth not what his lord doeth; but I have called you friends." The Negro loves his own and is satisfied to be with them, and yet, the man who would really help him must be a man who has seen the vision. Peter was unwilling to go to the Gentiles, being an orthodox Jew, until God put him in a trance upon the house top, let down the sheet from heaven with all manner of beasts, and bid him rise up, slay, and eat. Peter strenuously objected, saying, "Lord, I have touched nothing unclean." But God said, "What I have cleansed, call thou not unclean." Then Peter said, "I see of a truth that God is no respector of persons, but has made of one blood all men to dwell upon all the face of the earth."

I pray, I believe, that you have seen this vision, and in this spirit have come to help us. Sir Launfal, in searching for the Holy Grail, found it in ministering to the suffering and diseased at his own door. Ye who are in search of God's best gift can find it to-day in lifting up these ten millions of people at your door, broken by slavery, bound by ignorance, yet groping for the light. If we go down in sin and ignorance, we can not go alone, but must contaminate and curse millions unborn. If we go up, as in God's name we will, we will constitute the brightest star in your crown. What religion has done for others, it will do for us. See the triumphs of King Emanuel in Africa, Burmah, China, and the isles of the sea. It was Christianity that liberated four millions of slaves, and brought them to their better position. Christian men, North and South, are helping them to-day. We could not rise alone.

* * * * *

Has the Negro made improvement commensurate with the help he has received from North and South? I believe he has, and that each year finds him better than the last. Good Dr. Talmage was visiting a parishioner when a little girl sat on his knee. Seeing his seamed and wrinkled face, she asked, "Doctor, did God make you?" "Yes," was the reply. Then, looking at her own sweet, rosy face in a glass opposite, she asked, "Did God make me, too?" "Yes." "Did God make me after he made you?" "Yes, my child, why?" Looking again at his face and hers, she said, "Well. Doctor, God is doing better work these days."

God bless our mothers and fathers; no nobler souls ever lived under such circumstances; but God has answered their prayers, and with the young folks will do better work. The convention helps us to help ourselves, the only true help, and in this the conveners are investing in soul-power that pays the biggest dividends, and its bonds are always redeemable at the Bank of Heaven.

In a terrible storm at sea, when all the passengers were trembling with fear, one little boy stood calm and serene. "Why so calm, my little man?" asked one. "My father runs this ship," was the reply. I have too much confidence in what religion has done and too much faith in what it can do, to be afraid. "God's in his heaven, all's right with the world." Let each do his part to help on the cause.

"There is never a rose in all the world
But makes some green spray sweeter;
There is never a wind in all the sky
But makes some bird's wing fleeter;
There is never a star but brings to earth
Some silvery radiance tender,
And never a sunset cloud but helps
To cheer the sunset's splendor.
No robin but may cheer some heart,
Its dawnlight gladness voicing;
God gives us all some small sweet way
To set the world rejoicing."

America, I believe, is destined of God to be the land that shall flow with milk and honey, the King's Highway, when the "ransomed of the Lord shall return and come to Zion with songs and everlasting joy upon their heads; they shall obtain joy and gladness, and sorrow and mourning shall flee away."

I see gathered upon our fair western plain nations of all the earth. The Italian is there and thinks of "Italia, fair Italia!" The Frenchman sings his "Marsellaise." The solid, phlegmatic German sings his "Die Wacht am Rhein." The Irish sing "Killarney" and "Wearin' the Green"; the Scotchman his "Blue Bells"; the Englishman, "God save the King!"; the American, the "Star-spangled Banner." God bless the patriot, but the ultimate end of all governments is that the Kingdom of Christ may prevail. One towering Christian man thinks of this, and seeing a black man standing by without home or country remembers that "all are Christ's and Christ's is God's." He swings a baton high in air and starts a grand hallelujah chorus. Forgot is all else as the grand chorus, white and black, of every age and every clime, sing till heaven's arches ring again, while angels from the battlements of heaven listen and wave anew the palm-branches from the trees of paradise, and the angels' choir that sang on the plains of Bethlehem more than nineteen hundred years ago join in the grand refrain,

"All hail the power of Jesus' name,

Let angels prostrate fall;
Bring forth the royal diadem,
And crown him Lord of all."

WILLIAM LLOYD GARRISON: A CENTENNIAL ORATION[36]

BY REVERDY C. RANSOM, D. D.

Editor A. M. E. Church Review

Friends, Citizens:

We have assembled here to-night to celebrate the one hundredth birth of William Lloyd Garrison. Not far from this city he was born. Within the gates of this city, made famous by some of America's most famous men, he spent more than two-thirds of his long and eventful career, enriching its history and adding to the glory of its renown. This place, of all places, is in keeping with the hour. It is most appropriate that we should meet in Faneuil Hall, the cradle of American liberty, a spot hallowed and made sacred by the statesmen, soldiers, orators, scholars, and reformers who have given expression to burning truths and found a hearing within these walls. Of all people it is most fitting that the Negro Americans of Boston should be the ones to take the lead in demonstrating to their fellow-citizens, and to the world, that his high character is cherished with affection, and the priceless value of his unselfish labors in their behalf shall forever be guarded as a sacred trust.

Only succeeding generations and centuries can tell the carrying power of a man's life. Some men, whose contemporaries thought their title to enduring fame secure, have not been judged worthy in a later time to have their names recorded among the makers of history. Some men are noted, some are distinguished, some are famous,—only a few are great.

The men whose deeds are born to live in history do not appear more than once or twice in a century. Of the millions of men who toil and strive, the number is not large whose perceptible influence reaches beyond the generation in which they lived. It does not take long to call the roll of honor of any generation, and when this roll is put to the test of the unprejudiced scrutiny of a century, only a very small and select company have sufficient carrying power to reach into a second century. When the roll of the centuries is called, we may mention almost in a single breath the names which belong to the ages. Abraham and Moses stand out clearly against the horizon of thirty centuries. St. Paul, from his Roman prison, in the days of the Cæsars, is still an articulate and authoritative voice; Savonarola, rising from the ashes of his funeral-pyre in the streets of Florence, still pleads for civic righteousness; the sound of Martin Luther's hammer nailing his thesis to the door of his Wittenberg church continues to echo around the world; the battle-cry of Cromwell's Ironsides shouting, "The Lord of Hosts!" still causes the tyrant and the despot to tremble upon their thrones; out of the fire and blood of the French Revolution, "Liberty and Equality" survive; Abraham Lincoln comes from the backwoods of Kentucky, and the prairies of Illinois, to receive the approval of all succeeding generations of mankind for his Proclamation of Emancipation; John Brown was hung at Harper's Ferry that his soul might go marching on in the tread of every Northern regiment that fought for the "Union forever;" William Lloyd Garrison, mobbed in the streets of Boston for pleading the cause of the slave, lived to see freedom triumph, and to-night, a century after his birth, his name is cherished, not only in America, but around the world, wherever men aspire to individual liberty and personal freedom.

William Lloyd Garrison was in earnest. He neither temporized nor compromised with the enemies of human freedom. He gave up all those comforts, honors, and rewards which his unusual talents would easily have won for him in behalf of the cause of freedom which he espoused. He stood for righteousness with all the rugged strength of a prophet. Like some Elijah of the Gilead forests, he pleaded with this nation to turn away from the false gods it had enshrined upon the altars of human liberty. Like some John the Baptist crying in the wilderness, he called upon this nation to repent of its sin of human slavery, and to bring forth the fruits of its repentance in immediate emancipation.

William Lloyd Garrison was born in Newburyport, Mass., Dec. 10, 1805. He came of very poor and obscure parentage. His father, who was a seafaring man, early abandoned the family for causes supposed to relate to his intemperance. The whole career of Garrison was a struggle against poverty. His educational advantages were limited. He became a printer's apprentice when quite a lad, and learned the printing trade. When he launched his paper, *The Liberator*, which was to deal such destructive blows to slavery, the type was set by his own hands. The motto of *The Liberator* was "Our country is the world, our countrymen mankind."

Garrison did not worship the golden calf. His course could not be changed, nor his opinion influenced by threats of violence or the bribe of gold. Money could not persuade him to open his mouth against the truth, or buy his silence from uncompromising denunciation of the wrong. He put manhood above money, humanity above race, the justice of God above the justices of the Supreme Court, and conscience above the Constitution. Because he took his stand upon New Testament righteousness as taught by Christ, he was regarded as a fanatic in a Christian land. When he declared that "he determined at every hazard to lift up a standard of emancipation in the eyes of the nation, within sight of Bunker Hill and in the birthplace of liberty," he was regarded as a public enemy, in a nation conceived in liberty and dedicated to freedom!

Garrison drew his arguments from the Bible and the Declaration of Independence, only to be jeered as a wild enthusiast. He would not retreat a single inch from the straight path of liberty and justice. He refused to purchase peace at the price of freedom. He would not drift with the current of the public opinion of his day. His course was up-stream; his battle against the tide. He undertook to create a right public sentiment on the question of freedom, a task as great as it was difficult. Garrison thundered warnings to arouse the public conscience before the lightnings of his righteous wrath and the shafts of his invincible logic wounded the defenders of slavery in all the vulnerable joints of their armor. He declared: "Let Southern oppressors tremble—let their secret abettors tremble; let their Northern apologists tremble; let all the enemies of the persecuted blacks tremble." For such utterances as these his name throughout the nation became one of obloquy and reproach.

He was not bound to the slave by the ties of race, but by the bond of common humanity which he considered a stronger tie. In his struggle for freedom there was no hope of personal gain; he deliberately chose the pathway of financial loss and poverty. There were set before his eyes no prospect of honor, no pathways leading to promotion, no voice of popular approval, save that of his conscience and his God. His friends and neighbors looked upon him as one who brought a stigma upon the fair name of the city in which he lived. The business interests regarded him as an influence which disturbed and injured the relations of commerce and of trade; the Church opposed him; the press denounced him; the State regarded him as an enemy of the established order; the North repudiated him; the South burned him in effigy. Yet, almost single-handed and alone, Garrison continued to fight on, declaring that "his reliance for the deliverance of the oppressed universally is upon the nature of man, the inherent wrongfulness of oppression, the power of truth, and the omnipotence of God." After the greatest civil war that ever immersed a nation in a baptism of blood and tears, Garrison, unlike most reformers, lived to see the triumph of the cause for which he fought and every slave not only acknowledged as a free man, but clothed with the dignity and powers of American citizenship. William Lloyd Garrison has passed from us, but the monumental character of his work and the influence of his life shall never perish. While there are wrongs to be righted, despots to be attacked, oppressors to be overthrown, peace to find and advocate, and freedom a voice, the name of William Lloyd Garrison will live.

Those who would honor Garrison and perpetuate his memory and his fame must meet the problems that confront them with the same courage and in the same uncompromising spirit that Garrison met the burning questions of the day. Those who would honor Garrison in one breath, while compromising our manhood and advocating the surrender of our political rights in another, not only dishonor his memory, not only trample the flag of our country with violent and unholy feet, but they spit upon the grave which holds the sacred dust of this chiefest of the apostles of freedom.

The status of the Negro in this country was not settled by emancipation; the 15th Amendment to the Constitution, which it was confidently believed would clothe him forever with political influence and power, is more bitterly opposed to-day than it was a quarter of a century ago. The place which the Negro is to occupy is still a vital and burning question. The newspaper press and magazines are full of it; literature veils its discussion of the theme under the guise of romance; political campaigns are waged with this question as a paramount issue; it is written into the national platform of great political parties; it tinges legislation; it has invaded the domain of dramatic art, until to-day, it is enacted upon the stage; philanthropy, scholarship, and religion are, each from their point of view, more industriously engaged in its solution than they have been in any previous generation. If the life and labors of Garrison, and the illustrious men and women who stood with him, have a message for the present, we should seek to interpret its meaning and lay the lesson to heart.

The scenes have shifted, but the stage is the same; the leading characters have not changed. We still have with us powerful influences trying to keep the Negro down by unjust and humiliating legislation and degrading treatment; while on the other hand, the Negro and his friends are still contending for the same privileges and opportunities that are freely accorded to other citizens whose skins do not happen to be black. We, of this nation, are slow to learn the lessons taught by history; the passions which feed on prejudice and tyranny can neither be mollified nor checked by subjection, surrender, or compromise. Self-appointed representatives of the Negro, his enemies and his would-be friends, are pointing to many diverse paths, each claiming that the one they have marked for his feet is the proper one in which he should walk. There is but one direction in which the Negro should steadfastly look and but one path, in which he should firmly plant his feet—that is, toward the realization of complete manhood and equality, and the full justice that belongs to an American citizen clothed with all of his constitutional power.

This is a crucial hour for the Negro American; men are seeking to-day to fix his industrial, political, and social status under freedom as completely as they did under slavery. As this nation continued unstable, so long as it rested upon the foundation-stones of slavery so will it remain insecure as long as one-eighth of its citizens can be openly shorn of political power, while confessedly they are denied "life, liberty, and the pursuit of happiness." We have no animosity against the South or against Southern people. We would see the wounds left by the War of the Rebellion healed; but we would have them healed so effectually that they could not be trodden upon and made to bleed afresh by inhuman barbarities and unjust legislation; we would have the wounds of this nation bound up by the hands of those who are friendly to the patient, so that they might not remain a political running sore. We would have the bitter memories of the war effaced, but they cannot fade while the spirit of slavery walks before the nation in a new guise. We, too, would have a reunited country; but we would have the re-union to include not only white men North and South, but a union so endearing, because so just, as to embrace all of our fellow-countrymen, regardless of section or of race.

* * * * *

It is not a man's right, it is his duty to support and defend his family and his home; he should therefore resist any influence exerted to prevent him from maintaining his dependants in comfort; while he should oppose with his life the invader or despoiler of his home. God had created man with a mind capable of infinite development and growth; it is not, therefore, a man's right, it is his duty to improve his mind and to educate his children; he should not, therefore, submit to conditions which would compel them to grow up in ignorance. Man belongs to society; it is his duty to make his personal contribution of the best that is within him to the common good; he can do this only as he is given opportunity to freely associate with his fellow-man. He should, therefore, seek to overthrow the artificial social barriers which would intervene to separate him from realizing the highest and best there are within him by freedom of association. It is a man's duty to be loyal to his country and his flag, but when his country becomes a land of oppression and his flag an emblem of injustice and wrong, it becomes as much his duty to attack the enemies within the nation as to resist the foreign invader. Tyrants and tyranny everywhere should be attacked and overthrown.

This is a period of transition in the relations of the Negro to this nation. The question which America is trying to answer, and which is must soon definitely settle, is this: *What kind of Negroes do the American people want?* That they must have the Negro in some relation is no longer a question of serious debate. The Negro is here 10,000,000 strong, and, for weal or woe, he is here to stay—he is here to remain forever. In the government he is a political factor; in education and in wealth he is leaping forward with giant strides; he counts his taxable property by the millions, his educated men and women by the scores of thousands; in the South he is the backbone of industry; in every phase of American life his presence may be noted; he is also as thoroughly imbued with American principles and ideals as any class of people beneath our flag. When Garrison started his fight for freedom, it was the prevailing sentiment that the Negro could have no place in this country save that of a slave, but he has proven himself to be more valuable as a free man than as a slave. What kind of Negroes do the American people want? Do they want a voteless Negro in a Republic founded upon universal suffrage? Do they want a Negro who shall not be permitted to participate in the government which he must support with his treasure and defend with his blood? Do they want a Negro who shall consent to be set apart as forming a distinct industrial class, permitted to rise no higher than the level of serfs or peasants? Do they want a Negro who shall accept an inferior social position, not as a degradation, but as the just operation of the laws of caste based upon color? Do they want a Negro who will avoid friction between the races by consenting to occupy the place to which white men may choose to assign him? What kind of a Negro do the American people want? Do they want a Negro who will accept the doctrine, that however high he may rise in the scale of character, wealth, and education, he may never hope to associate as an equal with white men? Do white men believe that 10,000,000 blacks, after having imbibed the spirit of American institutions, and having exercised the rights of free men for more than a generation, will ever accept a place of permanent inferiority in the Republic? Taught by the Declaration of Independence, sustained by the Constitution of the United States, enlightened by the education of our schools, this nation can no more resist the advancing tread of the hosts of the oncoming blacks than it can bind the stars or halt the resistless motion of the tide.

The answer which the American people may give to the question proposed cannot be final. There is another question of greater importance which must be answered by the Negro, and by the Negro alone: *What kind of an American does the Negro intend to be?* The answer to this question he must seek and find in every field of human activity and endeavor. First, he must answer it by negation. He does not intend to be an alien in the land of his birth, nor an outcast in the home of his fathers. He will not consent to his elimination as a political factor; he will refuse to camp forever on the borders of the industrial world; as an American he will consider that his destiny is united by indissoluble bonds with the destiny of America forever; he will strive less to be a great Negro in this Republic and more to be an influential and useful American. As intelligence is one of the chief safeguards of the Republic, he will educate his children. Knowing that a people cannot perish whose morals are above reproach, he will ally himself on the side of the forces of righteousness; having been the object of injustice and wrong, he will be the foe of anarchy and the advocate of the supremacy of law. As an American citizen, he will allow no man to protest his title, either at home or abroad. He will insist more and more, *not only upon voting, but upon being voted for*, to occupy any position within the gift of the nation. As an American whose title to citizenship is without a blemish or flaw, he will resist without compromise every law upon the statute-books which is aimed at his degradation as a human being and humiliation as a citizen. He will be no less ambitious and aspiring than his fellow-countrymen; he will assert himself, not as a Negro, but as a man; he will beat no retreat in the face of his enemies and opposers; his gifted sons and daughters, children of genius who may be born to him, will make their contribution to the progress of humanity on these shores, accepting nothing but the honors and rewards that belong to merit. What kind of an American does the Negro intend to be? He intends to be an American who will never mar the image of God, reproach the dignity of his manhood, or tarnish the fair title of his citizenship, by apologizing to men or angels for associating as an equal, with some other American who does not happen to be black. He will place the love of country above the love of race; he will consider no task too difficult, no sacrifice too great, in his effort to emancipate his country from the un-Christlike feelings of race hatred and the American bondage of prejudice. There is nothing that injustice so much respects, that Americans so much admire, and the world so much applauds, as a man who stands erect like a man, has the courage to speak in the tones of a man, and to fearlessly act a man's part.

There are two views of the Negro question now at last clearly defined. One is that the Negro should stoop to conquer; that he should accept in silence the denial of his political rights; that he should not brave the displeasure of white men by protesting when he is segregated in humiliating ways upon the public carriers and in places of public entertainment; that he may educate his children, buy land, and save money, but he must not insist upon his children taking their place in the body politic to which their character and intelligence entitle them; he must not insist on ruling the land which he owns or farms; he must have no voice as to how the money he has accumulated is to be expended through taxation and the various forms of public improvement. There are others who believe that the Negro owes this nation no apology for his presence in the United States; that, being black, he is still no less a man; that he should not yield one syllable of his title to American citizenship; that he should refuse to be assigned to an inferior plane by his fellow-countrymen; though foes conspire against him and powerful friends desert him, he should refuse to abdicate his sovereignty as a citizen, and to lay down his honor as a man.

If Americans become surfeited with wealth, haughty with the boasting pride of race superiority, morally corrupt in the high places of honor and of trust, enervated through the pursuit of pleasure, or the political bondmen of some strong man plotting to seize the reins of power, the Negro American will continue his steadfast devotion to the flag, and the unyielding assertion of his constitutional rights, that "this government of the people, for the people, and by the people, may not perish from the earth."

It is so marvelous as to be like a miracle of God, to behold the transformation that has taken place in the position of the Negro in this land since William Lloyd Garrison first saw the light a century ago. When the Negro had no voice, Garrison pleaded his cause; to-night the descendants of the slave stand in Faneuil Hall, while from ocean to ocean every foot of American soil is dedicated to freedom. The Negro American has found his voice; he is able to speak for himself; he stands upon this famous platform here and thinks it no presumption to declare that he seeks nothing more, and will be satisfied with nothing less than the full measure of American citizenship!

I feel inspired to-night. The spirits of the champions of freedom hover near. High above the stars, Lincoln and Garrison, Sumner and Phillips, Douglass and Lovejoy, look down to behold their prayers answered, their labors rewarded, and their prophecies fulfilled. They were patriots; the true saviors of a nation that esteemed them not. They have left us a priceless heritage. Is there to be found among us now one who would so dishonor the memory of these sainted dead; one so lost to love of country and loyalty to his race, as to offer to sell our birthright for a mess of pottage? When we were slaves, Garrison labored to make us free; when our manhood was denied, he proclaimed it. Shall we in the day of freedom be less loyal to our country and true to ourselves than were the friends who stood for us in our night of woe? Many victories have been won for us; there are still greater victories we must win for ourselves. The proclamation of freedom and the bestowal of citizenship were not the ultimate goal we started out to reach, they were but the beginnings of progress. We, of this generation, must so act our part that, a century hence, our children and our children's children may honor our memory and be inspired to press on as they receive from us untarnished the banner of freedom, of manhood, and of equality among men.

The Negro went aboard the ship of state when she was first launched upon the uncertain waters of our national existence. He booked as through passenger until she should reach "the utmost sea-mark of her farthest sail." When those in command treated him with injustice and brutality, he did not mutiny or rebel; when placed before the mast as a lookout, he did not fall asleep at his post. He has helped to keep her from being wrecked upon the rocks of treachery; he has imperiled his life by standing manfully to his task while she outrode the fury of a threatening sea; when the pirate-craft of rebellion bore down upon her and sought to place the black flag of disunion at her masthead, he was one of the first to respond when the captain called all hands up on deck. If the enemies of liberty should ever again attempt to wreck our ship of state, the Negro American will stand by the guns; he will not desert her when she is sinking, but with the principles of the Declaration of Independence nailed to the masthead, with the flag afloat, he would prefer rather to perish with her than to be numbered among those who deserted her when assailed by an overwhelming foe. If she weathers the storms that beat upon her, outsails the enemies that pursue her, avoids the rocks that threaten her, and anchors at last in the port of her desired haven, black Americans and white Americans, locked together in brotherly embrace, will pledge each other to remain aboard forever on terms of equality, because they shall have learned by experience that neither one of them can be saved, except they thus abide in the ship.

For the present our strivings are not in vain. The injustice that leans upon the arm of oppression for support must fall; truth perverted or suppressed gains in momentum while it waits; generations may perish, but humanity will survive; out of the present conflict of opinion and the differences of race and color that divide, once the tides of immigration have ceased to flow to our shores, this nation will evolve a people who shall be one in purpose, one in spirit, one in destiny—a composite American by the co-mingling of blood.

ABRAHAM LINCOLN[37]

BY JAMES L. CURTIS, of New York

Since the curtain rang down on the tragedy of Calvary, consummating the vicarious sacrifice of Jesus of Nazareth, there has been no parallel in history, sacred or profane, to the deeds of Abraham Lincoln and their perennial aftermath.

For two hundred years this nation writhed in the pain and anguish of travail; and as a happy sequel to this long night of suffering, in the dawn of the nineteenth century, she bore a son who was destined to awaken a nation's somnolent conscience to a monstrous evil; to lead a nation through a fierce siege of fratricidal strife; to strike the shackles of slavery from the limbs of four millions of bondsmen; to fall a victim to the assassin's bullet; to be enshrined in the hearts of a grateful nation; and to have an eternal abode in the pantheon of immortals.

* * * * *

Abraham Lincoln! What mighty magic is this name! Erstwhile it made the tyrant tremble on his throne and the hearts of the down-trodden leap for joy. Now, over the chasm of two score years, it causes the drooping hopes of freemen to bud anew, and the smoldering embers of their ambition to leap into flame.

With talismanic power, it swerves the darts of hate and malice aimed at a defenseless race, so that though they wound, they do not destroy. With antidotal efficacy, it nullifies the virus of proscription so that it does not stagnate the blood nor paralyze the limb of an up-treading and on-going race.

When the nation was rent in twain, Lincoln, the propitiator, counselled conciliation. When the States of the South sought to secede, Lincoln, the concatenator, welded them into a solid chain, one and inseparable. When brother sought the life of brother and father that of son, Lincoln, the pacificator, advised peace with honor. When the nation was stupefied with the miasma of human slavery, Lincoln, the alleviator, broke its horrid spell by diffusing through the fire of war the sweet incense of liberty.

The cynic has sneered at the Proclamation of Emancipation. The dogmatist has called the great Emancipator a compromiser. The scholar, with the eccentricity peculiar to genius, has solemnly declared that the slaves were freed purely as a war necessity and not because of any consideration for the slave. The undergraduate, in imitation of his erudite tutors, has asserted that the freedmen owe more to the pride of the haughty Southerner than to the magnanimity of President Lincoln. But the mists of doubt and misconception have been so dissipated by the sunlight of history, that we, of this generation, may clearly see the martyred President as he really was.

* * * * *

All honor to Abraham Lincoln, the performer, not the preacher; the friend of humanity, the friend of the North, the friend of the South, the friend of the white man, the friend of the black man; the man whose heart, like the Christ's, was large enough to bring within the range of its sensibilities every human being beneath the stars. The man who, when God's clock struck the hour, swung back on its creaking hinges the door of opportunity that the slaves might walk over its portals into the army and into new fields of usefulness in civil life.

One hundred years have rolled into eternity since freedom's greatest devotee made his advent on this earth. One hundred years, as but a moment compared with the life of nations; yet, changes in our form of government, in the interpretation of our laws, in the relation between the North and the South, in the status of the Negro, have been wrought, that were beyond the wildest dreams of Lincoln. And wonderful as have been these changes to our advantage, in the acquisition of property, in moral and mental development, in the cultivation of sturdy manhood and womanhood, yet, all these have come to us as a direct result of the labors of Lincoln, who, with the ken of a prophet and the vision of a seer, in those dark and turbulent days, wrought more nobly than he knew.

From these prodigious tasks so well performed, I adjure you, my friends, that you catch inspiration; that you take no backward step in the future; that you prove worthy heirs and joint heirs to the heritage of golden opportunities bequeathed you; that you demand every right with which his labors have endowed you; and that the righteous sentiment of "Equal and Exact Justice" be emblazoned on a banner and flaunted in the breezes till every foe of justice is vanquished and right rules supreme.

That you will do this, I doubt not, for in my heart of hearts, I believe with Henry Clay that "Before you can repress the tendencies to liberty, or the tendencies to absolute emancipation from every form of serfdom, you must go back to the era of our independence and muzzle the cannon which thunders its joyous return; you must penetrate the human soul and eradicate there the love of liberty." Then, and not till then, can you stifle the ennobling aspiration of the American Negro for the unabridged enjoyment of every right guaranteed under the Constitution and the laws.

ABRAHAM LINCOLN AND FIFTY YEARS OF FREEDOM[38]

BY ALEXANDER WALTERS, D. D.,

Bishop of A. M. E. Zion Church

The distinguished person whom we pause to honor was not born great, if to be born great means to be born in a mansion, surrounded at the start of life with opulence, "dangled on the knee of indulgence and charmed to sleep by the voice of liveried servants"; if this is the measure of greatness, then Abraham Lincoln was not born great,—but if to be born great is to be ushered into the world with embryonic qualities of heart, elements calculated to unfold into the making of the stature of a complete man, a manly man, a brave, a God-fearing man—a statesman equal to the greatest emergency of a nation, then the little fellow of destiny who made his initial bow to the goddess of light in Hardin County, Kentucky, February 12, 1809, was born great.

If to achieve greatness is to win the hearts of one's youthful companions, one's associates in professional life, and to merit the confidence and genuine love of a nation to the extent of securing its greatest honors and to perform the mightiest work of a century, then Abraham Lincoln achieved greatness.

* * * * *

The assertion has been made that President Lincoln was not in favor of universal freedom. I beg to take issue with this view.

A careful study of this sincere, just, and sympathetic man will serve to show that from his earliest years he was against slavery. He declared again and again; "If slavery is not wrong, nothing is wrong; I cannot remember when I did not so think and feel."

Back in the thirties this young man clad in homespun was standing in the slave-mart of New Orleans, watching husbands and wives being separated forever, and children being doomed never again to look into the faces of their parents. As the hammer of the auctioneer fell, this young flat-boatman, with quivering lips, turned to his companion and said: "If ever I get a chance to hit that thing (slavery), I will hit it hard, by the Eternal God I will."

In March, 1839, he had placed upon the *House Journal of Illinois* a formal protest against pro-slavery resolutions which he could get but one other member beside himself to sign. Long before he was made President, in a speech at Charleston, Illinois, he said: "Yes we will speak for freedom, and against slavery, as long as the Constitution of our country guarantees free speech, until everywhere on this wide land the sun shall shine, and the rain shall fall, and the winds shall blow upon no man who goes forth to unrequited toil."

While in Congress in 1848 he offered a bill to abolish slavery in the District of Columbia. It was his opinion that Congress had control over the institution of slavery in the District of Columbia and the territories, and he evidenced his desire for the freedom of the slaves by offering a bill to abolish it in the District, and he afterwards strenuously advocated the elimination of slavery from the territories.

In 1864, about the time of the repeal of the Fugitive Slave Law, President Lincoln said to some gentlemen from the West: "There have been men base enough to propose to me to return to slavery our black warriors of Port Hudson and Olustee, and thus win the respect of the masters they fought. Should I do so, I should deserve to be damned in time and eternity."

Through all the mighty struggle of the Civil War when bowed in sorrow, and when it was truly said of him "That he was a man of sorrows and acquainted with grief," he was ever heard to say, "It is my desire that all men be free."

If President Lincoln were not in favor of the freedom of the slaves, why did he write the Emancipation Proclamation without the knowledge of his Cabinet and, when reading it to them, informed them that he did not do so to have them make any changes, but simply to apprise them of its contents? I answer, because he saw the time had come, the opportune time for which he had longed, when he, as President of these United States, could free the slaves. The South was so certain that it was Mr. Lincoln's intention to liberate the slaves, that, upon his election as President, they seceded from the Union. They felt that the institution which they had struggled so long to maintain was doomed.

His famous letter to Horace Greeley, so diplomatically written, shows him to be in favor of the emancipation of slaves. Said he; "My paramount object is to save the Union, and not either to save or destroy slavery. If I could save the Union without freeing any slaves I would do it; if I could save it by freeing all the slaves I would do it; and if I could do it by freeing some and leaving others alone, I would also do that. I shall try to correct errors when shown to be errors, and I shall adopt new views as fast as they shall appear to be true views. I have here stated my purpose according to my views of official duty, and I intend no modification of my oft-expressed personal wish that all men everywhere could be free."

Had President Lincoln not desired the freedom of the slaves would he have written this last sentence?

Professor Pickens, of Talladega College, says: "He was a patriot statesman; although he abhored slavery in his own inclination, he was wise enough to see that the question of slavery was subordinate to the immediate object of saving the Union. If slavery is not wrong, nothing is wrong; he declared as his private opinion; but it was his public duty and his oath to save the Union, regardless of slavery. His logic and clear seizure of the main point stood him in good stead against the over-zealous Abolitionists on the one hand, while on the other hand, as soon as the interests of Negro freedom and the interests of the Union coincided, the same unchanged and consistent logic answered those who assailed him on constitutional grounds."

Mr. Lincoln believed that the Constitution protected slavery in the States wherein it existed, and his aim was to let it alone where it had a constitutional right to exist. Not because he thought slavery right, but because of his respect for the law.

His original position was that, since slavery was protected by the law, the friends of freedom would have to abide their time and continue to create sentiment sufficient to change the law and thus overthrow the iniquitous institution. This is the only interpretation that can be put upon his doctrine. "The house divided against itself."

Is it reasonable to think that a man so thoughtful and sincere as was Mr. Lincoln could give a life to the advocacy of the freedom of the slaves, and in his heart not be in favor of their liberation. Mr. Lincoln often expressed ideas on the emancipation calculated to jeopardize his political future, which he would not have done but for the fact that in his heart of hearts he was committed to the cause of freedom.

The slaves hailed him as their savior, which he proved to be by emancipating 4,000,000 of them, and he will be held in loving remembrance by Afro-Americans as long as the world shall stand.

It is fitting that we assemble ourselves together on the anniversary of his birth to honor his memory, and tell of his noble deeds to the rising generation.

President Lincoln was truly a great man; a giant in intellect, a peerless diplomat, a fearless advocate of the rights of humanity and a wise ruler. In council he stood head and shoulders above the members of his Cabinet and other advisers, notwithstanding he was surrounded by some of the greatest scholars and statesmen of his time.

Allow me to apply to Lincoln the words of Wendell Phillips in his address "Toussaint L'Ouverture":

"Lincoln was greater than Cæsar; Cæsar fought to further his ambition and to extend a great empire. Lincoln was an advocate of principle, justice, and fair play. He was greater than Alexander; Alexander fought for glory—to conquer all the world, all at the sacrifice of happy homes and the desolation and ruin of countries. Lincoln sacrificed comfort and ease to save a nation and liberate an enslaved people. He was greater than Napoleon; Napoleon made wives to be widows, and children to be fatherless and homeless, and drenched Europe and Egypt in blood for fame and the desire to found a greater empire than the Roman dynasty; but Lincoln perished because he dared to defend an oppressed people."

When the last scarred veteran shall gather around the last campfire and shall rehearse stories of valor, he will close his tale of sorrow with the name of Lincoln.

When the last poet shall compose his last poem on America's greatest struggle,—yea of the victories of Vicksburg, Fort Donaldson, Lookout Mountain, Gettysburg, Appomattox, Petersburg, and the fall of Richmond, he will close it by paying a tribute to the memory of the sainted Lincoln.

When the last statesman of the world shall pronounce a farewell anathema upon the world's oppression, when he shall write the names of those foremost in the work of emancipation, after he shall have written the name of Moses,—long ere he reaches the name of Wilberforce or Clarkson, he shall have written high on the scroll of fame the name of Lincoln.

When the last flag bearing the "Stars and Stripes" shall wave over this great commonwealth, telling of its glory and tremendous influence, on the wings of the eagle upon the staff of that flag will be written for her to bear away on the eternal breezes the name of the immortal Lincoln,—the savior of his country, the Emancipator of its people.

* * * * *

The dying legacy bequeathed to the American nation by the martyred Lincoln was a united country and a free people. It gave us a nation which to-day stands first in the galaxy of the nations of the world—in character, thought, wealth, and all the qualities which make for the highest civilizations—a glorious country, whose natural resources stand unsurpassed.

All honor to Mr. Lincoln, the nation's Chieftain, the giant of the conflict, the statesman of the age, the immortal Emancipator; and all honor to the men who wore the blue, both white and black; and all honor to the men and women who gave their sons to the cause and furnished the sinews of war; and all praise be to the God of Heaven who was behind the conflict controlling all.

If we would properly honor this great and good man we must finish the work which he so nobly began,—the lifting up of the Negro race to the highest point of civilization. This can be accomplished; first, by being good and loyal citizens ourselves, and by teaching our children to be the same.

The groundwork of our material advancement is industry. As a race we are generally industrious, but we need to become more skillfully so. Unskilled labor cannot compete with skilled labor, neither North or South. In the past you gave us certain positions as the result of sympathy, not because we could perform the work as skillfully as others.

The sentiment which actuated you to help us was a noble one, but that kind of sentiment is a thing of the past; now we are required to stand or fall according to our merits. When goods are to be manufactured, machines constructed, houses and bridges built, clothing fashioned, or any sort of work performed, none but skilled workmen are considered; there are a great number of employers that care but little about the color of the workmen; with them the question is, Can he do the work?

We must continue the struggle for our civil and political rights. I have no sympathy with that class of leaders who are advising the Negro to eschew politics in deference to color prejudice.

Does it make for permanent peace to deny to millions of citizens their political rights when they are equal to the average electorate in intelligence and character? Fitness, and not color or previous condition of servitude, should be the standard of recognition in political matters. Indeed the Negro should not be denied any civil or political right on account of his color, and to the extent this is done there is bound to disquietude in the nation.

We have already seen that temporizing with slavery at the formation of the Union resulted in a hundred years of strife and bitterness, and finally brought on devastation and death. And may we not profit by this bitter experience? The enlightened American conscience will not tolerate injustice forever. The same spirit of liberty and fair play which enveloped the nation in the days of Mr. Lincoln and that was recognized by his astute mind, clear to his mental vision and so profoundly appreciated by his keen sense of justice and which he had the courage to foster against all opposition is abroad in our land to-day, will ultimately triumph.

Mr. Lincoln was the first to suggest to his party the enfranchisement of the Negro. He wrote Governor Hahn, of Louisiana, advising that the ballot should be given to the colored man; said he, "Let in, as for instance, the very intelligent and especially those who have fought gallantly in our ranks. They would probably help in some trying time in the future to keep the jewel of liberty in the family of freedom."

It seems to me right and proper on this memorable day, when the nation has stopped to consider the work of the man above all others who started the Negro on his upward way, that we should appeal to the enlightened conscience of the nation, to unloose further the fetters which bind the black man, especially the industrial bands placed upon him in the North. I appeal to the white people of the South, the sentiment-makers of that section, to create sentiment in favor of law and order, and that they demand a cessation of lynchings. I appeal to the legislature of the South to allow the civil and political door of hope to remain open to my people, and in all things which make for quietness and permanent peace, let us be brethren.

The Negro should no longer be considered a serf, but a citizen of this glorious Republic which both white and black alike have done so much to develop.

Mr. Edwin D. Mead, in the *New York Independent* of January 21, 1909, says, "Has the country been faithful to Lincoln's memory and task? Has the evolution of emancipation been pushed with proper persistence and earnestness? Are we ceasing our discrimination against men because they are black? It is not a question put by North to South. It is a question put to Springfield, Illinois, the old home of Lincoln himself, as directly as to men in Maryland busy with their pitiful disfranchising chicanery." To the still lingering cry of "black men down" this salutary Commemoration rings back, the "all men up," whose echoes after forty years were growing faint in too many American hearts.

Had they not grown faint in many, the recent words of Justice Harlan, so like Lincoln's own, upon the Berea College decision confirming the Kentucky law that, however, they themselves desired it, and even in private institutions, a black boy and a white boy may not study together the rule of three or the law of gravitation, the Golden Rule, or the Emancipation Proclamation,—would have aroused a vastly profounder and louder response.

"If the views of the highest court of Kentucky be sound, that commonwealth may, without infringing on the Constitution of the United States, forbid the association in the same private school of pupils of the Anglo-Saxon and Latin races respectively, or pupils of Christian and Jewish faith respectively. Have we become so inoculated with prejudice of race that any American government professedly based on the principles of freedom and charged with the protection of all citizens alike can make distinctions between such citizens in the manner of their voluntary meeting for innocent purposes, simply because of their respective races? If the court be right, then the State may make it a crime for white and colored persons to frequent the same market-places at the same time or to appear in an assemblage of citizens convened to consider questions of a public or political nature, in which all citizens without regard to race are equally interested; and other illustrations would show the mischievous, not to say cruel, character of the statute in question, and how inconsistent such legislation is with the principle of the equality of citizens before the law."

Mr. Mead further says that Abraham Lincoln was called upon to make his memorable and mighty protest with reference to a single race. In our time the problem becomes vastly more complex and pressing.

But, however complex, there is but one way of solving it—the simple, Christian, fraternal way. It is well for us that the Lincoln centennial comes to say this to us persuasively and commandingly.

ADDRESS ON THE OCCASION OF THE PRESENTATION OF A LOVING CUP TO HON. JOSEPH BENSON FORAKER, UNITED STATES SENATOR[39]

BY HON. ARCHIBALD H. GRIMKE

The Honorable Joseph Benson Foraker, and Colored Citizens:

A little more than two years ago the country was startled one November morning by a Presidential order for which there is no precedent in the history of the government. It was an act not only without precedent, but, as it appeared at the time to many Americans and as it appears to them now for that matter, not warranted either by law or justice. The punishment which that order inflicted on a whole battalion of American soldiers, without trial of any kind seemed unmerited and cruel in the highest degree, and a wanton abuse of executive power.

The history of this case is known of all men, thanks and yet again thanks and love without limit to the illustrious man whom we have met to honor to-night. For it is now and it must forever remain the history of the Black Battalion and of Senator Foraker. It is the history of the most masterly and heroic struggle in defense of the rights and liberties of the individual citizen against executive usurpation and oppression which this country has witnessed for a generation.

The act of the President, while it affected the rights of all Americans, bore with peculiar hardship, with crushing injustice, on the one hundred and sixty-seven men of the Black Battalion who were discharged from the Army without honor and on a mere assumption of their guilt in the "Brownsville" affray.

That act was a sad blow to the colored race of the country likewise, and fell upon them with cruel surprise. For they are people without many friends and are hard pressed in this boasted land of the free and home of the brave. They are hard pressed in every part of the Republic by an increasing race prejudice, by a bitter colorphobia which forgets that they are weak, forgets their claim at the hands of a Christian nation to just and equal treatment to the end that they may do and become as other men with a race and color different from their own. Blows they are receiving thick and fast from their enemies whose name is legion, blows against their right to life, liberty, and the pursuit of happiness in the South and in the North. We are accustomed as a race to such blows. Cruel as they are and hard to bear, yet they do not take us by surprise. For we have learned by long and bitter experience to look for them from a people who loudly proclaim, in season and out, their belief in the principles of democracy and of Christianity. But when an old friend turns against us, and strikes too like an ancient enemy, such a blow is more grievous to bear, and seems crueler than death itself. The blow of an old friend is always the unkindest blow of all. One is never prepared for it, and when it falls the wound which it inflicts cuts deeper than flesh and blood, for the iron of it enters the soul itself. And so it happened to us, when, two years ago, the cruel wrong of that executive order was done to our brave boys in blue by the hand of a trusted friend, the apostle of the "square deal."

Who can describe the shock of that first terrible amazement, the hot indignation felt by a race at the huge injustice, at the Draconian severity of that order which expelled from the American Army one hundred and sixty-seven men without trial of any kind and on a mere suspicion of their guilt, and which made them forever ineligible to employment thereafter in any department of the National Government, whether on its civil, military, or naval side, and the deep consternation which filled the homes of every colored man in the land—North and South alike? I for one can not describe those feelings, although I experienced in unison with the race at the time the amazement, the indignation, and the consternation which swept us together and caused us to feel and speak and act as one man under the wrong done us by the hand of an old friend whose golden words of hope and fair play we had sometime written in letters of light on the tablets of our hearts. It is no slight matter for any man, whether he be President or private citizen, so to wound the sense of right of a whole race, so to shock its faith in the justice and righteousness of its rulers and government, as that cruel blunder of the President of the United States produced among the colored people of the entire country.

We lifted up our voice as the voice of many waters from one end of the land to the other in loud protest against the wrong, in stern denunciation of it, and the press of the North came nobly to our assistance and swelled the volume of our protest and denunciation. But alas, all this volume of protest and denunciation on the part of the race and of the press would have passed over the nation and the Government like a summer storm of wind and rain—so little do our outcries against injustice and oppression excite the attention and sympathy of the Republic any more—had there not arisen in the Senate of the United States a man for the hour, had not God raised him up to defend his little ones against the slings and arrows of a sleepless energy, of an almost omnipotent power seated in the highest place of the Government. It was the genius, the grandcur of soul of a great man who was able to gather into thunderbolt after thunderbolt all the sense of outraged justice on the part of race and press, and to hurl them with marvelous precision and overwhelming might against that cruel executive order and the hosts of words and messages and other hordes of blood-dyed epithets which the President marshalled and sent forth from time to time in defense of his Draconian decree. If there was sleepless energy in the White House, there was an energy just as sleepless on the floor of the Senate. The almost omnipotent power wielded for the destruction of the Black Battalion by the formidable occupant of the executive mansion was met and matched, ay, overmatched again and again by an omnipotence in discussion which a just cause and genius as orator, lawyer, and debater of the first rank could alone have put into the strong right arm of the brave redresser of a race's wrongs on the floor of the Senate. For more than two years he carried the case of the Black Battalion in his big and tireless brain, in his big and gentle heart, as a mother carries under her bosom her unborn babe. God alone knows what sums of money, what deep thought and solicitude, what unflagging energy, what unceasing labor, he spent in his holy and self-imposed task to right the wrongs of those helpless and persecuted men. In the Senate their case pursued him like a shadow, and at home it sat with him like a ghost in his library, and slept for a few hours only when the great brain slept and the generous heart rested from the pain which was torturing it. Sir, did you know what love went out to you during those tremendous months of toil and struggle, and what prayers from the grateful hearts of ten millions of people?

Yes, he was one man against the whole power of the Administration and all that that meant. Perhaps we do not fully understand what a colossal power that was to confront and grapple with. Almost single-handed he met that power and threw it again and again in the arena of debate. Every speech he made in behalf of his clients, whether on the floor of the Senate or outside of that body, was as terrible as an army with banners to the enemies of the Black Battalion who had now, alas, become his enemies too, and who were bent on the destruction of both, the defender and the defended alike. But he did not hesitate or quail before that power and the danger which threatened his political life. As the battle thickened and perils gathered fast about his head he fought the fight of the Black Battalion as few men in the history of the Republic have ever fought for the weak, for a just cause against organized power and oppression in the high places of the Government. Senator Foraker was one man, but Senator Foraker was a host in himself. We know this, but the enemies of the Black Battalion know it better than we do, for wherever they appeared on the field of action during those two years, whether with their sappers and miners or assaulting columns, there they found him alert, dauntless, invincible—their sappers and miners hoisted with their own petard, their assaulting columns routed and driven to cover before the withering, the deadly fire from the flashing cannon of his facts, his logic, his law, and his eloquence. Sir, God knows that I would rather have fought the fight which you fought so gloriously than be a Senator of the United

States, day, than be President of the Republic itself. For it is better to be a brave and just and true man than to be either Senator or President, or both.

"Greater love hath no man than this that a man lay down his life for his friends." This is what Senator Foraker has done for the Black Battalion and for the principles of law and liberty which underlie their case. He has given his political life, his seat in the Senate, all the honor and power which were his had he chosen to defend the order of the President, discharging those one hundred and sixty-seven men without trial of any kind from the Army which their valor had helped to make glorious—instead of the soldiers whom he did not know but whose pitiful case, whose unjust and cruel punishment, enlisted the sympathy of his great heart and the masterly labors of his tireless brain. Yes, I repeat, and do not let it ever be forgotten by us as a race, that Senator Foraker might to-day be his own successor in the United States Senate had he chosen to play in the "Brownsville" affair the part of defender of President Roosevelt's wanton abuse and usurpation of executive power, instead of taking the side of the Black Battalion and the fundamental principle of our law and Constitution that each man accused of crime is entitled to trial before he is condemned and punished. He chose the side of the weak, of justice, and the Constitution in this great struggle, and not that of power and the Administration. This was the sin which brought upon him all the wrath of that power and of that Administration, but of which all good men and true absolve and for which they honor him, and for which, besides, a grateful race enshrines him in its heart of hearts. For he preferred to suffer affliction with the Black Battalion and to suffer defeat for the Senatorship rather than enjoy power and office as the price of his desertion of the cause of those helpless men.

No man can give as much as Senator Foraker has given to a just cause, give as generously, as unselfishly, gloriously as he has given of his very self in this "Brownsville" case and lose that which is best striving for in life. He may lose place in the Government and power as a political leader. But what are these but the ephemera of man's fevered existence and strivings here below? "What shadows we are," Burke said on a memorable occasion in his contest for a seat in Parliament, "and what shadows we pursue." Office, power, popularity; what are they but shadows of passing clouds which a breath blows to us and a breath blows from us again. No man loses anything in reality when he loses such fleeting, such shadowy possessions. But if for the sake of them he loses truth, justice, goodness, his love of the right and his hatred of the wrong, his sympathy for the oppressed, his passion to help God's little ones, such a man has bartered away his soul, the immortal part of him for a rood of grass, which to-day flourisheth and to-morrow withereth and is cast into the oven of all transitory and perishable possessions.

How many men who now hold seats in the United States Senate or the House of Representatives do we even know the names of? How many of all that long procession of them who have been passing for more than a century though those halls of power have we so much as heard the names of? They have filed through those stately chambers to dusty death and oblivion, and the places which knew them once know them no more forever. A few names only are remembered among all the multitude of them, not because of the places they occupied or the power they wielded, but because while in those houses they chose the better part—chose not to busy themselves with shadows, with the things which perish, but seized and held fast to the eternal verities of justice and freedom and human brotherhood. The vast majority of them magnified their brief authority and neglected the opportunity which their offices offered them to link their names and official lives with some noble movement or measure for the betterment of their kind, for the lifting up of those who were down, the strengthening of those who were weak, the succor of those who were hard pressed by man's inhumanity to man.

It is beautiful to defend those who can not defend themselves, to lift up the weak, to succor those who are ready to perish. It is heroic, divine, when the doing so involves peril and sacrifice of self. It is the essence of the Gospel preached and lived by one who spoke and lived as never man spoke and lived. It is simple and undefiled Christianity. Nothing avails to make Senator or President or people Christian but just this one thing—not race or color or creed, not learning and wealth and civilization—but kindness to God's poor, to Christ's little ones. Did you feed them when they were hungry; did you give them to drink when they were thirsty; did you visit and comfort them when they were in prison? Those who do these things to the humblest and the blackest of these little ones of the Republic have done them unto the divine Master, are in truth His disciples; and those who do them not are not His followers, whatever may be their profession, but quite the contrary. They have no part or lot with Him but belong to the evil forces of the world which are forever opposing the coming of His righteous Kingdom on earth when all men shall be brothers, when the strong shall everywhere bear the burdens of the weak.

Inasmuch as William Lloyd Garrison, Charles Sumner, Wendell Phillips, John Brown, and Abraham Lincoln did it to the least of His little ones in this Republic, they did it unto Him. They are a goodly company, the glorious company of the elect of the Republic, its prophets, its priests, and its kings. And, Sir, inasmuch as you, too, did it to the Black Battalion in their dire need, you did it unto Christ, and you are now henceforth and forevermore to enter into the supreme joy of that supreme service and sacrifice. You lost, Sir, your seat in the Senate, it is true, but you have won an enduring place in a race's heart, its enduring love and gratitude, and the plaudit of the divine Master,

"Well done, good and faithful servant," uttered from the lips of all good men and true the country over.

EQUALITY OF RIGHTS FOR ALL CITIZENS, BLACK AND WHITE, ALIKE[40]

BY REV. FRANCIS J. GRIMKE, D. D.

I Cor. 16:13. "Watch ye, stand fast in the faith, quit you like men, be strong."

It has been my custom for many years to speak during the inaugural week on some phase of the race question. I have done it because usually at such times there are representatives of our race here from all parts of the country, and an opportunity is thus afforded of reaching a larger number than would be possible at any other time. Such occasions, it seems to me, should be utilized in the interest of the race, in the discussion of matters pertaining to the race. The inauguration of a President is an event in which the whole nation is interested, and which emphasizes the fact of citizenship, as perhaps nothing else does, coming as it does after the election, and growing out of it. On such occasions it is well for us, therefore, especially at this juncture of our history, not to be unmindful of our own citizenship, of our own status in the body politic.

We have just been celebrating, all over the country, the centennial of the birth of Abraham Lincoln, our great war President, and this inauguration coming so soon after, makes it especially a good time to talk about some of the questions which grew out of the war, and which were settled by it. And this is what I want to do this morning.

Over forty years ago the great struggle ended, the "irrepressible conflict" came to a close. It marked an epoch in the history of our country, and in the history of the black race in this country. Certain great questions, which had agitated the country for years, were settled, and settled for all time.

* * * * *

It is now no longer a question as to whether we are a nation, or a confederation of sovereign and independent States. That question is settled, and settled once for all by the issue of the War. It is not likely that any Southern State will ever again attempt to withdraw from the Union, or to act on the assumption that it has the right to do so. Even if it is foolish enough to entertain such a view, it will be sure never again to act upon it. The issue of the War has removed forever from the field of serious discussion this question of the right of a State to secede. The ghost of secession will never again arise to disturb the peace of the Union. The Stars and Stripes, the old flag, will float, as long as it floats, over all these States, from the Atlantic to the Pacific, from the Lakes to the Gulf. If the time ever comes when we shall go to pieces, it will not be from any desire or disposition on the part of the States to pull apart, but from inward corruption, from the disregard of right principles, from the spirit of greed, from the narrowing lust of gold, from losing sight of the fact that "righteousness exalteth a nation, but that sin is a reproach to any people." It is here where our real danger lies—not in the secession of States from the Union, but in the secession of the Union itself from the great and immutable principles of right, of justice, of fair play for all regardless of race, color, or previous condition of servitude. The fact that the Union has been saved, that these rebellious States have been brought back into it, will amount to nothing unless it can be saved from this still greater peril that threatens it. The secession of the Southern States in 1860 was a small matter compared with the secession of the Union itself from the great principles enunciated in the Declaration of Independence, in the Golden Rule, in the Ten Commandments, in the Sermon on the Mount. Unless we hold, and hold firmly to these great fundamental principles of righteousness, of social, political, and economic wisdom, our Union, as Mr. Garrison expressed it, will be "only a covenant with death and an agreement with hell." If it continues to exist it will be a curse, and not a blessing.

Our brave boys in blue, whose bodies lie moldering in the grave, but whose souls are marching on, settled the question of the Union of the States. It is for the patriotic men who are living to-day, and those who are to follow in their footsteps, to deal with this larger and more important question. It isn't enough that these States are held together, they must be held together on right principles—principles of justice, of equity, of fair play, of equality before the law for all alike. Whether there is patriotism, political wisdom, moral insight and stamina enough to lead men to forget their differences on minor matters and to unite their forces for the attainment of this greater and more important end, remains to be seen. There are so many who are controlled by their petty prejudices, whose views are so narrow and contracted, that they seem incapable of appreciating the things of prime importance, the things that are fundamental in the life of the nation, and upon which its future peace and prosperity depend. The fear of rebellion is forever gone. It is not so, however, with regard to the danger of which I am speaking—the danger of the nation divorcing itself from sound political and moral principles.

* * * * *

In the scheme of citizenship of our country for years following the close of the war the Negro had no part; and he had no part because he was looked upon as an inferior. "Subordination to the superior race is declared to be his natural and moral condition." His inferiority was asserted to be a "great physical, philosophical, and moral truth."

And this is exactly the Southern view to-day; and is exactly the programme to which it is committed. Its whole attitude to-day is in harmony with the great principle upon which the Southern Confederacy was founded—the non-recognition of the Negro as an equal in any respect—socially, civilly, politically. The South holds to this view just as tenaciously to-day as it did when Mr. Stephens made his Great Cornerstone Speech in 1861. The Ku Klux Klan, the White Caps, the Red Shirt Brigade, tissue ballots, the revised constitutions with their grandfather clauses, Jim Crow Car legislation, the persistent effort of the South to disfranchise the Negro—all these things have grown out of the idea that the rightful place of the Negro is that of subordination to the white man, that he has no rightful place in the body politic.

* * * * *

But I cannot believe that the nation is always going to leave its loyal black citizens to be despoiled of their civil and political rights by the men who sought to destroy the Union. A better day is coming, and coming soon, I trust.

While we are waiting, however, for the nation to come to its senses—waiting for a revival of the spirit of justice and of true democracy in the land—it is important for us to remember that much, very much, will depend upon ourselves. In the passage of Scripture read in our hearing at the beginning of this discourse, three things we are exhorted to do, and must do, if we are ever to secure our rights in this land: We are exhorted to be watchful. "Watch ye," is the exhortation. We are to be on our guard. "Eternal vigilance is the price of liberty." There are enemies ever about us and are ever plotting our ruin—enemies within the race and without it. We have got to live in the consciousness of this fact. If we assume that all is well, that there is nothing to fear, and so relax our vigilance, so cease to be watchful, we need not be surprised if our enemies get the better of us, if we are worsted in the conflict.

(2) We are exhorted to stand fast in the faith. In the faith we feel that, as American citizens, we are entitled to the same rights and privileges as other citizens of the Republic. In this faith we are to stand, and stand fast. We are not to give it up; we are not to allow anyone, white or black, friend or foe, to induce us to retreat a single inch from this position.

(3) We are exhorted to quit ourselves like men, to be strong. And by this, I understand, is meant that we are to stand up in a manly way for our rights; that we are to seek by every honorable means the full enjoyment of our rights. It is still true—

"Who would be free himself must strike the blow."

And, if we are ever to be free from invidious distinctions in this country, based upon race, color, previous condition, we have got to be alive, wide-awake to our own interest. If we are not, we have no right to expect others to be; we have no right to expect anything but failure, but defeat. And we deserve defeat if ours is the spirit of indifference, of unconcern. We are not going to secure our rights in this land without a struggle. We have got to contend, and contend earnestly, for what belongs to us. Victory isn't coming in any other way. No silent acquiescence on our part in the wrongs from which we are suffering, contrary to law; no giving of ourselves merely to the work of improving our condition, materially, intellectually morally, spiritually, however zealously pursued, is going to bring relief. We have got, in addition to the effort we are making to improve ourselves, to keep up the agitation, and keep it up until right triumphs and wrong is put down. A programme of silence on the part of the race is a fool's programme. Reforms, changes in public sentiment, the righting of wrongs, are never effected in that way; and our wrongs will never be. A race that sits quietly down and rests in sweet content in the midst of the wrongs from which it is suffering is not worth contending for, is not worth saving.

This is not true of this race, however. We are not sitting down in sweet content, let it be said to our credit. I thank God from the bottom of my heart for these mutterings of discontent that are heard in all parts of the land. The fact that we are dissatisfied with present conditions, and that we are becoming more and more so, shows that we are growing in manhood, in self-respect, in the qualities that will enable us to win out in the end. It is our duty to keep up the agitation for our rights, not only for our sakes, but also for the sake of the nation at large. It would not only be against our own interest not to do so, but it would be unpatriotic for us quietly to acquiesce in the present condition of things, for it is a wrong condition of things. If justice sleeps in this land, let it not be because we have helped to lull it to sleep by our silence, our indifference; let it not be from lack of effort on our part to arouse it from its slumbers. Elijah said to the prophets of Baal, while they were crying to their god, "Peradventure he sleepeth." And it may be that he was asleep; but it was not their fault that he continued asleep, for they kept up a continual uproar about his altar. And so here, sleeping Justice in this land may go on slumbering, but let us see to it that it is due to no fault of ours. Even Baalam's ass cried out in protest when smitten by his brutal master, and God gave him the power to cry out, endowed him miraculously with speech in which to voice his protest.

It is not necessary for God to work a miracle to enable us to protest against our wrong; He has already given us the power. Let us see to it that we use it. If we are wise we will be able to take care of ourselves. If we are not wise, however, if we adopt the policy of silence, and if we continue to feel that it is our duty to follow blindly, slavishly, any one political party, we will receive only such treatment as is accorded to slaves, and will go on pleading for our rights in vain. The only wise course for us to pursue is to keep on agitating, and to cast our votes where they will tell most for the race. As to what party we affiliate with is a matter of no importance whatever; the important thing is our rights. And until we recognize that fact, and act upon it, we will be the football of all political parties. John Boyle O'Reilly, in speaking on the race question years ago, said: "If I were a colored man I should use parties as I would a club—to break down prejudice against my people. I shouldn't talk about being true to any party, except so far as that party was true to me. Parties care nothing for you, only to use you. You should use parties; the highest party you have in this country is your own manhood. That is the thing in danger from all parties; that is the thing that every colored man is bound in duty to himself and his children to defend and protect." And that is good advice. It embodies the highest political wisdom for us as a people.

The exhortation of the text is, "Watch ye, stand fast in the faith, quit you like men, be strong." And this is the message that I bring to you, who are here this morning, and to the members of our race all over the country. We must be watchful; we must hold firmly to our faith in our citizenship, and in our rights as citizens; and we must act the part of men in the maintenance of those rights. In the end the victory is sure to be ours. The right is bound, sooner or later, to triumph.

"Before the monstrous wrong he sits him down—
One man against a stone-walled city of sin.
For centuries those walls have been a-building;
Smooth porphyry, they slope and coldly glass
The flying storm and wheeling sun.

"No chinks, no crevice, lets the thinnest arrow in.
He fights alone, and from the cloudy ramparts
A thousand evil faces gibe and jeer him.
Let him lie down and die; what is the right
And where is justice in a world like this?

"But by and by earth shakes herself, impatient;
And down, in one great roar of ruin, crash
Watch-tower and citadel and battlements.
When the red dust has cleared, the lonely soldier
Stands with strange thoughts beneath the friendly stars."

And so, in the end, will it be with this great evil of race prejudice against which we are contending in this country, if, like the lonely soldier, we show the same earnestness, the same patient determination, the same invincible courage. A better day is coming; but we have got to help to bring it about. It isn't coming independently of our efforts, and it isn't coming by quietly, timidly, cowardly acquiescing in our wrongs.

IS THE GAME WORTH THE CANDLE?[41]

BY DR. JAMES E. SHEPARD

Founder and President of the National Religious Training School at Durham, N. C.

Students and Friends:

I am not unmindful of the vast opportunity that is mine as I stand before young men. The opportunity is great, but the responsibility is greater. It was the thought of the responsibility that decided me to speak on the subject, "Is the Game Worth the Candle?"; the meaning simplified being—Is the object pursued worth the price paid for its attainment.

Once during an all-night ride en route for Arkansas in the latter part of the year just closed, I fell into a retrospective mood, and the scroll of the past years unfolded itself before my memory, and as I reviewed it and marked the possibilities which had passed with the years, life took on even a greater aspect than it had already possessed. I shall not discuss my life, but life with its probabilities and possibilities of power and achievement; life in its earnestness and life that is merely drifting with the tide, of no benefit to itself or to humanity.

A man's life depends upon his emotions, his aspirations, his determinations.

A young man, somebody's son, starts out with the determination that the world is indebted to him for a good time. "Dollars were made to spend. I am young, and every man must sow his wild oats and then settle down. I want to be a 'hail fellow well met' with every one." So he is ever ready to drink a social glass, to give a pun and to be a "masher on the girls." With this determination uppermost in his life purpose he starts out to be a good-timer. Perhaps some mother expects to hear great things of her boy, some father's hopes are centered in him, but what does that matter? "I am a good-timer." From one gayety to another, from one glass to another, from one sin to another, and the good-timer at last is broken in health, deserted by friends, and left alone to die. Thus the "man about town" passes off the stage. When you ask some of his friends about him, the answer is, "Oh, John was all right, but he lived too fast. I like good time as well as anyone, but I could not keep up with John." Was the game worth the candle?

Two pictures come before my mind; two cousins, both of them young men. One started out early in life with the determination of getting along "easy," shirking work, and looking for a soft snap. His motto was, "The world owes me a living, and I am going to get mine." He was employed first by one firm and then by another; if anything that he considered hard came along, he would pay another fellow to do the work and he "took things easy." It was not long before no one would hire him. He continued to hold the idea that the world was indebted to him and furthermore, he arrogated a belief that what another man had accumulated he could borrow without his knowledge. He forged another's name, was detected, and sentenced to the penitentiary and is now wearing the badge of felony and shame—the convicts' stripes. Young men, the world owes no man a living, but those who work faithfully and make contributions to the happiness of mankind and the advancement of civilization. These will ever be honored and rewarded. Is the game worth the candle?

The other cousin started out with a determination altogether different. He believed with Lord Brougham, that if he were a bootblack, he would strive to be the best bootblack in England. He began in a store as a window-washer, and washed windows so well that they sparkled like diamonds under the sun. As a clerk, no customer was too insignificant to be greeted with a smile or pleasant word; no task was too great for him to attempt. Thus step by step, he advanced, each day bringing new duties and difficulties but each day also bringing new strength and determination to master them, and to-day that cousin is a man of wealth and an honored citizen, blessed too, with a happy home.

Some young men start life with the idea that every dollar made requires that one dollar and a half shall be spent; in order to be noticed they must make a big show, give big dinners, carriage drives, and parties, invite friends to the theatres, and have a "swell" time; must do like Mr. "So-and-So." They forget in their desire to copy, that Mr. "So-and-so," their pattern, has already made his fortune; that he began to save before he began to spend. But no, his name appears often in the papers and they think also that theirs must. So they begin their careers. A few years pass. The young men marry; their debts begin to accumulate and to press them, their countenances are always woe-begone; where once were smiles, now are frowns, and the homes are pictures of gloom and shadows. The lesson is plain.

Debt is the greatest burden that can be put upon a man; it makes him afraid to look honest men in the face. No man can be a leader in the fullest sense who is burdened by a great debt. If there is any young men in the audience who is spending more than he is making let him ask himself the question, Is the game worth the candle?

I know another young man who believed he could be happy by spending one-third of what he made and saving the other portion. He said to me, "some day I want to marry and I want to treat my wife better, if possible, than she was treated at home. I want the respect of my fellow man, I want to be a leader, and I know I can only do so by saving a part of what I make."

It was my good pleasure, a few weeks ago, to visit the city where this young man is practising medicine. He carried me over that town in an automobile, he entertained me in his $5000 home, he showed me other property which he owned. Ah, my friends, his indeed was a happy home. Life to him was blessedly real.

Some young men start life with the idea that Sunday school is a place for children, the church for old people and the Y. M. C. A. a place for young men with no life. What a wrong idea! Why, the young men who are alive in all walks of life, and who are in the forward ranks, are found in these places. The other young men with distorted views of life think that they must frequent places where the social glass is passed. They do so; after a while it becomes a necessity, the drink habit grows upon them; they die drunkards. Do you remember the story of Robert Ferguson who, better known as the "laureate of Edinburgh," was the poet of Scottish city-life? His dissipations were great, his tavern and boon companions hastening him on to a premature and painful death. His reason gave way. He was sent to an asylum for the insane. After about two months' confinement he died in his cell. What a sad climax to a promising career!

Young men, be masters of yourselves. Dare to do the right. Dare to say No. Have strong faith not only in yourself but faith in the Unseen Power, who holds the destinies of all in His hands. The world needs you.

A good many young men think that to be great they must go into the broad fields of politics, waiting for an office, waiting on the changing whims of men, instead of waiting upon self; waiting for something to turn up instead of turning up something; going to the Capital "because I helped to elect someone." "I leave behind me a good job but I have been promised something better." So the poor fellow starts out to the capital of the nation, spends what little money he has saved at home, because he is going to get a job and make barrels of money. The Mecca of his hopes is reached. He finds himself a little man at the great center of the nation, the few dollars he brings with him soon melt away; his friends run when they see him coming because he wants to borrow a dollar. At home he was a little king, but at the Capital he is a "would-be statesman seeking a job." Was the game worth the candle?

My friends, good men are needed in politics, men who are safe and tried, men who will not yield to prejudice or sentiment, but will do the right as they see the right. God give us such men. Politics for a helpless, dependent race will never prove a relief or blessing until we have strong, safe leaders who, losing sight of self and a few self-constituted leaders, will see the whole people. The race will never come into its own until we have such a condition.

A young man starts out in life with the determination to fight his way by physical force to the front ranks. Bruised, disfigured, or killed, he is forced back even beyond the lines again. A religiously inclined youth asked his pastor, "Do you think it would be wrong for me to learn the noble art of self-defense?" "Certainly not," replied the pastor, "I learned it in youth myself, and I have found it of great value in my life." "Indeed, sir, did you learn the Old English system or the Sullivan system?" "Neither; I learned Solomon's system!" replied the minister. "Yes, you will find it laid down in the first verse of the fifteenth chapter of Proverbs, 'A soft answer turneth away wrath'; it is the best system of self-defense I know."

Too many of us starting out on life's journey have a warped ambition. This ambition is a love of self in the desire that self might gain the ascendency over our fellows, not that we might be of benefit to humanity, but that we aim to derive personal gain only. We follow the standard of this or that man, not because we believe in him or his policies, but because he is on the successful top round of the ladder now, so away with principles, away with conscience, away with right,—I must follow the man who will give most! A sad awakening comes, the idol tumbles or else turns against you, and you are left like a stranded ship on some vast ocean, alone, amidst the lashing of the billows and the roaring of the waves. Remember Cardinal Wolsey's experience. You may recall these lines,

"Would that I had served my God
With half the zeal I served my king,
He would not in mine old age
Have left me naked to my enemies."

Was the game worth the candle?

Another young man starts life with a wrong idea regarding city and country life. Born in the country he is free, his thoughts and ambitions can feed on a pure atmosphere, but he thinks his conditions and his surroundings are circumscribed, he longs for the city, with its bigness, its turmoil, and its conflicts. He leaves the old homestead, the quiet village, the country people, and hies himself to the city. He forgets to a large extent the good boy he used to be, in the desire to keep up with the fashions and to make the people forget that he was once a country boy. City life, as is often the case, breaks up his youth, destroys his morals, undermines his character, steals his reputation, and finally leaves the promising youth a wrecked man. Was the game worth the candle?

Young men, never be ashamed of the old log-cabin in the country, or the old bonnet your mother used to wear, or the jean pants your father used to toil in. I had rather be a poor country boy with limited surroundings and a pure heart than to be a city man bedecked in the latest fashions and weighted down with money, having no morals, no character. I had rather have the religion and faith of my fathers than to have the highest offices. I had rather have glorious life, pure and lofty, than to have great riches. Sir Walter Scott was right when he said,

"Sound, sound the clarion, fill the fife,
To all the sensual world proclaim:
One crowded hour of glorious life
Is worth an age without a name."

Young men, what is the basis of your life and what is its goal? Have you digged deeply and thrown out all the waste material of follies and vice and built upon a substantial foundation of honest manhood and sterling character? If not, you are a failure. However, chords that are broken may vibrate once more; take up the angled threads again and weave another pattern. The book that will always be the best and safest guide for weaving life's pattern is the Bible,—the truest and best friend any young man can have. If you want oratory, you need not talk about Demosthenes walking along the shores of Greece with pebbles in his mouth, nor about that great American orator, Daniel Webster, but if you turn almost to the beginning of that wonderful Book and listen to the pleadings of Jacob's sons as they begged for the life of their father, it will surpass your Demosthenes or Webster in true eloquence. If you want logic, even though Aristotle may be world famous as the "father of logic," yet if you listen to the hunch-backed, red faced, crooked nosed, baldheaded Jew, Saul of Tarsus, you will find his logic stands unsurpassed in all the ages of the world. The history of four thousand years and more you will find there. You will discover the beginnings and the end of things. Reason, with her flickering torch, cannot point to any such sublime truths as are found in the Bible. Philosophy with her school stands amazed when confronted with the philosophy of the Bible. Science, itself the greatest contributor to the happiness of man, having penetrated the arcana of nature, sunk her shafts into earth's recesses, measured the heights of its massive pillars to the very pedestal of primeval granite, tracked the tornadoes, uncurtained the distant planets, and foretold the coming of the comets and the return of the eclipses, has never as yet been able to lift up a degraded man and point him to a higher path. I commend the Bible to you.

No life is great unless that life is good. Each day is a life, and that day is wasted that is not filled with lofty desire, with actual achievement, that does not bring us nearer to God, nearer to our fellow-man and nearer to the things God has created. In such a plan of life will we find real and lasting happiness. God means every man to be happy. He sends us no sorrows that have not some recompense.

There are two old Dutch words which have resounded through the world, "*Neen nimmer*," "No, never." The fleets of Spain heard it, and understood it fully, when they saw the sinking Dutch ships with the flags nailed to the shattered mainmast, crying "*Neen nimmer*," which indicated that they would never surrender.

Will the young men who are to be the leaders, spend their hours in riotous living? No, never! Will they be false to duty? No, never! Will they shirk? No, never! Will they be disloyal to self, to home, to country, and to God? No, never!

I close with an illustration. Croesus was a rich man, a king. One day Croesus said to Solon, the philosopher, "Do you not think I am a happy man?" Solon answered, "Alas, I do not know, Croesus; that life is happy that ends well." A few years later when Croesus had lost his wealth, his kingdom, and his health, and had been deserted by those who in his days of glory ran to do his slightest bidding, Croesus in anguish and misery exclaimed, "Solon, Solon, thou saidst truly that life is well and happy that ends well."

SOME ELEMENTS NECESSARY TO RACE DEVELOPMENT[42]

By Robert Russa Moton

Commandant of Cadets, Hampton Institute, Virginia

Students, Friends:

Among the most highly developed races we observe certain dominant characteristics, certain very essential elements of character, by which they have so influenced mankind and helped the world that they were enabled to write their names in history so indelibly as to withstand and endure the test of time.

Your education, your observation, your occupation, have brought you into close touch and into personal and vital relations with the fundamental problems of life. We may call it the truth problem, the labor problem, the Indian problem, or perhaps the Negro problem. I like to call it the "Human Race Problem."

The dawn of history breaks upon a world at strife, a universal conflict of man at war with his brother. The very face of the earth has been dyed in blood and its surface whitened with human bones in an endeavor to establish a harmonious and helpful adjustment between man and man. There can be no interest more fundamental or of greater concern to the human family than the proper adjustment of man's relations to his brother.

You and I belong to an undeveloped, backward race that is rarely for its own sake taken into account in the adjustment of man's relation to man, but is considered largely with reference to the impression which it makes upon the dominant Anglo-Saxon. The Negro's very existence is itself somewhat satellitious, and secondary only, to the great white orb around which he revolves. If by chance any light does appear in the black man's sphere of operations, it is usually assumed that it is reflected from his association with his white brother. The black is generally projected against the white and usually to the disadvantage and embarrassment of the former. It becomes very easy, therefore, to see in our minds and hearts what is so apparent in our faces, "Darkness there and nothing more."

But you must keep in mind that the Negro is a tenth part of a great cosmopolitan commonwealth; he is a part of a nation to which God has given many very intricate problems to work out. Who knows but that this nation is God's great laboratory which is being used by the Creator to show the rest of the world, what it does not seem thoroughly to understand, that it is possible for all God's people, even the two most extreme types, the black and the white, to live together harmoniously and helpfully?

The question that the American nation must face, and which the Negro as a part of the nation should soberly and dispassionately consider, is the mutual, social, civic, and industrial adjustment upon common ground of two races, differing widely in characteristics and diverse in physical peculiarities, but alike suspicious and alike jealous, and alike more or less biased and prejudiced each toward the other. Without doubt the physical peculiarities of the Negro, which are perhaps the most superficial of all the distinctions, are nevertheless the most difficult of adjustment. While I do not believe that a man's color is ever a disadvantage to him, he is very likely to find it an inconvenience sometimes, in some places.

We might as well be perfectly frank and perfectly honest with ourselves; it is not an easy task to adjust the relations of ten millions of people who, while they may be mature in passion and perhaps in prejudice, are yet to a large extent children in judgment and in experience, to a race of people not only mature in civilization, but the principles of whose government were based upon more or less mature judgment and experience at the beginning of this nation; and when we take into also account the wide difference in ethnic types of the two races that are here brought together, the problem becomes one of the gravest intricacy that has ever taxed human wisdom and human patience for solution. This situation makes it necessary for the Negro as a race to grasp firmly two or three fundamental elements.

The first is *race consciousness.*

The Negro must play essentially the primary part in the solution of this problem. Since his emancipation he has conclusively demonstrated to most people that he possesses the same faculties and susceptibilities as the rest of human mankind; this is the greatest victory the race has achieved during its years of freedom. Having demonstrated that his faculties and susceptibilities are capable of the highest development, it must be true of the black race as it has been true of other races, that it must go through the same process and work out the same problem in about the same way as other races have done.

We can and we have profited very much by the examples of progressive races. This is a wonderful advantage, and we have not been slow to grasp it. But we must remember that we are subject to the same natural factor in the solution of this problem, and that it cannot be solved without considering this factor. The Negro must first of all have a conscientious pride and absolute faith and belief in himself. He must not unduly depreciate race distinctions and allow himself to think that, because out of one blood God created all nations of the earth, brotherhood is already an accomplished reality. Let us not deceive ourselves, blighted as we are with a heritage of moral leprosy from our past history and hard pressed as we are in the economic world by foreign immigrants and by native prejudice; our one surest haven of refuge is in ourselves; our one safest means of advance is our belief in and implicit trust in our own ability and worth. No race that despises itself, that laughs at and ridicules itself, that wishes to God it were anything else but itself, can ever be a great people. There is no power under heaven that can stop the onward march of ten millions of earnest, honest, inspired, God-fearing, race-loving, and united people.

Secondly, we must have a *high moral ideal.*

With a strong race consciousness and reasonable prudence, a people with a low, vacillating, and uncertain moral ideal may, for a time, be able to stem the tide of outraged virtue, but this is merely transitory. Ultimate destruction and ruin follow absolutely in the wake of moral degeneracy; this, all history shows;—this, experience teaches. God visits the iniquities of the fathers upon the children unto the third and fourth generations. "The judgments of the Lord are true and righteous all together."

Not long ago I stood in the city of Rome amid its ruined fountains, crumbling walls, falling aqueducts, ancient palaces, and amphitheatres, to-day mere relics of ancient history. One is struck with wonder and amazement at the magnificent civilization which that people was able to evolve. It does not seem possible that the Roman people, who could so perfect society in its organic and civic relations and leave to the world the organic principles which must always lie at the base of all subsequent social development,—it does not seem possible that such a people should so decay as to leave hardly a vestige of its original stock, and that such cities as the Romans erected should so fall as to leave scarcely one stone upon another. Neither does it seem credible that a people who could so work out in its philosophical aspect man's relation to the eternal mystery, and come as near a perfect solution as is perhaps possible for the human mind to reach, that a people who could give to the world such literature, such art, such ideals of physical and intellectual beauty, as did the Greeks, could so utterly perish from the face of the earth; yet this is the case not only with Rome and Greece, but with a score or more of nations which were once masters of the world. The Greeks, Romans, Persians, Egyptians, and even God's chosen people, allowed corruption and vice to so dwarf their moral sense that there was, according to the universal law of civilization, nothing left for them but death and destruction.

It is no reproach to the Negro to say that his history and environment in this country have well-nigh placed him at the bottom of the moral scale. This must be remedied, if the Negro is ever to reach his full status of civilized manhood and womanhood. It must come through the united efforts of the educated among us. We must be united to stop the ravages of disease among our people; united to keep black boys from idleness, vice, gambling, and crime; united to guard the purity of black womanhood and, I might add, black manhood also. It is not enough to simply protest that ninety-five out of every hundred Negroes are orderly and law-abiding. The ninety-five must be banded together to restrain and suppress the vicious five.

The people must be impressed with the idea that a high moral character is absolutely essential to the highest development of every race, white quite as much as black. There is no creature so low and contemptible as he who does not seek first the approval of his own conscience and his God; for, after all, how poor is human recognition when you and your God are aware of your inward integrity of soul! If the Negro will keep clean hands and a pure heart, he can stand up before all the world and say, "Doubtless Thou, O Lord, art our Father, though Abraham be ignorant of us and Israel acknowledge us not."

Thirdly, and lastly, *the Negro needs intelligent industry.*

Slavery taught the Negro many things for which he should be profoundly thankful—the Christian religion, the English language, and, in a measure, civilization, which in many aspects may be crude in form, but these have placed him a thousand years ahead of his African ancestors.

Slavery taught the Negro to work by rule and rote but not by principle and method. It did not and, perhaps, could not teach him to love and respect labor, but left him, on the contrary, with the idea that manual industry was a thing to be despised and gotten rid of, if possible; that to work with one's hands was a badge of inferiority. A tropical climate is not conducive to the development of practical energy. Add to the Negro's natural tendency his unfortunate heritage from slavery, and we see at once that the race needs especially to be rooted and grounded in the underlying scientific principles of concrete things. The time when the world bowed before merely abstract, impractical knowledge has well-nigh passed; the demand of this age and hour is not so much what a man knows,—though the world respects and reveres knowledge and always will, I hope,—what the world wants to know is what a man can do and how well he can do it.

We must not be misled by high-sounding phrases as to the kind of education the race should receive, but we should remember that the education of a people should be conditioned upon their capacity, social environment, and the probable life which they will lead in the immediate future. We fully realize that the ignorant must be taught, the poor must have the gospel, and the vicious must be restrained, but we also realize that these do not strike the "bed-rock" of a permanent, lasting citizenship.

If the Negro will add his proportionate contribution to the economic aspect of the world's civilization, it must be done through intelligent, well-directed, conscientious, skilled industry. Indeed, the feasible forms of civilization are nothing but the concrete actualization of intelligent thought applied to what are sometimes called common things.

The primary sources of wealth are agriculture, mining, manufacturing, and commerce. These are the lines along which the thoughtful energy of the black race must be directed. I mean by agriculture, *farming*—the raising of corn, cotton, peas, and potatoes, pigs, chickens, horses, and cows.

Land may be bought practically anywhere in the South almost at our own price. Twenty years hence, with the rapidly developing Southern country and the strenuous efforts to fill it up with foreign immigrants, it will be difficult, if not impossible, for us to buy land. God gave the children of Israel the "Land of Canaan" but, Oh, what a life and death struggle they had to take possession of it and hold on to it. God has given to the Negro here in this Southern country two of the most fundamental necessities in his development—*land* and *labor*. If you don't possess this land and hold this labor, God will tell you as He has often told other races—"to move on."

The Creator never meant that this beautiful land should be forever kept as a great hunting-ground for the Indian to roam in savage bliss, but he intended that it should be used. The Indian, having for scores of generations failed to develop this land, God asked the Anglo-Saxon to take possession and dig out the treasures of wheat, corn, cotton, gold and silver, coal and iron, and the poor Indian was told "to move on."

The Negro in Africa sits listlessly in the sunshine of barbarous idleness while the same progressive, indomitable, persevering, white man is taking possession; the same edict has gone forth to the native African—he is being told "to move on."

The same God will tell the white man in America and in Africa, if he does not mete out absolute justice and absolute fairness to his weaker and less-advantaged brother, black or red or brown, if he cannot do justly and love mercy, just as he told the patricians of Rome, he will tell the white man "to move on."

Whatever question there may be about the white man's part in this situation, there is no doubt about ours. Don't let us delude ourselves but keep in mind the fact that the man who owns his home and cultivates his land and lives a decent, self-respecting, useful, and helpful life is no problem anywhere. We talk about the "color line," but you know and I know that the blackest Negro in Alabama or Mississippi or Africa or anywhere else who puts the same amount of skill and energy into his farming gets as large returns for his labor as the whitest Anglo-Saxon. The earth yields up her increase as willingly to the skill and persuasions of the black as of the white husbandman. Wind, wave, heat, stream, and electricity are absolutely blind forces and see no race distinction and draw no "color line." The world's market does not care and it asks no question about the shade of the hand that produces the commodity, but it does insist that it shall be up to the world's requirements.

I thank God for the excellent chance to work that my race had in this Southern country; the Negro in America has a real, good, healthy job, and I hope he may always keep it. I am not particular what he does or where he does it, so he is engaged in honest, useful work. Remember always that building a house is quite as important as building a poem; that the science of cooking is as useful to humanity as the science of music; that the thing most to be desired is a harmonious and helpful adaptation of all the arts and sciences to the glory of God and the good of humanity; that whether we labor with muscle or with brain, both need divine inspiration. Let us consecrate our brain and muscle to the highest and noblest service, to God, and humanity.

* * * * *

There is no reason why any Negro should become discouraged or morbid. We believe in God; His providence is mysterious and inscrutible; but his ways are just and righteous altogether. Suffering and disappointment have always found their place in divine economy. It took four hundred years of slavery in Egypt and a sifting process of forty years in the "Wilderness" to teach Israel to respect their race and to fit them for entrance into the "Promised Land." The black man has not as yet thoroughly learned to have the respect for his race that is so necessary to the making of a great people. I believe the woes that God has sent him are but the fiery furnace through which he is passing, that is separating the dross from the pure gold, and is welding the Negroes together as a great people for a great purpose.

There is every reason for optimism, hopefulness. The Negro never had more the respect and confidence of his neighbors, black and white, than he has to-day. Neither has he because of his real worth deserved that respect more than he does to-day. Could anybody, amid the inspiration of these grounds and buildings, be discouraged about the future of the Negro? The race problem in this country, I repeat, is simply a part of the problem of life. It is the adjustment of man's relation to his brother, and this adjustment began when Cain slew Abel. Race prejudice is as much a fact as the law of gravitation, and it is as foolish to ignore the operation of one as of the other. Mournful complaint and arrogant criticism are as useless as the crying of a baby against the fury of a great wind. The path of moral progress, remember, has never taken a straight line, but I believe that, unless democracy is a failure and Christianity a mockery, it is entirely feasible and practicable for the black and white races of America to develop side by side, in peace, in harmony, and in mutual helpfulness each toward the other; living together as "brothers in Christ without being brothers-in-law," each making its contributions to the wealth and culture of our beloved country.

* * * * *

I close with these lines, from an anonymous poet, on "The Water Lily":

"O star on the breast of the river,
O marvel of bloom and grace,
Did you fall straight down from heaven,
Out of the sweetest place?
You are white as the thought of the angel,
Your heart is steeped in the sun;
Did you grow in the golden city,
My pure and radiant one?

"Nay, nay, I fell not out of heaven;
None gave me my saintly white;
It slowly grew in the blackness,
Down in the dreary night,
From the ooze of the silent river
I won my glory and grace;
While souls fall not, O my poet,
They *rise* to the sweetest place."

THE TWO SEALS[43]

BY PROFESSOR GEORGE WILLIAM COOK

Secretary of Howard University

Mr. Toastmaster and Friends:

Let me first thank the Committee and you all for your generosity in tendering me this evidence of good wishes and good will. It is stated in your invitation, "In honor of George William Cook, Secretary of Howard University"—a double compliment, at once personal and official. Surely it is an honor to find so many men of varied occupations and duties turning aside to spend time and money to express appreciation of one's character. Dull indeed must the creature be who cannot find gratitude enough to return thanks; for grateful minds always return thanks. To be direct I deeply feel the personal and non-official side of the compliment you pay me, but will you pardon me, gentlemen, if I confess that to compliment me as Secretary of Howard University touches me in a tender and vulnerable spot. "I love old Howard," and always have been and am now anxious to be in the team to tug at the administrative phase of Howard's movements. Accept then, my sincere thanks.

Now let us then turn aside in sweet communion as brothers to talk about our alma mater. Let us trace her from foundation to present eminence; re-affirm our family pledges and form resolutions new. Howard men will spring up with both money and spirit, not far in the future, when the mother's cry in want will be met with a generous hand from her sons and daughters. A little more time for preparation and accumulation; then will be the time when endowment will precede request for preferment. When black philanthropists can turn desert spots into oases of learning and build halls of culture, then will Howard be reaping the reward in her own harvest and justify her being in the great family of Universities.

Though I wax warm in sentiment, I crave your indulgence but for a short while, for I pledge you my honor, and I say it seriously, that there is an affection underlying my words that makes Howard but second in love to my wife and child. She has been a gracious mother to me, supplying my necessities and defending me in my adversities, for which I have ever sought with might and main to return loyalty and service. When I am referred to as a Howard man, I have an uplift in the consciousness of relationship and fealty to an institution which to honor is but to be honored.

Visible manifestations of thought and idea have ever marked the purposes of man. Monuments and cities but express precurrent mental objects. God, in His message to Moses, directed that a tabernacle be built and that it should be the sign of his pleasure and approbation, a veritable indwelling of the spirit of God. Living thought can be said to have habitation. Greek and Roman art, Egyptian architecture, Catholic grandeur, or Quaker simplicity, all speak some great and noble soul-moving and world-moving power. Within the temple area was centered the devotion of the Jew, both political and religious. The Hebrew theocratic system of government made it so. St. Peter's at Rome, no more nor less than St. Paul's at London, speaks of God and the mission of His son. The Mosque of Omar, Saint Sophia at Constantinople, point that Allah is God and Mohammed is His Prophet; the Taj-Mahal is at once the emblem and creation of love; the Sistine Chapel teaches the glories and joys of maternity and God incarnate in man. The Pan-American Building at Washington, the Carnegie Peace Building at The Hague, teach unity of mankind, and but heighten the angelic chorus of "Peace and good will to men."

From yon Virginia hill, a galaxy of institutions may be discerned, bringing lessons to a listening world. As one may stand on Arlington's sacred heights, looking about him, he will find the indices in the graves and monuments there of sacrifice for a national union "indissoluble and forever"; and as his eyes sweep the horizon, scanning through mist and sunshine, the emblem and insignia of thought and policy will block the view. He will see the gold-tipped dome of the Library of Congress glinting in the light, and know its scintillations but herald the purpose to keep the light of learning and knowledge bright. Yon stately Capitol dome interrupts his line of vision but to remind him that it covers the chancel of legislation, and that representative government is a fixed and permanent fact. That single towering shaft on yon Potomac bed speaks of individual and unselfish devotion to a nation—Washingtonian patriotism, unique in history—and at the same time reflects the appreciation of a grateful and worshipful people. Hast thou seen it in its lonely grandeur on a moonlight night? It is well worth a trip across the ocean to read its message. Sweeping westward, the eye sees planted on a hill-top Georgetown College, the outward symbol of tenet and propaganda. Raising the visual angle and dropping back to the northwest, the white marble walls of the American University come to view, planted that Methodism with justification by faith might preach the Gospel for the redemption of man. Turning to the northeast, the great Catholic University presents itself as a repository and, at the same time, a vehicle of Catholic love of learning; and in juxtaposition towers high in alabastine whiteness the Spanish architecture of the Soldiers Home; though standing mute in immaculate marble, expressing to the defenders of a country an appreciation of their patriotism and sacrifice; the *ensemble* preaching to an active world. Then, the line of vision is obtruded upon by the stately main building of Howard University, of her structures the noblest. Observed from the high palisades or the low bed of the Potomac, that ever-present object of view from any point of the

District is veritably "a city on a hill that cannot be hid,"—symbolic and typical of her mission. And then the inquiry comes as to her significance. Why standeth thou there absorbing space?

Vying in sunshine and moonshine with the Capitol in conspicuous aspect, the two stand as twin sentinels on opposite ramparts of the Potomac Valley, overlooking in midnight vigil the slumbering city, each challenging the attention of the wayfarer. What art thou to justify thyself to man? What mission hast thou to excuse thy being? What road of profit? What principle of uplift hast thou to send forth? Thy halls resound to the murmur of what message from the Divine? What, we ask, is thy mission? The answer is echoed from the archives: "Consult her founders; learn of them if thou wouldst know." Therefore, friends, we turn to the records of Howard University and the declaration of her founders—her founders, men fresh from the fortunes of war, battle-scarred and blood-stained, desiring further to perpetuate the object of their militant victories by the forces of peace and brotherhood; men who failed to die at Gettysburg, Chancellorsville, and Lookout Mountain, and continued the fight on this hill; men who, not satisfied with loosening the shackles of bondage, turned their powers to driving darkness from human souls, though encased in ebony; men who wrought under God's hand, and dying dissatisfied that the full fruition of their labors were not yet come to pass, leaving to survivors and posterity an unmistaken task and warfare.

Howard has had two seals. The first reading "Equal rights and knowledge for all"; the second, "For God and the Republic"; the former breathing the spirit of the Civil War period and the Pauline doctrine declared before the Areopagus, announced in the preaching and work of Christ and emphasized by the Declaration of Independence; the latter pregnant with reverence, piety, and patriotism; the twain compassing man's duty higher than which human conception is lost. Privileged indeed is one to live under the ægis of such twin declarations. Fortunate indeed to have the authorization of official acts blessed by the benediction of such battle-cries.

The preamble to the charter explains comprehensively, though not in detail, the great purpose of Howard University:

"Section 1. That there be established, and is hereby established in the District of Columbia, a university for the education of youth in the liberal arts and sciences, under the name, seal, and title of Howard University," stated as simple and plain as the decalogue itself.

I glean from the Fourth Annual Report on Schools for Freedmen for July 1, 1867, by J. W. Alvord, then General Superintendent of Schools, Bureau for Refugees and Abandoned Lands, what I conceive to be the first catalogue of Howard University, and, if you will bear with me, I will read the entire catalogue.

"Howard University. A charter has been granted by Congress for the Howard University, which is to be open to all of both sexes without discrimination of color. This institution bids fair to do great good. Its beautiful site, so opportunely and wisely secured, is an earnest of success. Large and commodious buildings are soon to be erected thereon. The normal and preparatory departments of the university were opened on the first of May, under the instruction of Rev. E. F. Williams, an accomplished scholar and a thorough teacher. At the close of the month the school numbered thirty-one scholars; it has now increased to about sixty. Miss Lord, so long a popular teacher of this city, has been appointed assistant. The grade of this school is low for its name, but the students are making good advancement."

It may be thought by casual consideration, as was said by eminent men, that the name was the largest thing about it, but I prefer to disagree and to say that the purpose as set forth in the charter is the greatest thing about it. These are the words:

"We urge all friends of the freedmen to increasing confidence and to look forward with assured expectation to greater things than these. This people are to be prepared for what is being prepared for them. They are to become a 'people which in time past were not a people'; and there is increasing evidence that 'God hath made of one blood all the nations of men.' Equal endowments substantially, with equal culture, will produce that equality common to all mankind."

In them we get the quintescence, we get the crystallization, we get the high purpose, we get the spiritual foundation, of Howard University.

Conceived in prayer, born of the faith and convictions as embodied in its original seal which reads, "Equal rights and knowledge for all," an offspring of Plymouth Rock, Howard University is set before you—a cross between religious fervor and prophetic educational enthusiasm. She is, then, the essence filtrating from the declaration of Paul at Athens, that "of one blood hath God created all men to dwell upon earth."

For forty-five years, Howard has been living her life. She has been more or less doing her work as circumstances allowed and dictated, but now we ask of you "Watchman, what of the night?" How far has this work been progressing along the line of basal principles that we find embodied in all these authoritative extracts? Unfortunate I think it is that the discussions in the early meetings of the Board of Trustees were not preserved in stenographic report, for the time will come when the spiritual history of Howard University must be written as well as its material history, and then the historian will be at a loss to find the true afflatus that gave birth to our alma mater, unless we keep it in evidence.

The imagination has oft painted Howard University as a temple—a temple of knowledge,—a temple for the teaching of justice; a temple for the upbuild of mankind. Let us then hold its form to our imagination, pearly white as the palaces of the South, straight in its construction as rectitude, and let us present it to an admiring world, not only for æsthetic culture but ethical grandeur, religious progress, and political righteousness; and let us say to all, be he high or low, "who touches a stone in yon God-given edifice" is guilty of vandalism, is an iconoclast not at any time to be tolerated. He is tampering with the rights and privileges of a worthy people and deserves to have visited upon him the excoriation of a fiery indignation. Howard was created to meet the dire needs of a meritorious class, and insensible indeed must the man be who for sentimental or personal reasons or for profit, swerves one degree from the line of the highest form of education in administration or instruction. There should be launched upon him the anathema of an outraged people.

Sound the alarm that no man must hinder the true mission of Howard University. It were better for him that a millstone were hung about his neck and that he be cast into the deep. For him there is punishment even after death in the sure infamy that will attach to his name.

The old motto, "Equal rights and knowledge for all," is a necessary constituent of the Howard University life and purpose. There can be no Howard University without equal rights and highest culture for all, based upon merit and capacity. To be plain, we know of no Negro education. Political rights and civic privileges are accompaniments of citizenship and are therefore part of the warp and woof of Howard University's curricula; the salt and savor without which wherewith will it be salted? Mathematics has no color; ethics and philosophy are of no creed or class; culture was not fashioned for race monopoly; knowledge is in no plan or department an exclusive goal; justice is universal. Freedom in striving for the acquisition of God's bounty as revealed by nature is the birthright of all and an inalienable right of all. These are God-given privileges, and any contravention of them is born of evil and belongs to the evil powers.

Our privileges have imposed a trust and we are the trustees. Let no man deceive himself. Whatever the opportunity of approval now for betrayal of trust bequeathed to us, the time will come for the court of public opinion to find whom to blame and whom to thank. What the founders demanded for Howard, we must still demand. What William Clark and Martha Spaulding by their gifts meant, must still be meant by Howard's activities. Being justified in the past, it must be maintained in the future. Then to-night let us re-baptize in Howard spirit and issue the mandate of loyalty and endeavor.

* * * * *

Let no Howard man ever expatriate himself. Necessity driving him from Howard, let him consider himself domiciled elsewhere, but his scholastic citizenship intact in Howard.

We will sing the old song of Howard, though there be other songs greater. Yale, Cambridge, Oxford, and Leipsic may sing their songs, but, for me and my house, we will sing "Howard, I love old Howard."

Let us imitate the psalmist: "We will meditate also of all thy work, and talk of thy doings." We will exalt Howard and delight in her good work. Where she is weak we will endeavor to strengthen, and where she is strong we will direct to the uplift of the race. She may be lacking in equipment; that can be tolerated; but as to principle, she must not be weak at any point. From stem to stern she must carry the marks of her purpose, and at mast-head must float the pennant of her seals.

Neither time nor purpose can ever erase the fitness of "Equal rights and knowledge for all," "For God and the Republic,"—*the two seals.*

A SOLUTION OF THE RACE PROBLEM[44]

BY J. MILTON WALDRON, S. T. D.

J. MILTON WALDRON, D.D., *of Washington, D. C. Noted as having erected and operated the first Institutional Church among Negroes in America in Jacksonville, Florida, 1890-1907.*

That fearless, able, and broad-minded author of "The Negro and the Sunny South"—a book, by the way, every American citizen should read—Samuel Creed Cross, a white man of West Virginia, takes up an entire chapter in giving with the briefest comments even a partial list of the crimes committed by the whites of the South against the Negroes during the author's recent residence of six months in the section. Last year eighty or ninety colored persons, some of them women and children, were murdered, lynched, or burned for "the nameless crime," for murder or suspected murder, for barn-burning, for insulting white women and "talking back" to white men, for striking an impudent white lad, for stealing a white boy's lunch and for no crime at all—unless it be a crime for a black man to ask Southern men to accord him the rights guaranteed him by the Constitution.

Within the last twelve months Georgia disfranchised her colored citizens by a constitutional subterfuge and Florida attempted the same crime. And within the same period almost every white secular newspaper, and many of the religious journals, of the South contained in every issue of their publications abusive and malicious articles concerning the Negro in which they inflamed the whites against the brother in black and sought to justify the South in robbing him of his labor, his self-respect, his franchise, his liberty, and life itself. Many of the officials of Southern States, including numerous judges and not a few Christian ministers, helped or sanctioned these Negro-hating editors and reporters in their despicable onslaught upon the Negro, while tens of thousands of white business men of the South fattened upon Negro convict labor and the proceeds of the "order system."

Not satisfied with the wrongs and outrages she has heaped upon the colored people in her own borders the South is industriously preaching her wicked doctrine of Negro inferiority, Negro suppression, and Negro oppression everywhere in the North, East, and West. And yet, in the face of this terrible record of crime against the liberty, manhood, and political rights and the life of the colored man which is being rewritten in the South every day, there are those in high places who have the temerity to tell us that "The Southern people are the Negro's best friends," and that the Negro problem is a Southern problem and the South should be allowed to solve it in her own way without any interference on the part of the North.

The North and the South together stole the black man from his home in Africa and enslaved him in this land, and this whole nation has reaped the benefits of his two hundred and fifty years of unrequited toil, and this whole nation must see to it that the black man is fully emancipated, enfranchised, thoroughly educated in heart, head, and hand, and permitted to exercise his rights as a citizen and earn, wherever and however he can, an honest and sufficient living for himself, his wife, and children—this the South cannot do alone and unaided.

Nearly three millions of the ten million Negroes in this country live north of Mason and Dixon's line, and thousands of others are coming North and going West every month; over four hundred thousand of the three millions mentioned above live in Washington, Baltimore, Philadelphia, New York, St. Louis, and Chicago; if the Negro problem was ever a Southern problem, the colored brother has taken it with him into the North and the West and made it a national problem.

The life, liberty, and happiness of the black man and of the white man of this country are so wrapped up together that it is impossible to oppress the one without eventually oppressing the other. The white man of the South was cursed by slavery as much almost as the black man whom he robbed of life, liberty, and virtue. In many parts of the South to-day the masses of poor white men are no better off in any sphere of life than the colored people, with the single exception that their faces are white. The rights and liberties of the common people of this entire country have grown less secure, and their ballots have steadily diminished in power, while the colored man has been robbed of his franchise by the South. The trusts and the favored classes of this country have seen the rights of millions of loyal black citizens taken from them by the South in open violation of the Federal Constitution, and that with the indirect approval of the highest courts of the land. And these trusts and interests have come to feel that constitutions and laws are not binding upon them, and that the common people—white and black—have no rights which they are bound to respect. The South alone cannot right these gigantic wrongs nor restore to the white people (not to mention the Negroes) within her own borders the liberties and privileges guaranteed them by the Constitution of the United States.

In discussing the South's attitude towards the colored man we seek only to hold up to scorn and contempt the spirit which pervades the majority of the people who live in that section; and we desire to condemn only the men of the South who hate their fellow men; we wish to bear testimony now and here to the truth that there is an undercurrent in the South which is making for righteousness, and that there are a few noble and heroic souls in every Southern State who believe that the Negro ought to be treated as a man and be given all the rights and privileges accorded any other man. This righteous spirit must, however, be encouraged and strengthened, and the number of noble and fair-minded men and women in the South must be greatly augmented, or the battle for human liberty and the manhood and political rights of both races in that section will never be won.

We beg to say that all the enemies of human rights in general, and of the rights of black men in particular, are not in the South; the wrongs complained of by the Negro in that section are, for the most part, the same as those bewailed by him in the North, with this difference: the Northern Negro's right to protest against the wrongs heaped upon him is less restricted, and, his means of protection and defense are more numerous in the North than in the South. Already in at least one State north of Mason and Dixon's line Herculean efforts are being put forth to disfranchise the colored man by constitutional enactment; the discrimination against a man on account of his color, and the lynching of Negroes and the burning of their houses by infuriated mobs of white men, are not unheard of things in the North and West. Most of the labor-unions of these sections are still closed to the brother in black, and most white working-men in the Northern and Western States are determined that the Negro shall not earn a living in any respectable calling if they can prevent it. Many of the newspapers North and West (and a few right here in New York City) often use their columns to misrepresent and slander the colored man, and it was only last week when one of the highest courts in the Empire State rendered a decision in which it justified discrimination against a man on the grounds of his color and his condition of servitude. Verily, the Negro problem is not a Southern, but a national problem!

* * * * *

Many solutions for the Negro problem have been proposed, but to our mind there is one and only one practical and effective answer to the question. In the first place we claim that the early friends of the Negro grasped the true solution, which is that his needs and possibilities are the same as those of the other members of the human family; that he must be educated not only for industrial efficiency and for private gain, but to share in the duties and responsibilities of a free democracy; that he must have equality of rights, for his own sake, for the sake of the human race, and for the perpetuity of free institutions. America will not have learned the full lesson of her system of human slavery until she realizes that a rigid caste system is inimical to the progress of the human race and to the perpetuity of democratic government.

In the second place, the Negro must make common cause with the working class which to-day is organizing and struggling for better social and economic conditions. The old slave oligarchy maintained its ascendency largely by fixing a gulf between the Negro slave and the white free laborer, and the jealousies and animosities of the slave period have survived to keep apart the Negro and the laboring white man. Powerful influences are at work even to-day to impress upon the Negro the fact that he must look to the business men of the South alone for protection and recognition of his rights, while at the same time these very same influences inflame the laboring white man against the black man with fears of social equality and race fusion. The Negro, being a laborer, must see that the cause of labor is his cause, that his elevation can be largely achieved by having the sympathy, support, and co-operation of that growing organization of working men the world over which is working out the larger problems of human freedom and economic opportunity.

In the third place, wherever in this country the Negro has the franchise, and where by complying with requirements he can regain it, let him exercise it faithfully and constantly, but let him do so as an independent and not as a partisan, for his political salvation in the future depends upon his voting for men and measures, rather than with any particular party.

For two hundred and fifty years the black man of America toiled in the South without pay and without thanks; he cleared her forests, tunneled her mountains, bridged her streams, built her cottages and palaces, enriched her fields with his sweat and blood, nursed her children, protected her women and guarded her homes from the midnight marauder, the devouring flames, and approaching disease and death. The colored American willingly and gladly enlisted and fought in every war waged by this country, from the first conflict with the Indians to the last battle in Cuba and the Philippines; when enfranchised he voted the rebellious States back into the Union, and from that day until this he has, as a race, never used his ballot, unless corrupted or intimidated by white men, to the detriment of any part of America. When in power in the South, though for the most part ignorant and just out of slavery and surrounded by vindictive ex-slave owners and mercenary, corrupted and corrupting "carpet baggers," he did what his former masters had failed for centuries to do—he established the free school system, erected asylums for the insane and indigent poor, purged the statute-books of disgraceful marriage laws and oppressive and inhuman labor regulations, revised and improved the penal code, and by many other worthy acts proved that the heart of the race was, and is, in the right place, and that whenever the American Negro has been trusted, he has proven himself trustworthy and manly. And when the colored man is educated, and is treated with fairness and justice, and is accorded the rights and privileges which are the birthright of every American citizen, he will show himself a man among men, and the race problem will vanish as the mist before the rising sun.

THE SOCIAL BEARINGS OF THE FIFTH COMMANDMENT

BY JAMES FRANCIS GREGORY, B. D.

Vice Principal Manual Training and Industrial School, Bordentown, New Jersey

"Honor thy father and thy mother that thy days may be long in the land which the Lord thy God giveth thee."

While obedience to parents is the primary significance of this command, its widening scope is seen in the comprehensive authority of the father of the old Hebrew family. He was the ruler and the protector of the family, and as human society enlarged and much of the original authority of the parent passed from him, the child was prepared to give honor to such authority and wisdom as he had recognized in the father. Thus generically the command may cover the wide range suggested by the Westminster Assembly: "The Fifth Commandment requireth the preserving the honor and performing the duties belonging to every one in their several places and relations as superiors, inferiors or equals." And this honor idea in the home not only spreads out, but it climbs, and we may say that as the Hebrew family contained the beginning of government, all other authorities of this world wind up and out of the home, ascending in spiral form until the little coil of the domestic circle eventuates.

* * * * *

Last summer, while seated in a crowded train, my attention was attracted by a little family group. The heat-worn mother held a baby in one arm, and the other hand was steadying a toddling boy. She had repeatedly reproved her half-grown daughter and finally spoke sharply to her, when the child suddenly lifted the heavy umbrella in her hand and struck her mother!

These are the facts that impressed me: the unmasked powerlessness of the mother, the cool unconcern of the father, but above all the apathetic indifference of the passengers.

The modern family is without discipline, all of the elements in the home having a tendency to wander from the hearth center. There is the father whose absence, because of occupational absorption, is lengthened by many extraneous interests. The mother, too, is receding from the home center in her misguided enthusiasm for so-called equality in business, professional, and political life. And the children? As one sad-faced mother said to me the other day, "They get out of the home so early!"

* * * * *

All the reverence for parents in the world's history, is hallowed by the lofty example of Jesus in his dutiful subjection to his earthly parents, and in the marvelous solicitude of his dying words, "Son, behold thy mother!"

* * * * *

A great light is thrown on this economic relation of the commandment by the attitude of the Centurion pleading with the Master for his servant's life. Here was an employer whose stretched-out arm of authority could be transformed into a gesture of appeal, for his servant lying sick at home. Indeed only as the spirit of this commandment makes itself felt in our business life will the clenched hands of capital and labor relax from the hilts of their dripping blades and grasp each other with the warm pressure of brotherly sympathy.

* * * * *

Then there are the mutual relations between the young and the aged. Oh, for a return in our youth to that ancient bowing deference to old age a beautiful instance of which Cicero preserves for us. Into the crowded amphitheatre at Athens, with the multitudes' expectant hush, there staggered an aged man, who made his tottering progress, beneath tier after tier of indifferent or averted faces, looking in vain for a place, until finally he came in front of the section occupied by the Lacaedemonians, who rose as one man and offered him a seat!

* * * * *

Then there are the superiors and inferiors in wisdom. As we look back through the mists of years to our student years, there stand out sharply distinguished the kindly figures of our intellectual fathers. I recall at this moment that man of infinite reserve behind the desk at Yale, whose eye could flash with authority and yet kindle with concern at the sight of the necessity of one of his boys—in Browning's thought, "As sheathes a film the mother eagle's eye when her bruised eaglet breathes!"

* * * * *

I need scarcely suggest the obvious pertinence of this command to the relations of the pastor and his congregation. We cling very jealously to the term, "Father," as it has been applied to the men of God in the history of the Church. The picture is beautiful of the Roman Catholic priest, conscious of the reluctance of her neighbors to bear to the poor widow the evil news of the sudden death of her only son, walking quietly up the gravel path, and covering with his healthy hands the two withered ones as he met her at the doorway, answering her searching inquiry, "Father?" with an unmistakable inflection of the words, "My child!" That also of the American Protestant

Episcopal bishop, leaving his little birthday gathering already interrupted for three successive years, and foregoing a breath of country air, after weary months of toil in the hot city, to comfort a simple family hovering piteously about a little white casket:—these are attitudes far more impressive than the ceremonious exercise of their loftiest ecclesiastical functions.

* * * * *

Many lines of evidence from the side of reason converge on the Biblical teaching that civil government is a divine institution. Perhaps one of the most striking features of our later American growth is the colossal selfishness of our people. The habit of freedom from restraint is fast hardening into a lawlessness of character.

* * * * *

Listen to some of the palliating expressions with which our legal atmosphere is permeated: "indiscreet and untactful," "the unwritten law," "swift justice," "murder a fine art," and remember that these are the terms that play around that triangle of corrupt judge, dallying lawyer, and bribed and illiterate jury—all conspiring to "shove by justice" with technicalities. And what are those sinister figures, flitting and stalking through the land—the law-maker with his spoils, the rioter with his rock, the anarchist with his bomb, the assassin thrusting out his black hand, the lyncher with his battering ram, his rope and his rifle; these are some of the outside lawless who conspire with the inside lawless to make a scarecrow of American law, making it the perch and not the terror of the birds of prey. And who knows how soon all of these lawless ones may stand up together and, with a monarch's voice cry, Havoc in the confines of this Republic!

* * * * *

But we must be conscious of our Heavenly Father behind the earthly type. This unmistakably is the significance of the Biblical words: "To obey your parents in the Lord"; "To be obedient unto your masters as unto Christ"; "To fear God in honoring the face of the old man"; "To be subject unto rulers as the ministers of God." And this leads us to the great levelling truth, that we are all equally accountable to our Heavenly Father, that we are nations and individuals, in the high thought of Lincoln, "Under God."

* * * * *

This command carries with it the promise of a reward restated by Paul, "Honor thy father and thy mother that it may be well with thee and that thou mayest live long on the earth." In fact this is the logic of life. This retributive justice is bound up in the laws of nature. Plants that array themselves against these laws wither and die. And higher up in the animal kingdom, Kipling's verse tells us that this inexorable sequence prevails:

"And these are the laws of the Jungle,
And many and mighty are they;
But the head and the hoof of the law is,
And the haunch and the hump is—obey."

And it is true that obedience in a human being conduces to a long and prosperous life. The beautiful truth is gradually emerging in science and theology that religion is healthful. As one of my discerning fathers was often wont to say, "The whole Bible is a text-book of Advanced Biology, telling men how they may gain the fuller life."

* * * * *

Here and there the obedient die early, you say.—Yes; and this fact sounds the deeper spiritual import of this promise, for they, sooner than we, enter upon that eternal life, and pass over into that greener Canaan, to that inheritance incorruptible and undefiled.

Standing one afternoon in the Gallery of the Louvre in Paris, a vision of the perfect adjustment of our seemingly conflicting relations to Cæsar and to God shone forth to me, in the divine gesture of the Master in Da Vinci's wonderful painting of the Last Supper, where the hand turned downward lays hold of the things of earth, and the hand turned upward grips the things which are eternal, both of which obligations are glorified in those later words of the Saviour spoken out of the agony of the Cross: "Son, behold thy mother! Father, into thy hands I commend my spirit."

LIFE'S MORN[45]

By William C. Jason, D. D.

Principal State College for Colored Students, Dover, Delaware

"Nature," says one, "is like a woman; in the morning she is fresh from her bath, at noon she has on her working-dress, and at night she wears her jewels."

Nature is most charming in the morning. The following extract from "A Picture of Dawn" is a tribute Edward Everett pays to the morning.

"As we proceeded, the timid approach of the twilight became more perceptible; the intense blue of the sky began to soften; the smaller stars, like little children, went first to rest; the sister beams of the Pleiades soon melted together; but the bright constellations of the west and north remained unchanged. Steadily the wondrous transfiguration went on. Hands of angels, hidden from mortal eyes, shifted the scenery of the heavens; the glories of the night dissolved into the glories of the dawn. The blue sky now turned more softly gray; the great watch-stars shut up their holy eyes; the east began to kindle. Faint streaks of purple soon blushed along the sky; the whole celestial concave was filled with the inflowing tides of the morning light which came pouring down from above in one great ocean of radiance; till at length, as we reached the Blue Hills, a flash of purple fire blazed out from above the horizon, and turned the dewy teardrops of flower and leaf into rubies and diamonds. In a few seconds, the everlasting gates of the morning were thrown wide open, and the lord of day, arrayed in glories too severe for the gaze of man, began his state."

Nothing but the morning itself is more beautiful than this sublime description.

The best of the day is the morning. The brain is clearer, the nerves more steady, the physical powers at their best before the sun reaches its zenith. Weariness waits for noon, and the wise man chooses the morning as the period for his most exacting toil.

Of all the year, the spring-time is the fairest. Nature wakes from the restful sleep of winter. Grasses grow, flowers bloom, trees put forth their leaves, birds build their nests, and he who hopes for harvest lays the foundations of his future gain. The whole year is lost to him who sleeps or idles away the seed-time. Late planting will grow, perhaps, if excessive heat does not kill the seed or wither the shoot; but before it comes to fruitage the frosts of autumn will blight it, flower and stem and root. Man cannot alter God's plan. There is a time to sow and a time to reap.

Life has its seasons also—its spring-time, its winter; morning, noon, and night. The Scriptures enjoin us to work while it is called day; for the night cometh when no man can work. In the parable the rich man who went on a journey appointed each servant a task. To each of us is entrusted some treasure; each is commanded to work. To labor is man's appointed lot. This is his supreme mission in the world. He cannot avoid it. Even the servant who sought to evade his responsibility went and *digged* in the earth.

Resisting the forces which tend to destroy life; surmounting the obstacles to substantial success; breaking down barriers, commercial, civil, social, political, and becoming a factor in the best life of his community—the peer of any in mental and moral qualities, a representative and an advocate of the principles of justice and equality—this is the work of a man.

Such efforts do not tax the muscles only. They call forth the energies of the entire being. Foresight, calculation, enterprise, courage, self-control; fertility in resources; the ability to recognize and embrace an opportunity, are all required. The inspiration must come from above. All the powers of mind and body must be enlisted. Flagging energies, lashed by an indomitable will, must persevere.

"Life is real and life is earnest" wrote the poet. He who does not take life seriously has woefully failed to comprehend its significance. Toil, service, sacrifice—these are the words which tell the true story of a life. Willingly, it should be, but if not so, then reluctantly man must toil, serve, sacrifice. For noble ends, it should be, but if not so, then for base ends, he must toil, serve, sacrifice. With buoyant, hopeful spirit, or with cheerless, heavy heart; toil, service, sacrifice is the Divine decree, irrevocable, eternal.

* * * * *

It is my privilege to address the members of the Epworth League but my thought embraces young people everywhere, especially those of my own race.

You live. A definite responsibility is thereby placed upon you. Not as a burden to be borne with sadness, but rather as an act of beneficence has the Creator called you into being and sent you forth upon your mission in the world. He sends you to a world full of beauty. Sunshine, fragrance, and melody are about you. Yet you may not be conscious of it. Blindness or perverted vision may cloud the sky and fill the earth with shadows. The clamors of selfish interest or lawless passion may change the harmony into perpetual discord and din. Evil associations, impure thoughts, and unholy practises create false ideas of life.

"Faults in the life breed errors in the brain,

And these reciprocally those again;
The mind and conduct mutually imprint,
And stamp their image in each other's mint."

Yet for him who hath eyes to see, the world is full of beauty. Nor beauty only; but design is everywhere manifested, revealing the presence of a supreme Intelligence and immeasurable love in fitting out for man a perfect habitation. Whatever of wretchedness the world holds is man-made. It is proof positive of a purpose to make man happy that so many instruments of pleasure are placed at his hand. Each sense and organ has its objects of exercise and enjoyment. Every natural instinct, desire, and appetite is recognized, and its proper, legitimate indulgence provided for. Blessed are they who find life joyous and who choose it, not from a fear of death, but for what there is in life—who can say: "I find death perfectly desirable, but I find life perfectly beautiful."

You have life and you have youth. You live in life's morn; the spring-time of your existence is upon you. Quick perceptions, swift and keen intelligence, strong limbs, rich, pure blood, and a hope that "springs eternal," are a portion of the heritage of youth. With faculties unimpaired by age or excesses, you awake to an existence which shall never end, and begin a destiny which shall be whatever you, by the use or abuse of those faculties, shall determine.

Hereditary influences count for something. Environment has much to do with the shaping of a life. Yet a responsibility without evasion rests upon each individual soul. Not one is saved or lost without his own voluntary contribution toward that end. It is an awful responsibility, commensurate with the rewards offered to integrity and fidelity. The thought that you must stand at the judgment-seat and answer for this life should impress the most thoughtless with the importance of seed-time.

Young people are the life-blood of the nation, the pillars of the state. The future of the world is wrapped up in the lives of its youth. As these unfold, the pages of history will tell the story of deeds noble and base. Characters resplendent with jewels and ornaments of virtue will be held up for the admiration of the world and the emulation of generations not yet born. Others, thoughtlessly or wilfully ignoring the plain path of duty, dwarfed, blighted, rejected of God and man, will be sign-posts marking the road to ruin.

Think not that moderation will escape notice; you cannot slip by with the crowd. Exceptional instances of vice or virtue attract more temporary notice; but the thought, tone, and general sentiment of a community give the inspiration and the impulse to those who outstrip the masses in the race for the goal of honor or of shame. None so humble but he has his share in moulding the destiny of the race. At the last, a just balance will determine your share of praise or blame.

Young people should recognize their own worth and resolve to act a noble part. "Let no man despise thy youth," says the Word. Despise not thou thy youth. Fully appreciating your high privilege and your rich estate, go forth into the world's broad field of battle, determined to make no misuse of your day of opportunity. Be bold, vigilant, and strong. Be true to the noblest instincts of your nature and have strong faith in God.

"Call up thy noble spirit;
Rouse all the generous energies of virtue,
And, with the strength of Heaven-endued man,
Repel the hideous foe."

"Manhood, like gold, is tested in the furnace:
A fire that purifies is fierce and strong;
Rare statues gain art's ideal of perfection,
By skilful strokes of chisel, wielded long."

AN ADDRESS DELIVERED BEFORE THE HOUSE OF REPRESENTATIVES OF MASSACHUSETTS[46]

BY WILLIAM H. LEWIS

Assistant Attorney-General of the United States

Mr. Speaker and Members of the House of Representatives:

The power of the House to summons forthwith any citizen of the Commonwealth has never been resisted; and so by designation of the Honorable Speaker, in accordance with the order of the House, I am here in answer to your summons. You have invited me, as a member of the liberated race, to address you upon this Lincoln's Birthday in commemoration of the 50th Anniversary of the Emancipation Proclamation. Words would be futile to express my deep appreciation of this high honor, however unworthily bestowed. Twice before have I met this honorable House. I came first as an humble petitioner seeking redress against discrimination on account of color. You then granted my prayer. Some years later, I came as a member of this House, the last representative of my race to sit in this body. You treated me then as a man and an equal. And now the honors of an invited guest I shall cherish as long as memory lasts.

To-day is the anniversary of the birth of Abraham Lincoln, the preserver of the Union, the liberator of a race. "The mystic chords of memory," stretching from heart to heart of millions of Americans at this hour, "swell the chorus of thanksgiving" to the Almighty for the life, character, and service of the great President.

Four brief, crucial years he represented the soul of the Union struggling for immortality—for perpetuity; in him was the spirit of liberty struggling for a new birth among the children of men.

"Slavery must die," he said, "that the Union may live."

We have a Union to-day because we have Emancipation; we have Emancipation because we have a united country. Though nearly fifty years have elapsed since his martyr death and we see his images everywhere, yet Lincoln is no mere legendary figure of an heroic age done in colors, cast in bronze, or sculptured in marble; he is a living, vital force in American politics and statecraft. The people repeat his wise sayings; politicians invoke his principles; men of many political stripes profess to be following in his footsteps. We of this generation can almost see him in the flesh and blood and hear falling from his lips the sublime words of Gettysburg, the divine music of the second inaugural and the immortal Proclamation of Emancipation. We see this man of mighty thews and sinews, his feet firmly planted in mother earth, his head towering in the heavens. He lived among men but he walked with God. He was himself intensely human, but his sense of right, of justice, seemed to surpass the wisdom of men. A true child of nature, he beheld the races of men in the raw without the artificial trappings of civilization and the adventitious circumstances of birth or wealth or place, and could see no difference in their natural rights.

"The Negro is a man," said he, "my ancient faith tells me that all men are created equal."

As a man he was brave yet gentle, strong yet tender and sympathetic, with the intellect of a philosopher, yet with the heart of a little child. As a statesman he was prudent, wise, sagacious, far-seeing and true. As President he was firm, magnanimous, merciful, and just. As a liberator and benefactor of mankind, he has no peer in all human history.

As Lowell said in his famous commemoration ode, it still must be said:

"Great captains, with their guns and drums,
Disturb our judgment for the hour,
But at last silence comes;
These are all gone, and, standing like a tower,
Our children shall behold his fame,
The kindly-earnest, brave, foreseeing man,
Sagacious, patient, dreading praise, not blame,
New birth of our new soil, the first American."

There are only three great charters of freedom among Anglo-Saxon peoples: the Magna Charta, which the barons wrung from King John at Runnymede; the Declaration of Independence, which a few colonials threw at the head of an obstinate king; the Emancipation Proclamation, which Lincoln cast into the balance for the Union. The Magna Charta gave freedom to the nobility; the Declaration of Independence brought freedom down to the plain people; the Proclamation of Abraham Lincoln set free the under-man, and proclaimed liberty to the slave and the serf throughout the world.

Massachusetts had no small part in the second great charter of liberty. This is attested not only by the signatures of Hancock, the Adams's, Paine, and Gerry to that great document, but here are Boston, Concord, Lexington, and Bunker Hill, and a thousand memorials of the Revolution besides. Great indeed as was the part that Massachusetts played in achieving independence, greater still was her share in the Emancipation of the slave. Lincoln himself said that Boston had done more to bring on the war than any other city; and when Emancipation had been achieved he generously credited the result "to the logic and moral power of Garrison and the anti-slavery people."

This day, therefore, belongs to Massachusetts. It is a part of her glorious history. Emancipation was but the triumph of Puritan principle—the right of each individual to eat his bread out of the sweat of his own brow or not at all. The history of the abolition of slavery in America could not be written with Massachusetts left out; the history of Massachusetts herself, since the Revolution, would be but a dreary, barren waste without the chapter of her part in the Emancipation.

The House does well to pause in its deliberations to commemorate this anniversary. In 1837 your predecessors threw open the old Hall of Representatives to the first meeting of the New England Anti-Slavery Society. A year later, the legislature adopted resolutions against the slave-trade, for the abolition of slavery in the District of Columbia, and the prohibition of slavery in the territories.

The fathers early enacted that there should be neither bond slaves nor villeinage amongst us except captives taken in just wars and those condemned judicially to serve. When it was attempted to land the first cargo of slaves upon her soil, the people seized them and sent them back to their own country and clime. In spite of the prayers and resolutions and acts of the early fathers, a form of slavery grew up here, but it was milder than the English villeinage: it resembled apprenticeship except in the duration. The slave had many of the rights of free men; the right to marry and the right to testify in court. Either with the decision of Somerset's case in England or the adoption of the first Constitution of the Commonwealth, during the Revolution, that institution passed away forever. The voices of freedom were first raised here. Whittier, Lowell, and Longfellow sang the songs of Emancipation. Garrison, Phillips, and Parker were the prophets and disciples of Lincoln. In the darkest days of slavery, John Quincy Adams held aloft the torch of liberty and fed its flame with his own intrepid spirit. Sumner was the scourge of God, the conscience of the state incarnate.

The people of Massachusetts were not only idealists, dreamers, and molders of public opinion, but when thirty years of agitation had reached its culmination in the Civil War, Massachusetts sent 150,000 of her sons to sustain upon the battle-fields of the Republic the ideals which she had advocated in the Halls of Congress, in the forum and the market-place. The people of Massachusetts, true to their history and traditions, have abolished here, so far as laws can do so, every discrimination between race and color, and every inequality between man and man.

I have recalled these things for no vainglorious purpose. We should remind ourselves constantly that we have a history behind us, that we have a character to sustain. Are we of this generation worthy descendants of tea spillers and abolitionists? Are we living up to the traditions of the Commonwealth, to the principles of the fathers in relation to the treatment of citizens of color? I have observed with aching heart and agonizing spirit during the last twenty years not only the growing coldness and indifference on the part of our people to the fate of the Negro elsewhere; but here in our own city the breaking up of the old ties of friendship that once existed between people of color and all classes of citizens, just after Emancipation; the gradual falling away of that sympathy and support upon which we could always confidently rely in every crisis. I have watched the spirit of race prejudice raise its sinister shape in the labor market, in the business house, the real-estate exchange, in public places, and even in our schools, colleges, and churches.

I say all this with pain and sorrow. I would be the last to "soil my own nest" or to utter one word that would reflect in the slightest degree upon Massachusetts or her people. I love inexpressibly every foot of Massachusetts soil, from the Berkshires to Essex, from the Capes to the islands off our southern coast. I have studied her history; I know her people, and when I have played out the little game with destiny, I want to rest upon some Massachusetts hillside.

I can never forget the emotions that filled my breast when first I set foot in Boston just a quarter of a century ago, a Negro lad in search of education, freedom, and opportunity. As I walked these sacred streets I lived over the Revolution, I saw them peopled with the mighty men of the past. I hastened to make my obeisance first to the spot where Attucks fell, the first martyr of the Revolution. I next looked out upon Bunker Hill where Peter Salem stood guard over the fallen Warren. I said to myself "here at last no black man need be ashamed of his race, here he has made history." And then to scenes of still another period I turned my gaze. I looked upon the narrow streets where Garrison was mobbed for my sake. I viewed the place where a few brave men gave Shadrach to freedom and to fame. The pictured walls of the old "cradle of liberty" seemed still to echo to the silvery tones of Phillips. The molded face of Governor Andrew spoke a benediction: "I know not what record of sins awaits me in that other life, but this I do know, I never despised any man because he was ignorant, because he was poor or because he was black."

I felt that here at last was liberty, and here I would make my home.

You say to me, "certainly you can find no fault." I gratefully acknowledge the debt which I owe the people of Massachusetts, but I cannot forget my brethren here. I cannot forget my children too, who were born here and by the blessings of God and your help I will leave to them and their children a freer and better Massachusetts even than I have found her.

"Eternal vigilance is the price of liberty."

I want upon this day to remind Massachusetts of her old ideals of liberty, justice, equality for all beneath her pure white flag. Laws, customs, institutions are nothing unless behind them stands a vital, living, throbbing public sentiment in favor of their enforcement in the spirit as well as in the letter. My friends, unless we can stay the rising tide of prejudice; unless we can hark back to our old ideals and old faiths, our very statues and memorials will some day mock us and cry shame upon us.

National Emancipation was the culmination of a moral revolution, such as the world has never seen. It was not as Garrison intended, a peaceful revolution, the unanimous verdict of an awakened national conscience. Thirty years of fierce agitation and fiercer politics made an appeal to arms absolutely certain. A conflict of arms brought on by a conflict of opinion was bound to be followed by a conflict of opinion, whichever side won. So for fifty years since Emancipation, there has been more or less conflict over the Negro and his place in the Republic. The results of that conflict have in many instances been oppressive and even disastrous to his freedom. Many things incidental to Emancipation and vital to complete freedom are unfortunately still in the controversial stages. The right of the Negro to cast a ballot on the same qualifications as his other fellow citizens is not yet conceded everywhere. Public sentiment has not yet caught up with the Constitution, nor is it in accord with the principles of true democracy. The right of the Negro to free access to all public places and to exact similar treatment therein is not universal in this country. He is segregated by law in some sections; he is segregated by custom in others. He is subjected to many petty annoyances and injustices and ofttimes deep humiliation solely on account of his color.

The explanation of this reactionary tendency sometimes given is that the Negro is only a generation from slavery. It should not be forgotten that individuals of every other race in history have at some time been held slaves. The bondage of Israel is to-day only an epic poem. The Greek Slave adorns simply a niche in some palace of art. The Servii of Rome instructed the masters of the world. The Anglo-Saxon has not only worn the Roman and Norman collars, but individuals of that race were sold as slaves in the West Indies as late as the seventeenth century. White men have enslaved white men, black men have enslaved black men. The place of human slavery in the divine economy I do not understand, nor do I defend it; I am glad that the human race has long since passed that stage in its development. No race has a right to lord it over another or seek to degrade it because of a history of servitude; all have passed through this cruel experience; the history of the black race is a little more recent, that is all. The fact of slavery, therefore, should not impose the slightest limitation upon the liberty of the Negro or restriction upon his rights as a man and citizen.

The one great phase of the race question agitating the country to-day is that of intermarriage and miscegenation. It is a serious question; it is a vital question. No one will deny the right of any man to protect his family stock, or the right of a group to preserve its racial integrity. The facts show, however, that laws, however stringent, will not accomplish it. I submit for the serious consideration of the American people that the only danger of infusion from the Negro side is simply one thing, and that is summed up in one word "injustice." Why is it that thousands of colored men and women go over to the other side, "pass" as we say? It is for no other purpose than to escape the social ostracism and civic disabilities of the Negro. Why is it that we see so many pathetic attempts to be white? It is simply to escape injustice. In a country where every opportunity is open to the white, in business, in society, in government, and the door shut against or reluctantly opened to the black, the natural unconscious effort of the black is to get white. Where black is a badge of an inferior caste position in society, the natural effort of the black is to find some method of escape. I do not advocate intermarriage; I do not defend miscegenation. The same thing is true to-day as it was true in the time of Lincoln. In his debates with Douglass in 1858, he noted "that among the free States, those which make the colored man the nearest equal to the white have proportionally the fewest mulattoes, the least amalgamation."

I submit therefore, that the only sure way to put an end to this tendency or desire, so far as the Negro is concerned, is to accord him all his public and political rights and to treat each individual upon his merits as a man and citizen, according to him such recognition as his talents, his genius, his services to the community or the state entitles him. Make black, brown, yellow, the "open sesame" to the same privileges and the same opportunities as the white, and no one will care to become white.

Upon this day which commemorates the emancipation of the black and the larger freedom of the white race, the redemption of the state and the birth of a new nation, I would bring to you a message not of blackness and despair but of hope—hope triumphant, hope, that Watts has pictured as blind with one string to her lyre, that sees not the star just ahead, but sits supreme at the top of the world.

Emancipation redeemed the precious promises of the Declaration of Independence. It rid the Republic of its one great inconsistency, a government of the people resting upon despotism; it rescued the ship of state from the rocks of slavery and sectionalism, and set her with sails full and chart and compass true once more upon the broad ocean of humanity to lead the world to the haven of true human brotherhood. We have encountered storms and tempests at times; the waves of race antipathy have run high, and the political exigencies of the hour seem to overcast the heavens with clouds of darkness and despair, yet I have never lost faith, because the fathers set her course, and God, the Master Mariner, has ever been at the helm. "In giving freedom to the slave we insured freedom to the free." In a country where all men were free none could be slaves. Emancipation raised labor to its true dignity and gave a new impetus to industry, commerce, and civilization. Under free labor men of many climes have come here to help develop the natural resources of the country, and the nation has entered upon a period of progress such as the world has never before witnessed in any time or place.

What of the Negro himself? Has he justified Emancipation? The statistics of his physical, intellectual, and material progress are known to all. He has increased his numbers nearly threefold. The Negro population is to-day nearly three times that of the whole country at the time of the adoption of the Constitution. It is nearly three times that of New England in 1860. He has reduced his illiteracy to thirty per cent. He owns nearly $700,000,000 worth of property including nearly one million homes. He has shown that his tutelage in American civilization has not been vain; that he could live under the most trying and oppressive conditions.

Three milestones in his progress have been reached and passed:

First: The North and South agree that the abolition of slavery was right and just.

Second: The people of the North and South agree that every industrial opportunity shall be given to the Negro.

Third: The right of the Negro to be educated and the duty of the state to see to it that he has every opportunity for education are established. Public opinion has settled forever the right of the Negro to be free to labor and to educate. These three things constitute no slight advance; they are the fundamental rights of civilization.

The prophecy of Lincoln has been fulfilled, that Emancipation would be "An Act, which the world will forever applaud and God must forever bless." Moreover it should not be forgotten, as Bancroft the historian has said, that "it is in part to the aid of the Negro in freedom that the country owes its success, in its movement of regeneration—that the world of mankind owes the continuance of the United States as an example of a Republic." The American Negro in freedom has brought new prestige and glory to his country in many ways. Tanner, a Georgia boy, is no longer a Negro artist, but an American artist whose works adorn the galleries of the world. Paul Laurence Dunbar, an American poet, who singing songs of his race, voicing its sorrows and griefs with unrivalled lyric sweetness and purity, has caught the ear of the world. The matchless story of Booker Washington, the American educator, is told in many tongues and in many lands.

The history of the world has no such chapter as the Negro's fifty years of freedom. *The duty of the hour is to unshackle him and make him wholly free.* When the Negro is free from the vexatious annoyances of color and has only the same problems of life as any other men, his contribution to the general welfare of his country will be greater than ever before.

Whatever be his present disadvantages and inequalities, one thing is absolutely certain, that nowhere else in the world does so large a number of people of African descent enjoy so many rights and privileges as here in America. God has not placed these 10,000,000 here upon the American Continent in the American Republic for naught. There must be some work for them to do. He has given to each race some particular part to play in our great national drama. I predict that within the next fifty years all these discriminations, disfranchisements, and segregation will pass away. Antipathy to color is not natural, and the fear of ten by eighty millions of people is only a spook of politics, a ghost summoned to the banquet to frighten the timid and foolish.

I care nothing for the past; I look beyond the present; I see a great country with her territories stretching from the rising to the setting sun, with a climate as varied as a tropical day and an Arctic night, with a soil blessed by the fruits of the earth and nourished by the waters under it; I see a great country tenanted by untold millions of happy, healthy human beings; men of every race that God has made out of one blood to inherit the earth, a great human family, governed by righteousness and justice, not by greed and fear—in which peace and happiness shall reign supreme.

Men more and more are beginning to realize that the common origin and destiny of the human race give to each species the right to occupy the earth in peace, prosperity, and plenty, and that the duty of each race is to promote the happiness of all. The movements for social and industrial justice and the right of the people to rule are world-wide.

The American people are fast losing their provincial character. They are to-day a great world power with interests and possessions upon every part of the globe. Their horizon is the world; they are thinking in terms of the universe, and speaking in the tongues of all men.

With the widening of men's visions they must realize that the basis of true democracy and human brotherhood is the common origin and destiny of the human race; that we are all born alike, live alike, and die alike, that the laws of man's existence make absolutely no distinction.

I wandered recently into Westminster Abbey. I beheld all around me the images and effigies of the illustrious and the great,—kings, rulers, statesmen, poets, patriots, explorers, and scientists; I trampled upon the graves of some; I stood before the tombs of kings, some dead twelve centuries; there the wisest and merriest of monarchs and the most pious and dissolute of kings slept side by side. As illustrating the vanity of triumphs of personal glory, on one side of the Chapel of Henry VII, rests Mary, Queen of Scots, and almost directly opposite, all that remains of Elizabeth, her executioner. I stood before the tomb of the great Napoleon; I wandered through his palaces at Versailles and Fontainebleau with all of their magnificence and splendor, and I recalled the period of his power and glory among men, and yet, he too died. Then I passed a Potter's field and I looked upon the graves of the unknown, graves of the pauper and the pleb, and I realized that they were at last equal, those who slept in Valhalla and those who slept in the common burying-ground, and that they would each and all hear the first or the second trump of the resurrection "according to the deeds done in the body and the flesh, according to whether they were good or evil." In the democracy of death all are equal. Then men, my brothers, our duty is to make life in human society the same great democracy of equality of rights, of privileges, of opportunities, for all the children of men. There is nothing else worth while.

God grant to the American people this larger view of humanity, this greater conception of human duty. In a movement for democracy, for social and industrial justice, for the complete Emancipation of the Negro from the disabilities of color, Massachusetts must now, as in the past, point the way. If we fail here, with traditions and history such as are ours behind us, can we succeed elsewhere? The Great Emancipator speaks to us at this hour and furnishes the solution for all our race problems. "Let us discard all this quibbling about this man and the other man, this race and the other race, and the other race being inferior and therefore must be placed in an inferior position. Let us discard all these things and unite as one people throughout this land, until we shall once more stand up declaring that 'all men are created equal.'"

God grant that the American people, year by year, may grow more like Lincoln in charity, justice, and righteousness to the end that "the government of the people, for the people, by the people, shall not perish from the earth."

THE LIFE OF SOCIAL SERVICE AS EXEMPLIFIED IN DAVID LIVINGSTONE[47]

BY ALICE MOORE DUNBAR

Hamilton Wright Mabie says that the question for each man to settle is not what he *would* do if he had means, time, influence, and educational advantages, but what he *will* do with the things he has. In all history there are few men who have answered this question. Among them none have answered it more effectively than he whom we have gathered to honor to-night—David Livingstone.

The term "social service," which is on every one's lips now, was as yet uncoined when David Livingstone was born. But it was none the less true, that without overmuch prating of the ideal which is held up to the man of to-day as the only one worth striving for, the sturdy pioneers of Livingstone's day and ilk realized to the highest the ideal of man's duty to his fellow-man.

The life of David Livingstone is familiar to all of you. From your childhood you have known the brief data of his days. He was born in Lanarkshire, Scotland, March 19, 1813. He began working in a cotton-factory at the age of ten, and for ten years thence, educated himself, reading Latin, Greek, and finally pursuing a course of medicine and theology in which he graduated. In 1840, firmly believing in his call, he offered his services to the London Missionary Society, by whom he was ordained, and sent as a medical missionary to South Africa, where he commenced his labors. In 1849, he discovered Lake Ngami; in 1852, he explored the Zambezi River. In 1856, he discovered the wonderful Victoria Falls, and then returned to England, where he was overwhelmed with honors. In 1857, he published his first book, hardly realizing that it was an epoch-making volume, and that he had made an unprecedented contribution alike to literature, science, and religion. In the same year, he severed his connection with the Missionary society, believing that he could best work unhampered by its restrictions. He was appointed British Consul for the East Coast of Africa, and commander of an expedition to explore Eastern and Central Africa. He discovered the Lakes Shirwa and Nyassa in 1859; published his second book during a visit to England, 1864-65. He returned to Africa, started to explore the interior, and was lost to the world for two years. He re-appeared in 1867, having solved the problem of the sources of the Nile. From then until 1871, when he was found by Stanley, suffering the most pitiful privations, his was a record of important discoveries and explorations. After parting with Stanley in 1872, he continued his explorations, and died in 1873. His body was interred in Westminster Abbey in 1874.

This is a meagre account of the life of David Livingstone. The romance and wonder of it do not appear on the surface; the splendor of the heroic soul is lost in the dry chronology of dates; the marvelous achievement of self-sacrifice is not visible. Yet the wildest fantasies of medieval troubadours pale into insignificance when placed side by side with the life-story of David Livingstone.

What has this modern romance in it for the man of to-day? An infinity of example, of hope, of the gleam to follow. The most salient thing about Livingstone's early life is the toil and the privation which he endured gladly, in order to accomplish that which he had set himself to do. Listen to his own words in describing the long hours spent in the cotton-mill. Here he kept up his studies by placing his book on the top of the machine, so that he could catch sentence after sentence as he passed his work, learning how completely to abstract his mind from the noises about him. "Looking back now on that life of toil, I cannot but feel thankful that it formed such a material part of my early education, and were it possible, I would like to begin life over again in the same lowly style, and to pass through the same hardy training."

I wonder how many of the modern men, whose privations in early life in no wise approached those of our hero look back with gratitude upon their early days? Are we not prone to excuse and condone our shortcomings, either of character or of achievement, by murmuring at the hard fate which deprived us of those advantages which more fortunate brothers and sisters enjoyed in infancy and youth? Do we not to-day swing too far in the direction of sickly sentimentality and incline to wrap ourselves, and those about us, in the deadening cotton-wool of too much care? Were it not better if a bit more of the leaven of sturdy struggle were introduced into the life of the present-day youth? Strength of character and strength of soul will rise to their own, no matter what the struggles be to force them upward.

In keeping with this studious concentration which is shown in his work in the cotton-mill, was Livingstone's ideal of thorough preparation for his work. On his first missionary journey, before penetrating into the interior, he stopped at a little station, Lepelole, and there for six months cut himself off from all European society in order to gain an insight into the habits, ways of thinking, laws, and language of the natives. To this he ascribed most of his success as a missionary and explorer, for Livingstone's way was ever the gentle method of those who comprehend—not the harsh cruelty of those who feel superior to the ones among whom they work. In a day whose superficiality is only equalled by the ease with which we gloze over the faults of the unprepared, this bit of information of Livingstone's preparation comes like a refreshing reminder that true worth is always worth while.

When Livingstone gave up his purely missionary labors and turned his life channel into the stream of scientific investigation, the same thoroughness of preparation is shown. He did not work for immediate results, attained by shallow touching of the surface, or for hasty conclusions. His was the close observation and careful and accurate deductions of the mind trained by science to be patient and await results. Rather than be inaccurate, he would wait until he knew he was correct. A quarter of a century after Livingstone died a compatriot of his, Robert Louis Stevenson, said that among the hardest tasks that life sets for a man is "to await occasions, and hurry never." Livingstone learned this thoroughly.

In keeping with the quietness, simplicity, and thoroughness of this truly great man was the meeting between him and Stanley when that redoubtable youth found him in the heart of the Dark Continent. Life is essentially a dramatic thing, for as Carlyle says, "Is not every deathbed the fifth act of a tragedy?" But I sometimes think that we miss the drama and poetry of every-day life because it seems so commonplace. We look abroad and afar for great moments, and great moments pass unheeded each hour. So to those two—the toil-worn and weary explorer and the youthful Stanley, full of enthusiasm, albeit dimmed by the hardships and disappointments of his long search, that moment of first meeting must have seemed essentially commonplace. There was a wonder in the encounter, but like all great emotions and great occasions there was a simplicity, so that the greetings were as commonplace as if occurring in a crowded street. Thirty years had passed since the explorer had dedicated himself to the task of making the world know Africa, and he was an old man, worn-out, bent, frail, and sorrow-stricken. But courage was unfaltering, faith undimmed, power unabated. Had Stanley been a few months later, much of his work would have been lost, and his death even more pitiful than it was—yet he could smile and be patient and unhurried.

As Stanley phrases it, "Suppose Livingstone, following the custom of other travellers, had hurried to the coast, after he had discovered Lake Bangweolo, to tell the news to the geographical world; then had returned to discover Moero, and run away again, then come back once more to discover Kamolondo, and to race back again. But no, he not only discovers the Chambezi, Lake Bangweolo, Luapula River, Lake Moero, Lualaba River, and Lake Kamolondo, but he still tirelessly urges his steps forward to put the final completion to the map of the grand lacustrine river system. Had he followed the example of ordinary explorers, he would have been running backwards and forwards to tell the news, instead of exploring, and he might have been able to write a volume upon the discovery of each lake and earn much money thereby."

This was no negative exploration. It was the hard, earnest labor of years, self-abnegation, enduring patience, and exalted fortitude, such as ordinary men fail to exhibit. And he had achieved a wonderful deed. The finding of the poles, north and south, is no greater feat than his. For, after all, what is it to humanity that the magnetic pole, north or south, is a few degrees east or west of a certain point in the frozen seas and barren ice mountains? What can humanity offer as a reward to those whose bodies lie under cairns of ice save a barren recognition of their heroism? What have their lives served, beyond that of examples of heroism and determination? Bronze tablets will record their deeds, but no races will arise in future years to call them blessed. Cold marble will enshrine their memory; but there will be no fair commerce, nor civilization, nor the thankful prayers of those who have been led to know God.

In his earlier years of exploration, Livingstone became convinced that the success of the white missionary in a field like Africa is not to be reckoned by the tale of doubtful conversions he can send home each year, that the proper work of such men was that of pioneering, opening up, starting new ground, leaving native agents to work it out in detail. The whole of his subsequent career was a carrying out of this idea. It was the idea of commerce, bringing the virgin country within the reach of the world, putting the natives in that relation to the rest of humanity which would most nearly make for their efficiency, if not in their own generation, at least in the next. Shall we not say that this is the truest ideal of social service—to plan, not for the present, but for the future; to be content, not with the barren achievement of exploration, the satisfaction that comes with the saying, "I am the first who has trod this soil!" but to be able to say, "Through me, generations may be helped?"

Says a biographer of Dr. Livingstone, "His work in exploration is marked by rare precision and by a breadth of observation which will make it forever a monument to the name of one of the most intrepid travellers of the nineteenth century. His activity embraced the field of the geographer, naturalist, benefactor of mankind, and it can justly be said that his labors were the first to lift the veil from the 'Dark Continent.'"

During the thirty years of his work he explored alone over one-third of the vast continent; a feat which no single explorer has ever equalled. But it must be remembered that even though he had severed his connection with the missionary society that he regarded himself to the last as a "Pioneer Missionary."

One of the most fascinating subjects of controversy since the time of Herodotus was the problem of the source of the Nile. Poetry, from the description of the Garden of Eden and the writings of Ptolemy to the Kubla Kahn of Coleridge, ran rife over the four fountains out of which flowed the wonderful river. To Livingstone was reserved the supreme honor of settling for all time the secret of this most poetic river of mystery. Long ere this he had been honored with a gold medal from the Royal Geographical Society. How futile must the bit of metal have seemed to this dark, silent man, whose mind had grown away from bauble and tinsel, and who had learned in the silences the real value of the trinkets of the world.

When he had discovered the Victoria Falls, he had completed in two years and a half the most remarkable and most fruitful journey on record, reconstructed the map of Africa, and given the world some of the most valuable land it ever could possess. The vast commercial fields of ivory were opened up to trade; the magnificent power of the Victoria Falls laid bare to the sight of civilized man. We can imagine him standing on the brink of the thunderous cataract of the Victoria gazing at its waters as they dashed and roared over the brink of the precipice,

"—Like stout Cortez—when with eagle eyes
He stared at the Pacific, and all his men
Look'd at each other with a wild surmise,
Silent, upon a peak in Darien."

To this man, who had opened up a continent; who had penetrated not only into the heart of the forest, but had made himself one with the savages who were its denizens; who knew and understood them as human beings, and not as beasts, the slavery trade was, as he expressed it, "the open sore of Africa." Over and again he voiced his belief that the Negro freeman was a hundred times more valuable than the slave. He repeatedly enjoined those who had the fitting out of his expeditions not to send him slaves to accompany him on his journeys, but freemen, as they were more trustworthy. He voiced the fundamental truth that he who is his own master is he who obeys and believes in his master.

The slave trade in Africa was dealt its death-blow by Dr. Livingstone. Portugal had foisted the shame of centuries upon the Dark Continent, and openly defied decency and honor. Livingstone's example and his death acted like an inspiration, filling Africa with an army of explorers and missionaries, and raising in Europe so powerful a feeling against the slave trade that it may be considered as having received its death-blow. Dear to his heart was Lincoln, the Emancipator, an ideal hero whom he consistently revered. Away to the southwest from Kamolondo is a large lake which discharges its waters by the important river, Lomami, into the great Lualaba. To this lake, known as the Chobungo by the natives, Dr. Livingstone gave the name of Lincoln, in memory of him for whom your noble institution was named. This was done because of a vivid impression produced on his mind by hearing a portion of Lincoln's inauguration speech from an English pulpit, which related to the causes that induced him to issue the Emancipation

Proclamation. To the memory of the man whom Livingstone revered he has contributed a monument more durable than brass or stone.

This strange, seemingly almost ascetic man sets before us of to-day an almost impossible standard of living. One idea mastered him—to give Africa to the world. His life was a success, as all lives must be which have a single aim. Life was clear, elemental almost to him, and to the man whose ambition is a unit; who sees but one goal, shining clearly ahead, success is inevitable, though it may be masked under the guise of poverty and hardship. Livingstone had a higher and nobler ambition than the mere pecuniary sum he might receive, or the plaudits of the unthinking multitude; he followed the dictates of duty. Never was such a willing slave to that abstract virtue. His inclination impelled him home, the fascinations of which it required the sternest resolves to resist. With every foot of new ground he travelled over, he forged a chain of sympathy which should hereafter bind all other nations to Africa. If he were able to complete this chain, a chain of love, by actual discovery and description of the people and nations that still lived in darkness, so as to attract the good and charitable of his own land to bestir themselves for their redemption and salvation—this, Livingstone would consider an ample reward. "A delirious and fatuous enterprise, a Quixotic scheme!" some will say. Not so; he builded better than even he knew or dared hope, and posterity will reap the reward.

The missionary starting out must resolve to bear poverty, suffering, hardship, and, if need be, to lose his life. The explorer must resolve to be impervious to exquisite little tortures, to forget comforts, and be a stranger to luxuries; to lose *his* life, even, in order that the world may add another line or dot to its maps. The explorer-missionary must do all these things, and add to them the zeal for others that shall illumine his labors, and make him at one with God. David Livingstone had all these qualities, coupled with the sublime indifference of the truly great to the mere side issues of life. You and I sit down to our comfortable meals, sleep in our well-appointed beds, read our Bibles with perfunctory boredom, and babble an occasional prayer for those who endure hardships—when we are reminded from the pulpit to do so. When we read of some awful calamity, such as has blazoned across the pages of history within the past few weeks, we shudder that men should lay down their lives in the barren wastes of ice. When we read of the thirty years of steady suffering which Livingstone endured in the forests of Africa, the littleness of our own lives comes home to us with awful realization. You who fear to walk the streets with a coat of last year's cut, listen to his half whimsical account of how he "came to the Cape in 1852, with a black coat eleven years out of fashion, and Mrs. Livingstone and the children half naked." You who shudder at the tale of a starving child in the papers, and lamely wonder why the law allows such things, read his recital of the sufferings of his wife and little ones during the days without water under a tropic sun, and of the splendid heroism of the mother who did not complain, and the father who did not dare meet her eye, for fear of the unspoken reproach therein.

He was never in sufficient funds, and what little means he could gather here and there were often stolen from him, or he found himself cheated out of what few supplies he could get together to carry on his travels. Months of delay occurred, and sometimes it seemed that all his labors and struggles would end in futility; that the world would be little better for his sufferings; yet that patient, Christian fortitude sustained him with unfaltering courage through the most distressing experiences. Disease, weakening, piteous, unromantic, unheroic, wasted his form; ulcers, sores, horrible and hideous, made his progress slow and his work sometimes a painful struggle over what many a man would have deemed impossible barriers. The loss of his wife came to him twelve years after she had elected to cast in her lot with his, but like Brutus of old, he could exclaim,

"With meditating that she must die once,
I have the patience to endure it now.

Stanley could but marvel at such patience. On that memorable day when they met, and the younger man gave the doctor his letters, he tells how "Livingstone kept the letter-bag on his knee, then, presently opened it, looked at the letters contained there, read one or two of his children's letters, his face in the meanwhile lighting up. He asked me to tell him the news, "No, Doctor," said I, "read your letters first, which I am sure you must be impatient to read." "Ah," said he, "I have waited years for letters, and I have been taught patience."

To you, of the younger generation, what a marvel, what a world of meaning in those words—"I have been taught patience." We, who fret and chafe because the whole world will not bend its will to our puny strivings, and turn its whole course that we might have our unripe desires fulfilled, should read and re-read of the man who could wait, because he knew that time and all eternity would be bent to meet his desires in time.

Livingstone's is a character that we cannot help but venerate; that calls forth all one's enthusiasm; that evokes nothing but sincerest admiration. He was sensitive, but so is any man of a high mind and generous nature; he was sensitive on the point of being doubted or criticised by the easy-chair geographers, lolling comfortably in their clubs and scanning through their monocles the maps which the hard working travellers had made. He was humble-souled, as are all the truly great. His gentleness never forsook him; his hopefulness never deserted him. No harassing anxiety, distraction of mind, long separation from home and kindred, could make him complain. He thought all would come out right at last, such faith had he in the goodness of Providence. The sport of adverse circumstances; the plaything of the miserable slaves, which were persistently sent him from Zanzibar, baffled and worried, even almost to the grave; yet he would not desert the charge imposed upon him. To the stern dictates of duty alone did he sacrifice his home and ease, the pleasures, refinements, and luxuries of civilized life. His was the Spartan heroism, the inflexibility of the Roman, the enduring heroism of the Englishman—never to relinquish his work, though his heart yearned for home; never to surrender his obligations, until he could write "Finis" to his work.

Yet who shall say that the years spent alone at the very heart of Nature had not made him the possessor of that "inward eye," which, as Wordsworth says, "is the bliss of solitude." For many years he lived in Africa deprived of books, and yet when Stanley found him, he learned to his surprise, that Livingstone could still recite whole poems from Byron, Burns, Tennyson, Longfellow, and other great poets. The reason is found in the fact that all his life he lived within himself. He lived in a world in which he revolved inwardly, out of which he awoke only to attend to his immediate practical necessities. It was a happy inner world, peopled with his own friends, acquaintances, relatives, readings, ideas, and associations. Blessed is the man who has found the inner life more real than the trivial outer one. To him mere external annoyances are but as the little insects, which he may brush away at will. No man can be truly great who has not built up for himself a subjective world into which he may retire at will. The little child absorbed in a mythical land peopled by fairies and Prince Charmings is nearest to possessing such an inner life; and we must become as little children. To some it is a God-given gift; others may acquire it, as Jack London tells us, by "going into the waste places, and there sitting down with our souls." There comes then, the overwhelming realization of the charms and beauties of nature—man is a pygmy, an abstraction, an unreality. This had come to our hero. Added to the strength of his inner life Livingstone had the deep sympathy with Nature in all her moods. He became enthusiastic when he described the beauties of the Moero scenery. The splendid mountains, tropical vegetation, thundering cataracts, noble rivers, stirred his soul into poetic expression. His tired spirit expanded in the presence of the charms of nature. He could never pass through an African forest, with its solemn stillness and serenity, without wishing to be buried quietly under the dead leaves where he would be sure to rest undisturbed. In England, there was no elbow-room, the graves were often desecrated, and ever since he had buried his wife in the woods of Shupanga, he had sighed for just such a spot, where his weary bones would receive the eternal rest they coveted. But even this last wish was denied him, and the noisy honors and crowded crypt of Westminster Abbey claimed him, far away from the splendid solitude he craved. All Africa should have been his tomb. He should never have been forced to share with hundreds of others a meagre and scant resting-place. Yet there is food for rejoicing in the knowledge, that though his body was borne away, his heart was buried by his beloved natives in the forest.

The study of Dr. Livingstone would not be even superficially complete if we did not take the religious side of his character into consideration. By religion, we do not mean the faith he professed, the particular tenets he believed, the especial catechism he studied, or any hair-splitting doctrine he might have upheld, but that deeper ethical side of manhood, without which there can be no true manhood. Livingstone's religion was not of the theoretical kind, but it was a constant, earnest, sincere practise. It was neither demonstrative nor loud, but manifested itself in a quiet, practical way, and was always at work. It was not aggressive, nor troublesome, nor impertinent. In him, religion exhibited its loveliest features; it governed his conduct not only towards his servants, but towards the natives, the bigoted Mohammedans, and all with whom he came in contact. Without it, Livingstone, with his ardent temperament, his enthusiasm, his high spirit and courage, must have become uncompanionable, and a hard master. Religion had tamed him, and made him a Christian gentleman; the crude and wilful were refined and subdued; religion had made him the most companionable of men and indulgent of masters—a man whose society was pleasurable to a high degree.

If his life held for us no other message than this, it would hold enough. Unfortunately the youth of to-day is apt to chafe when the ideal of Christianity and manly religion is held up to him. He thinks of the religious man as a milksop, a mollycoddle. He cannot associate him in his mind with the doing of great deeds, the thinking of great thoughts. His ideal of manhood is the ruthless Man on Horseback, with too often a disregard of the sacred things of life. Sometimes, if the youth of to-day thinks at all, he runs riot into ethics, forgetting that, after all, there could be no ethics without a firm base of religion. And so he wastes many precious years before he learns that all the greatest men whom the world has known drew their strength and power from the unseen and the spiritual.

We have noticed that Livingstone's religion was not aggressive nor impertinent. Early in his career as a missionary, he recognized the truth that if he were to exercise any influence on the native Africans, it would not be by bringing to them an abstraction in place of their own savage ideals. His influence depended entirely upon persuasion, and by awakening within their minds the sense of right and wrong. "We never wished them to do right," he says, "because it would be pleasing to us, nor think themselves to blame when they did wrong." Worldly affairs, and temporal benefits with the natives were paramount, so he did not force abstractions upon them but, with a keen insight into human nature, as well as into savage human nature, he reached their higher selves through the more worldly.

His was a pure and tender-hearted nature, full of humanity and sympathy, modest as a maiden, unconscious of his own greatness, with the simplicity we have noted before, the simplicity of the truly great. His soul could be touched to its depths by the atrocities of the Arab slave-traders, yet he forgot his own sufferings in the desire to make others immune from suffering. He had but one rule of life, that which he gave to the Scotch school children, whom he once addressed:

"Fear God and work hard!"

* * * * *

It is one hundred years since this quiet, high-souled man was given the world, in the little Scotch village, and yet another hundred may pass away and still his life will be as a clarion call to the youth of the world to emulate his manhood. For the world needs men now, as it never needed them before,

"Men, high-minded men,
With powers as far above dull brutes endued
In forest brake or den, as beasts excel cold rocks and rambles rude."

Such a man was Livingstone, not afraid to be meek in order to be great; not afraid to "fear God and work hard;" not ashamed to stoop in order that he might raise others to his high estate. He gave the world a continent and a conscience; with the lavishness almost of Nature herself he bestowed cataracts and rivers, lakes and mountains, forests and valleys, upon his native land. He stirred the soul of the civilized world to the atrocities of the slave trade, and he made it realize that humanity may be found even in the breast of a savage. When he laid down his life in the forest he loved, he laid upon the altar of humanity and science the costliest and sweetest sacrifice that it had known for many a weary age.

What message has this life for us to-day, we the commonplace, the mediocre, the unknown to fame and fortune? Shall we fold our hands when we read of such heroes and say, "Ah, yes, he could be great, but I? I am weak and humble, I have not the opportunity?" Who was more humble than the poor boy spinning in the cotton-mill; who was less constrained by Fortune's frowns than the humble missionary? His life brings to us the message of doing well with that little we have.

We cannot all be with Peary at the North Pole, nor die the death of the hero, Scott, on the frozen Antarctic continent. It is not given to us to be explorers; it is not given us to be pioneers; we may not discover vast continents, name great lakes, nor gaze with wonder-stricken eyes upon the rolling of a mighty unknown river. But to each and all of us comes the divine opportunity to carve for himself a niche, be it ever so tiny, in the memories of men. We can heed the admonition of Carlyle, "Be no longer a Chaos, but a World, or even a Worldkin. Produce! Produce! Were it but the pitifullest infinitesimal fraction of a Product, produce it in God's name! 'Tis the utmost thou hast in thee, out with it then!"

The life of service; the life of unselfish giving—this must Livingstone's life mean to us. Unselfish, ungrudging lavishing of life and soul, even to the last drop of heart's blood. Service that does not hesitate because the task seems small, or the waiting weary; service that does not fear to be of no account in the eyes of the world. Truly, indeed, might Wordsworth's apostrophe to Milton be ascribed to him:

"Thy soul was like a star and dwelt apart;
Thou hadst a voice whose sound was like the sea;
Pure as the naked heavens, majestic, free,
So didst thou travel on life's common way
In cheerful godliness, and yet thy heart
The lowliest duties on itself did lay."

EDUCATION FOR MANHOOD[48]

BY KELLY MILLER

We must keep clearly in mind the proposition that the educational process is always under domination of contemporary opinion. The education prescribed for any class is likely to be conditioned upon the presumed relationship of that class to the social body. When woman was regarded as an inferior creature, whose destiny was to serve as a tool and plaything of man, she was accorded only such education as would fit her for this subsidiary function. Any other training was regarded as unnecessary and mischievous. It is only within comparatively recent times, when man began to realize the essential human quality and powers of the female sex, and deemed it not mockery to place her on the same footing with himself, that the comprehensive education of woman has become a possibility.

The traditional relation of the American Negro to the society of which he forms a part is too well known to need extensive treatment in this connection. The African slave was introduced into this country as a pure animal instrumentality to perform the rougher work under dominion of his white lord and master. There was not the remotest thought of his human personality. No more account was taken of his higher qualities than of the higher susceptibilities of the lower animals. His mission was considered to be as purely mechanical as that of the ox which pulls the plow. Indeed, his human capabilities were emphatically denied. It was stoutly contended that he did not possess a soul to be saved in the world to come nor a mind to be enlightened in the world that now is. Under the dominion of this dogma, education was absolutely forbidden him. It became a crime even to attempt to educate this *tertium quid* which was regarded as little more than brute and little less than human. The white race, in its arrogant conceit, constituted the personalities and the Negro the instrumentalities. Man may be defined as a distinction-making animal. He is ever prone to set up barriers between members of his own species and to deny one part of God's human creatures the inalienable birthright vouchsafed to all alike. But the process was entirely logical and consistent with the prevailing philosophy.

The anti-slavery struggle stimulated the moral energy of the American people in a manner that perhaps has never had a parallel in the history of vicarious endeavor. "One touch of nature makes the whole world kin." In dealing with fundamental principles of human rights and human wrongs involved in the issue of slavery, these moral reformers found that the Negro was a human being, endowed with heart and mind and conscience like as themselves; albeit these powers of personality had long been smothered and imbruted by centuries of suppression and harsh usage. These philanthropists believed in the essential manhood of the Negro. This belief was the chief dynamic of their endeavor. Upon this foundation they not only broke the Negro's chain, but clothed him with political and civic prerogative as an American citizen. They established schools and colleges and universities for him because they believed in his higher susceptibilities. To-day we are almost astounded at the audacity of their faith. They projected a scheme of education comparable with the standards set up for the choicest European youth for a race which had hitherto been submerged below the zero point of intelligence. These schools and colleges founded and fostered on this basis were the beginnings of the best that there is in the race and the highest which it can hope to be.

But, alas, as the passion engendered by the war grew weaker and weaker, the corresponding belief in the Negro has also declined, and the old dogma concerning his mission as a human tool has begun to reassert itself. In certain sections the white race has always claimed that the Negro should not be encouraged in the development of personality. The denial of the designation "mister" is suggestive of this disposition. With them the term "mister" is made to mean a direct designation of personality. There is no objection to such titles as "doctor," "reverend" or "professor," as these connote professional rather than personal quality.

Our whole educational activities are under the thrall of this retrograde spirit. We are marking time rather than moving forward. The work is being carried on rather than up. Our bepuzzled pedagogues are seriously reflecting over the query, *Cui bono?*—Is it worth while? Few, indeed, are left who have the intensity of belief and the intrepidity of spirit to defend the higher pretentions of the Negro without apology or equivocation. The old form of appeal has become insipid and uninspiring; the ear has become dull to its dinging. The old blade has become blunt and needs a new sharpness of point and keenness of edge. Where now is heard the tocsin call whose key-note a generation ago resounded from the highlands of Kentucky and Tennessee to the plains of the Carolinas calling the black youths, whose hopes ran high within their bosoms, to rise and make for higher things? This clarion note, though still for the nonce, shall not become a lost chord. Its inspiring tones must again appeal to the youth to arise to their higher assertion and exertion. If you wish to reach and inspire the life of the people, the approach must be made not to the intellectual, nor yet to the feelings, as the final basis of appeal, but to the manhood that lies back of these. That education of youth, especially the suppressed class, that does not make insistent and incessant appeals to the smothered manhood (I had almost said godhood) within, will prove to be but vanity and vexation of spirit. What boots a few chapters in Chemistry, or pages in History, or paragraphs in Philosophy, unless they result in an enlarged appreciation of one's own manhood? Those who are to stand in the high places of intellectual, moral, and spiritual leadership of such a people in such a time as this must be made to feel deep down in their own souls their own essential manhood. They must believe that they are created in the image of God and that nothing clothed in human guise is a more faithful likeness of the original. This must be the dominant note in the education of the Negro. If the note itself is not new, there must at least be a newness of emphasis and insistence. The Negro must learn in school what the white boy absorbs from association and environment. The American white man in his ordinary state is supremely conscious of his manhood prerogative. He may be ignorant or poor or vicious; yet he never forgets that he is a man. But every feature of our civilization is calculated to impress upon the Negro a sense of his inferiority and to make him feel and believe that he is good for nothing but to be cast out and trodden under foot of other men. A race, like an individual, that compromises its own self-respect, paralyzes and enfeebles its own energies. The motto which should be engraved upon the conscience of every American Negro is that which Milton places in the mouth of His Satanic Majesty: "The mind is its own place and of itself can make a heaven of hell; a hell of heaven." To inculcate this principle is the highest mission of the higher education. The old theologians used to insist upon the freedom of the will, but the demand of the Negro to-day is for the freedom and independence of his own spirit. Destroy this and all is lost; preserve it, and though political rights, civil privileges, industrial opportunities be taken away for the time, they will all be regained.

By the development of manhood on the part of the Negro nothing is farther from my thought than the inculcation of that pugnacious, defiant disposition which vents itself in wild ejaculations and impotent screaming against the evils of society. I mean the full appreciation of essential human qualities and claims, and the firm, unyielding determination to press forward to the mark of this calling, and not to be swerved from its pursuit by doubt, denial, danger, rebuff, ridicule, insult, and contemptuous treatment. While the Negro may not have it within his power to resist or overcome these things, he must preserve the integrity of his own soul.

The higher education of the Negro up to this point has been very largely under the direction and control of philanthropy. The support has come almost wholly from that source. The development of this sense of manhood should be the highest concern of a wise, discriminating philanthropy, for if this is once developed the Negro will be able to handle his own situation and relieve his philanthropic friends from further consideration or concern; but, if he fails to develop this spirit of manhood, he will be but a drag upon the resources of philanthropy for all times to come.

The Negro must develop courage and self-confidence. A grasp upon the principles of knowledge gives the possessor the requisite spirit of confidence.

To the timid, the world is full of mystery manipulated and controlled by forces and powers beyond their ken to comprehend. But knowledge convinces us that there is no mystery in civilization. The railroad, the steamship, and the practical projects that loom so large to the unreflecting, are but the result of the application of thought to things. The mechanical powers and forces of Nature are open secrets for all who will undertake to unravel the mystery. And so it is with essential and moral principles. The one who will have himself rooted and grounded in the fundamental principles of things can look with complacence upon the panorama of the world's progress. The Negro should plant one foot on the Ten Commandments and the other on the Binomial Theorem: he can then stand steadfast and immovable, however the rain of racial wrath may fall or the angry winds of prejudice may blow and beat upon him.

The educated Negro must learn to state his own case and to plead his own cause before the bar of public opinion. No people who raise up from out their midst a cultivated class, who can plead their own cause and state their own case, will fail of a hearing before the just judgment of mankind.

The educated Negro to-day represents the first generation grown to the fullness of the stature of manhood under the influence and power of education. They are the first ripened fruit of philanthropy, and by them alone will the wisdom or folly of that philanthropy be justified. The hope of the race is focused in them. They are the headlight to direct the pathway through the dangers and vicissitudes of the wilderness. For want of vision, the people perish; for want of wise direction, they stumble and fall. There is no body of men in the world to-day, nor in the history of the world, who have, or ever have had, greater responsibilities or more coveted opportunities than devolves upon the educated Negro to-day. It is, indeed, a privilege to be a Negro of light and leading in such a time as this. The incidental embarrassments and disadvantages which for the time being must be endured are not to be compared with the far more exceeding weight of privileges and glory which awaits him if he rises to these high demands. For such a privilege well may he forego the pleasure of civilization for a season.

His world consists of 10,000,000 souls, who have wrapped up in them all the needs and necessities, powers and possibilities, of human nature; they contain all the norms of civilization, from its roots to its florescence. His is the task to develop and vitalize these smothered faculties and potentialities. His education will prove to be but vanity and vexation of spirit, unless it ultimates in this task. He is the salt of the earth, and if the salt lose its savor, wherewith shall it be salted? If the light within the racial world be darkness, how great is that darkness?

The highest call of the civilization of the world to-day is to the educated young men of the belated races. The educated young manhood of Japan, China, India, Egypt, and Turkey must lift their own people up to the level of their own high conception. They must partake of the best things in the civilization of Europe and show them unto their own people. The task of the educated American Negro is the same as theirs, intensified, perhaps, by the more difficult and intricate tangle of circumstances and conditions with which he has to deal.

He cannot afford to sink into slothful satisfaction and enjoy a tasteless leisure or with inane self-deception hide his head under the shadows of his wings, like the foolish bird, which thereby hopes to escape the wrath to come. The white race, through philanthropy, has done much; but its vicarious task culminated when it developed the first generation of educated men and women. They must do the rest.

These philanthropists spoke for us when our tongues were tied. They pleaded our cause when we were speechless; but now our faculties have been unloosed. We must stand upon our own footing. In buffeting the tempestuous torrents of the world we must either swim on the surface or sink out of sight. The greatest gratitude that the beneficiary can show to the benefactor is, as soon as possible, to do without his benefaction. The task of race statesmanship and reclamation devolves upon the educated Negro of this day and generation. Moral energy must be brought to bear upon the task, whether the Negro be engaged in the production of wealth or in the more recondite pursuits which minister to the higher needs of man.

The white race is fast losing faith in the Negro as an efficient and suitable factor in the equation of our civilization. Curtailment of political, civil, and religious privilege and opportunity is but the outward expression of this apostasy. As the white man's faith decreases, our belief in ourselves must increase. Every Negro in America should utter this prayer, with his face turned toward the light: "Lord, I believe in my own inherent manhood; help Thou my unbelief." The educated Negro must express his manhood in terms of courage, in the active as well as in the passive voice: courage to do, as well as to endure; courage to contend for the right while suffering wrong; the courage of self-belief that is always commensurate with the imposed task. The world believes in a race that believes in itself; but justly despises the self-bemeaned. Such is the mark and the high calling to which the educated Negro of to-day is called. May he rise to the high level of it. Never was there a field whiter unto harvest; never was there louder cry for laborers in the vineyard of the Lord.

A FEW REMARKS ON MAKING A LIFE[49]

BY ROBERT E. JONES, LL. D.

Editor Southwestern Christian Advocate, New Orleans, La.

I have a story to relate, and at once I want to present to you my hero,—a hero more inspiring than Achilles of the "Iliad," or Odysseus of the "Odyssey," or Æneas of the "Æneid."

My hero is not a myth, not a creation of literature, not a tradition, but not unlike the Grecian hero in that he sprung from the union of a god and a mortal. My hero is not reckoned among the high and mighty nor will his name ever be carved on stone or raised on bronze. Neither has my hero accomplished startling feats. As a hero he may be a paradox. Inconspicuous, humble in station, modest, hid far away from the maddening, jealous, curious, bickering, taunting, striving, restless crowd of life. Too long already I have held him from you. His name? I do not know. His birthplace? I do not know. His age? I do not know. Is he living now? Here my ignorance is painful. I do not know. My hero, however, is an actual man of flesh and blood. I met him but twice in life, but was so charmed I did not ask his name. His personality thrilled and he in a measure has become my patron saint. He is not a hero of large and commanding stature, but a cripple—doubly so. His arms were palsied and turned in so that he could not use a crutch, his lower limbs turned in also. He sat in an ordinary cane-bottomed chair and could easily move himself about by throwing the weight of his body from one back leg of the chair to the other, lifting the front legs at the same time. I saw him along the train side at Spartanburg, S. C.

A beggar? No, my young friends, beggars are seldom heroes. He was a merchant prince. He carried his goods around his neck and shoulders and in his outer coat pockets. He was selling shoe-strings and pencils. If you gave him a dime he would insist on your taking one or both of the articles he had for sale. In his activities he was a fine lesson of the first requirement of life. He was self-sustaining. By the sweat of his brow he earned his bread.

Did he complain of his lot? Not a bit of it. His handicap he did not make nor could undo. He therefore accepted his condition philosophically; he was self-respecting. He knew his limitations; he knew what he could do and what he could not do; he was self-knowing. Knowing his handicap and that it was quite unlike any other man's and that he needed a means of locomotion, he found it; he had, therefore, initiative. He leaned not upon the strength of others, but used his own resources; he was therefore self-reliant. He did not wait for business to come to him, he put himself in the path of business; he was a hustler. He saw life through a cheerful lens and kept a stout heart; he was optimistic. He recognized his own personality apart from the personalities of the crowded throng through which he passed; he was a self-contented individual. He had but one life to live and he was making the most of life. When I left him I crowned him, honored him, and I love him for his worth as a true man.

"I like a man who faces what he must,
With step triumphant and a heart of cheer;
Who fights the daily battles without fear;
Nor loses faith in man; but does his best,
Nor ever murmurs at his humble lot,
But, with a smile, and words of hope, gives zest
To every toiler; he alone is great
Who by a life heroic conquers fate."

When once away from my hero, as I thought of him in my deepest soul, I cried:

"Thou art my chastiser and my inspirator. Thou art simple yet great; untaught thyself, thou art the teacher of all. Henceforth thou shalt be my hero and guide. Doubting myself, bemoaning my limitations, depressed by my failure, ashamed of my achievements, my seeing you has given me a new interpretation of life. I own you my friend, my life's inspiration and hero."

There is my hero. You ask his color? What difference does it make? Men have often refused to recognize worth because of color. But to satisfy you I will tell you. He is a Negro. Give a seat of honor to my hero. Gather inspiration and learn from him the lessons of life, if you will. Here is an individual doubly afflicted, without a word of complaint, or a fret or whine, depending upon his own initiative and resources, making the most of life under the circumstances which surround him.

Upon the basis of what has been said, in closing this address to the graduating Class of 1913 of the Tuskegee Normal and Industrial Institute I desire to offer a personal word:

In the first place, you will know a year from now, more than you can realize at this present moment, that this is a commencement. This is not the climax of your life. It is but the beginning, and however paradoxical it may seem, you are not at the top of the ladder, you are at the foot. We are here to applaud you to-day not so much on what you have already accomplished as to give you a send-off for the strenuous tasks that lie before you. To be frank with you, young men and young women, the life in earnest that awaits you without will tax every bit of your strength. Your moral strength will be drawn upon, as well as your intellectual resources.

Secondly; had I my way I would have each of you burn your diploma and never refer to it as an indication of what you are and what you know. Do not attempt to pass through the world on your diploma or your class standing. The world cares little for these. I would urge that you prove to the world what you are by what you can do—that you let your achievements point to your diploma.

Thirdly; you go forth to-day as a representative of this institution, mantled with all the sacred honors, prestige, and commendation that this institution, State, and your admirers can bestow. See to it that you keep the honors of this hour unsoiled and that you disgrace not the noble history of your alma mater.

Fourthly; I do not believe that this institution is fostered with the idea that the few students who gather here from time to time only shall be reached. I rather suspect that the dollars that come from the State and generous friends come with the hope that as you have been helped and lifted to culture and refinement, you in turn will carry culture to those who may never be permitted to stay in these walls. You are to carry light into dark places and unto those who sit in darkness. By your arm of strength you are to lift the poor who are beneath you. And then your education comes not for self-culture, not for self-enjoyment, not for self-use, but for the betterment of those who are about you.

Fifthly; you go forth as the embodiment of a new generation. You stand to-day upon the foundation built by those who have gone before you. They have wrought well. By their toil and suffering you are blest. You are to carry your generation one notch higher and thus help the onward march of the world's progress. Be thou faithful. Lift your eyes heavenward and aspire to do the best and be the noblest according to God's heritage to you. There are no chosen depths, no prescribed heights to which you may climb.

"Honor and shame from no condition rise,
Act well your part, there all the honor lies."

Make the most of life!

EMANCIPATION AND RACIAL ADVANCEMENT[50]

BY THE REV. ERNEST LYON, D.D., LL.D.

Mr. Chairman, Members of the Celebration Committee, Ladies and Gentlemen:

We are not here to-day in the capacity of the priest performing the funeral rights over the graves of the dead; neither are we here simply to offer tribute to their memory, by the time-honored custom of decorating their graves with the faded tokens of a nation's love and gratitude; but we are here, ladies and gentlemen, to cheer the hearts of the living—not by an optimism impossible of realization—but by a candid and truthful report of the conduct of that legacy of freedom, which came to us fifty years ago, through the sacrifice and death of the patriots, living and dead, whose memories are honored to-day all over this broad land of ours.

The civilized world will watch for the newspaper reports of to-morrow to learn the sentiments of the American people uttered to-day upon many of the burning issues before the Congress of the United States, relating to our domestic and foreign policies. The opportunities, which this day gives, will be seized by national orators to record their convictions upon matters of morality, politics, and diplomacy. Japan will listen with keen, diplomatic interest to every utterance, official or unofficial, touching the vexing problems involved in the so-called "Yellow Peril" and in the Anti-Alien Land legislation, which, like Segregation and the Jimcrowism of the South, have been enacted into laws discriminating against citizens, not aliens, but citizens of the United States of America, such as we are.

Many to-day believe that the gravity of these international matters will force the Decoration Day orators to ignore the Negro question, which, in some form or other, has been the livest question in American politics for nearly three centuries. In this belief I think they will be disappointed, for no question before the American people to-day, whether national or international, can overshadow the Negro question in America, and no day as historic as this would be complete in its observance without some reference to it.

We, therefore, gladly welcome the Japanese, or any other members of the colored race in the earth, to come and share with us that notoriety which our presence begets in this country, for no other people on the face of the globe, so far as the United States is concerned, will be able to dispossess us from the limelight of public discussion. We have not only helped, but we have made history in this country. We are wrapped up in the history of the United States of America, despite the attempt in certain quarters to deny us a respectful place therein. There is not a single page, from the period of its colonial existence to its present standard of greatness and renown, from which we are absent. From the landing of the Pilgrims at Plymouth Rock to the advent of the Cavaliers at Jamestown; from the stirring periods of the Revolution, which resulted in the emancipation of the colonists from British imperialism, to the Rebellion in 1860—resulting in the salvation of the Federal Union—we have ever and always been a potent factor in the history of this country.

Our presence here has made this day possible. There would have been no Decoration Day had the American kidnappers left us in Africa—our fatherland. The world must, therefore, hear from us upon these special occasions. So, like other elements of the population, we come to-day to make our annual report. We come, in company with the others, to review the past, to study the present, and, if possible, to forecast the future. In measuring the progress of any successful commercial enterprise, the mode of procedure is to compare beginnings with balance-sheets. Commercially speaking, it is to take an inventory. What, therefore, is true of any commercial enterprise is equally true of races and individuals. The *modus operandi* is the same. In fact, we proceed by comparing beginnings with beginnings; environments with environments, and the advantages and disadvantages of the past and present. This is the mode by which the progress of a race or the attainments of an individual must be measured, and the Negro race offers no exception to this rule.

It was Wendell Phillips, one of America's greatest statesmen, jurists, and orators, who said in that marvellous lecture on Toussaint L'Ouverture—beyond doubt the greatest military genius of the nineteenth century—that there are two ways by which Anglo-Saxon civilization measures races. First, by the great men produced by that race; secondly, by the average merit of the mass of that race. In support of the first he bravely summoned to his presence, from the regions of the dead, the immortal Bacon, Shakespeare, Hampden, Hancock, Washington, and Franklin, offering them as stars, who, in their day, had lent lustre in the galaxy of history. And with equal pride he gloried in the average merit of Anglo-Saxon blood, since it first streamed from its German home, in support of the contention of the second way.

As a race, we shall offer no objection to this principle of judgment. In fact, we cannot even if we so desired. We shall, therefore, accept it without any reluctance. We think it is a good principle upon which to base a judgment. The only consideration we demand, in connection with it, is that the white American, in his judgment of the Afro-American, shall strictly observe the rule which the race he represents has set for itself; that is to say, let him measure our race by the great and useful men it has produced, since the immortal Abraham Lincoln issued that Proclamation, whose fiftieth anniversary we celebrate to-day, giving freedom to four and one-half millions of human beings. Let him measure us by the average merit of Afro-American blood, since it first streamed from the land of the Pharaohs, whose wills were inscribed in hieroglyphics—long before Ph[oe]nicia invented the alphabet; long before the conquest of Alexander the Great had enabled Eratosthenes and Appollodorus to construct their synchrony of Egyptian antiquity; long before the construction of the Pyramids (those silent but eloquent tributes to the grandeur and majesty of the African intellect) had proclaimed the immortality of the soul.

Our record in this country, Mr. Chairman, must begin with the Emancipation period. The Emancipation is our birthday. Mankind, therefore, in measuring our progress, must, in order to be just, make Emancipation its starting point. Previous to that period we were like the earth in its primeval condition, as described by Moses, the great Lawgiver, in the Book of the Generations; namely, that the "Earth was without form, and void, and darkness was upon the face of the deep." So, too, were we before the issuance of the Emancipation Proclamation; we were without national form; void of civic rights; and moral and intellectual darkness covered the minds and souls and spirits of the race.

What was the condition of the race when the Emancipation Proclamation was first issued, a half century ago? Commercially speaking, what were the assets of this race? Had it anything to its credit in the balance-sheets of human progress, save the evils accruing from a long period of bondage? The facts will prove that it had nothing to its credit but the virtues of patience and endurance, under trials and afflictions, the horrors of which will form one of the darkest chapters in the history of this country.

The twenty Africans, brought by the slave-traders to Jamestown, in 1620, representing the introduction of African slavery into the United States, in two hundred and forty-three years had increased to four and one-half millions of human souls; and it is fair to presume that an equal, if not a greater number than this, had perished on account of the rigors of transmission in crossing the Atlantic Ocean and the indescribable cruelties of the slave system at home.

The Proclamation of Emancipation found these four and one-half millions of human beings practically homeless, penniless, and friendless, and absolutely dependent upon the very same people to whom they were in bondage for two hundred and forty years, and against whom they had taken up arms in a civil war. The forty acres of land and two mules, which were promised by the Federal Government, never materialized. That promise was like the proverbial pie-crust, made to be broken; and the descendants of these four and a half millions are to-day entitled, by every humane consideration, to all the benefits and the equities in the case. The Federal Government at Washington can only purge itself of this breach of promise by paying the bill, with legal interest; if not, according to the legal terms of the agreement (forty acres and two mules), then in its just equivalents, either by pensioning the survivors of the slave system—many who are to-day in abject squalor and want—or by a liberal grant of money to the schools of the land charged with the educational development of their much proscribed posterity.

What of the race's mental condition at the time of its civic birth? There were scarcely any at that time who could either read or write with any degree of proficiency. Not because they were incapable of learning; not because of any mental inferiority; but because of the cruel and unjust law prohibiting their education and making it a criminal offense, not only for the Negro himself, but for any white man who should undertake to instruct him. Punishment was so severe along this line that the very sight of a book awed him into fear and fright. The very existence of such a law was, indeed, an admission of the educational possibilities of the race. In the year 1863 there were about twenty members of the race who had received collegiate training. Mathematically speaking, it took three hundred years to pull twenty Negroes through the colleges of the land, so great was the combination against our mental development.

What was our status in the business pursuits and gainful occupations at that time? The year 1863 is as far back as we desire to go for this enquiry, when the entire race, with but a few exceptions, were servants, restricted to menial employment and plantation occupations.

What was the moral status of the race at that period? Here there are two sides involved in any answer which might be given to this question. The evidences of unlawful miscegenation present themselves to every traveler throughout this country, and is in itself a pertinent answer to this query. Our women have had to fight against indescribable odds in order to preserve their womanhood from the attacks of moral lepers, who, very often, were their masters and overseers. Yet, in spite of these well-known facts, we have produced women among us of pure and good morals, with unimpeachable reputation for virtue and purity. Sometimes it is a little amusing to hear the white American expatiate on the immorality of Negro women. They certainly cannot forget their own record in their dealings with the helpless Negro women of this country. But here, we will let the curtain of secrecy fall upon such a scene, while we shall advance to a higher and nobler plane upon this day when nothing but good feeling must be allowed a place on the programme.

"Watchman, what of the night?" What tidings does the morning bring, if any? Has the future nothing in store for America's greatest factors in her industrial and commercial development?

Let us turn from the past; what of the present? In spite of the dehumanizing and other efforts to destroy the fecundity of the race, the twenty Africans of 1620, by the close of the Revolution, had increased to 650,000, and these 650,000, at the close of the Civil War, had reached the alarming number of four and one-half millions; and these four and a half millions, had, according to the last Federal Census, reached the astonishing number of ten millions or more of native-born citizens—entitled, though sometimes denied, to every right and privilege granted by the Constitution of the United States and by the Fourteenth and Fifteenth Amendments thereof; the making and sustaining of which our fathers contributed much of their blood and sacrifice, in peace, as well as in war.

For we have been present, not only as spectators, but as active participants in every trying crisis in the history of this nation. In the beginning of the seventeenth century, when labor troubles threatened the very life of the infant colony and continuing to the founding of the Republic—when white men were held in peonage or actual bondage for the uncanceled financial obligations due to the nobility of Great Britain—who furnished the labor which solved the vexed problem? Who furnished the brawn and muscle which cleared the forests, leveled the hills, tunneled the mountains, bridged the rivers, laid the tracks and cultivated the fields, until this broad land had become as beautiful as the lily of the valley and as fragrant as the rose of Sharon?

In 1776, when despotism was enthroned and liberty languished in the streets of Boston, was it not the blood of a Negro—Crispus Attucks—which animated the sinking spirit of the Goddess, who was almost ready to die under the oppression of King George and the despotism of Cornwallis?

In the Sixties—when Lincoln, despairing of the outcome of the Civil War, on account of the treachery in his own ranks and repeated reverses on the battle-field, called for 75,000 volunteers to suppress the Rebellion in the South—who came to the rescue of the Union? In spite of the effort of McClellan and his company of 50,000 soldiers, who went to Richmond to prevent "niggers," as they were called, from enlisting, who came to the rescue of the Union? Whose blood helped to render the testament of liberty valid? Ask Port Hudson and Milligan's Bend, and Fort Wagner, and Fort Pillow, and Pittsburg Landing, how the nearly 200,000 Negro soldiers behaved themselves under the fire of the enemy on these memorable battlefields—rendered sacred by their patriotic blood.

Who saved the Rough Riders and Colonel Roosevelt in the late Spanish-American War, when San Juan was illuminated with the fire of Spanish cannonading? Hark! Methinks I hear the tramp of the black boys of the 24th and the 25th Cavalry, chanting to the strains of martial music,—"Glory Hallelujah, we are going to have a hot time in the old town to-night," as they dashed up the dangerous parapet to defend the honor of their country, and to keep "Old Glory" from trailing in the dust.

At the close of the Civil War we were without homes, lands, or money. To-day, according to the last census of the United States, we own 600,000 homes, 20,000,000 acres of farm land, covering an area equal to the political dominions of the kingdoms of Belgium and Holland. We have under cultivation 40,000,000 acres of farm lands, including those farms rented by our people and those owned in fee-simple, and worth $500,000,000. The gross incomes from the farms conducted by Negroes amount to $250,000,000 annually. We own 10,000 business establishments, 300 drug stores, and 57 banks.

At the close of the Civil War we were without schools, without men of letters, without men in the various professions and lucrative avocations of life. To-day, we have 200 universities, colleges, and schools of lower grade supported by the race. We have 3,000,000 Negro children attending these schools and the public schools of the land. We have written 2,000 books. We edit and conduct 200 periodicals and magazines. In forty years we have contributed, as levies for school purposes, $45,000,000. With a membership of 4,000,000 we have 35,000 churches, valued at $56,000,000, and contribute annually $7,500,000 to their support. We contribute annually $6,000,000 to secret and benevolent societies. We have about 40,000 teachers, 1,500 lawyers, 2,500 doctors, 20,000 preachers, and 80,000 business men—Marvellous!—Marvellous!

A race that can produce in fifty years, beginning with nothing, such a report as this, whose minutest detail is supported by official statistics, needs no pity, Mr. Chairman. A race that can produce a Douglass, a Langston, a Hood, a Scott, a Turner, a Harvey Johnson, a Bruce, a Payne, an Arnett, a Revells, a Price, an Elliott, a Montgomery, a Bowen, a Mason, a Dunbar, a Du Bois, and last but not least, a Booker T. Washington—the foremost genius of our vocational and industrial training—asks not for pity. It only asks for an equal opportunity in the race of life; it asks not for special legislation to accommodate any necessity; it simply asks for a just application of existing laws to all citizens alike, without any reference to race or color or previous condition of servitude. The representatives of this race, in this year of Our Lord, 1913, ask the American people to judge them upon the record of their great and useful men and women which the race has produced in less than a half century—and upon the average merit of the mass of the race since the Emancipation Proclamation was issued by the immortal Lincoln.

In concluding this brief summary—for at best it can only be regarded as a brief summary of the doings of the race—and standing on the threshold of a new era in politics, in commerce, in religion and in ethics—a new era in the feeling and temper of the white American towards the Afro-American, I ask you, ladies and gentlemen, what shall be our conduct in the future? Watchman, what shall be the forecast?

Mr. Chairman, the forecast is bright—brighter than it has ever been in any previous period of the race's history in this nation—and I make this statement in the fullest appreciation of the efforts which are being made all over this land, by adverse legislation, to weed us out of politics and other public preferments; to push us into a corner to ourselves, in both Church and State—a propaganda which has brought gloom to many of our leaders, producing a pessimism inimical to progress.

But why a pessimistic outlook, Mr. Chairman? Is it possible to deprive ten million native-born American citizens from the enjoyment of their rights and privileges, guaranteed alike to all by the Constitution of the United States? I think not. Such a condition, Mr. Chairman, would be like an established government with no diplomatic representative at court. No matter what methods are adopted, some of the representative men of our race, unexpectedly or otherwise, in the final analysis, will slip in; if not in the Congress of the United States, then in the legislatures and in the municipal governments of the State—such, for example, as Lawyer Bass in Philadelphia, Pa.; Councilman Cummings in Baltimore; Smith in the legislature of Ohio; Fitzgerald in New Jersey, and Jackson in Illinois. No arrangement, no matter how planned, can ultimately defeat this logical result which *patience* alone will produce.

God and Time, ladies and gentlemen, are important factors in the solution of these questions. Fifty years are not sufficient to determine the possibilities of a race. No seer who knew the ancestors of the Anglo-Saxons as Cæsar knew them, would have foretold such a future as they now enjoy. This Anglo-Saxon race, whose ancestors worshipped the mistletoe, offered human sacrifices, and drank wine out of human skulls, have now become the conquerors and the dominant race on the earth. Their literature is the cream of the human intellect, and their tongue promises to become the official lingua of the earth. *God and Time* have wrought these things for them, and what God and Time have wrought for one race, *God and Time* can accomplish for another race—if that race remain true to itself and to God.

If you ask me for the ground of my optimism, I reply it is based upon two things, namely, the ability of the race itself to overcome difficulties and obstacles, and the over-ruling Providence of God, based upon His justice and His righteousness. It is hardly possible for this Negro race to experience any greater difficulties and obstacles in the future than it has already experienced in the past. It has overcome every obstacle with heroic courage—from slavery to the present period of its marvellous success. Without discounting the human efforts of the race, it has accomplished all of this by an heroic faith in God and in the justice and righteousness of His character as practised by our ancestors in the days of their bitterest afflictions—when weakness characterized the arm of flesh. Personally, I believe in God and in His justice and righteousness, and I have never lost faith in the benevolent brotherhood of mankind. I believe that "Right, like God is eternal and unchangeable; and since Right is Right and God is God, Right must ultimately prevail; though its final triumph may be retarded by the operation of wicked devices—nevertheless—it must prevail."

THE FUTURE OF THE NEGRO CHURCH[51]

BY HON. JOHN C. DANCY, LL.D.

Secretary Church Extension Society, A. M. E. Church

There is only one safe way to judge the future of the Negro Church, and that is by its past. And the past of this Church, despite its shortcomings, is safe.

To the curious it would seem strange that the Negro Church as such should exist at all. But in the light of its history, covering almost the entire history of this Government, its existence has been proved a necessity, as its records abundantly testify.

Until we had the Negro Church we had nothing of which the race could boast. We early discovered that it was religious rights which first opened our eyes to all our rights, but until we were secure in the enjoyment of our religious liberty, we were not fully aroused to the importance and value of civil liberty. We had not learned that they were twin blessings often dearly bought, but of inestimable value.

The Negro Church, therefore, became the basis upon which would be reared the superstructure of all our subsequent achievements. The men who laid the foundation for the Negro Church, whether of Methodist, or Baptist, or Episcopalian, or Presbyterian, or of Congregational predilection, were wise in their day and generation, and paved the way for the best work of Negro development ever undertaken in this country. Until we had the Negro Church, we had not the Negro school, and the one was the natural forerunner and concomitant of the other, opening up avenues for the preacher, the teacher, the lawyer, the physician, the editor, the orator, and the spokesman of and for the race.

* * * * *

The Negro Church has passed the experimental stage. It is no longer in a stage of incubation. It is an actuality,—an active, aggressive, and progressive reality. It has thoroughly established its rights to existence and its indispensability as a religious force and influence. Our religious fervor may at times appear to be unduly emotional and lacking in solemnity, but even this is pardonable, and we are reminded that this is an emotional age, and we must not forget that the great Penticostal awakening, in the early days of Christianity, provoked a similar criticism from the unaroused and unaffected unbelievers. The Negro Church of the future may be less emotional, but if the Church is to survive and throw off a cold formality which threatens to sap its very life-blood, it must not get away from its time-honored, deep spirituality, for without the Spirit the seemingly religious body is dead. Our Church of the future as well as our Church of the present will take care that no new dogmas of exotic growth will deprive it of those eternal verities which constitute the fundamentals of our Christian faith. These verities of our religion have their foundation in the teachings of our Great Redeemer himself, who is the very embodiment of all Truth.

The Negro Church of the future will address itself to the correction of present-day evils in both Church and State. It will emphasize the teaching that the highest form of virtue is the purest form of love. It will demand that men and women, and Christian professors especially, exemplify in their own lives and habits the religion they make bold to proclaim. It will insist upon the remedying of great wrongs from which countless numbers suffer,—whether these wrongs be unfair and unjust discriminations in public places, on the common thoroughfares, in the courts and halls of justice, in the Congress, the legislature or the municipal councils,—everywhere the Church will condemn and protest and fulminate against these injustices, until they melt away with the certainty of April snow. The Church of the future will more fully realize that where great principles are involved, concessions are dangerous and compromises disastrous.

The future will disclose a Negro Church with men in all its pulpits equal to the great task which the responsibilities thereof impose. They will be qualified men from every viewpoint—deeply spiritual, well trained, pious, influential, impressive, strong. They will lead their people, and be a part of their life, their indomitable spirit, their ambitions, their achievements. They will be absolutely trusted and trustworthy. They will be an inspiration to our youth, to our manhood and our womanhood. They will speak as one having authority and they will boldly assert their authority to speak. They will take up where the fathers left off, and they in their possession of so great an inheritance of religious fervor and unshrinking faith, will arouse Christianity from its lethargy, and start as a nation of believers, arousing, as it were, from its spell of years. They will be as bold as lions, wise as serpents, and harmless as doves. They will win their way because the things for which they stand and the gospel which they preach, will deserve to win. They will not seek so much to impress their own personality, but their cause, and they will lose themselves in the cause by magnifying the cause.

* * * * *

The Negro Church of the future will take greater interest in the young people, will give greater attention to the Sunday-school work, to the young people's societies, to the Young Men's Christian Association, to the full development of all the departments of all the churches of whatever denomination, to the end that the churches will be thoroughly organized for work, and such work as will lead eventually to the thorough evangelization of the world. The redemption of Africa, one of the forward movements of the world to-day, must come largely through the efforts, the service, and the personal sacrifices of our own churches, our own ministers and teachers, our own men and women. Once fully aroused to the importance of the obligation we owe to the land of our forefathers, we will enter upon the task with all the zest and spirit of David Livingstone, whose one hundredth anniversary we are celebrating this year, as we are also celebrating the first half century of our emancipation from human slavery. Livingstone sacrificed himself in the heart of Africa in order to give life and light to the aborigines of the Dark Continent. Our Church of the future must take up the task so grandly undertaken by him, and cease not until the work he so nobly began finds its full fruitage in Africa's redemption from heathendom, superstition, and ignorance, that she may take her place among the civilized and enlightened people of the world.

* * * * *

The Church of the future will have to do with the life of its membership. It will take heed to its health, and will teach hygiene and the laws which safeguard one's health in the home, in the Church, in the public schools and public places, in the open air and where not. It will impress the lesson of a sound mind in a sound body, and the great need of a sound body in order to have a sound mind. It will not fear to declare in favor of pure athletics as a means of developing the physical system, which is so essential to sound health and a strong manhood. The boys and young men will be urged to identify themselves with Young Men's Christian Associations so as to have advantage of the reading-rooms, the swimming-pools, the gymnasiums, and other young men's society, thus eschewing the dens of vice and haunts of infamy which might otherwise attract them and blight their precious young lives for all time, it may be. It will take knowledge of human life and its means of existence everywhere. It will seek to know what the man and woman in the alley as well as those on the broad thoroughfare are doing,—whether they are oppressed or distressed in body or in mind, and to go to their relief. It will discover that man *is* his brother's keeper, and is largely responsible for him and must seek to take care of him. The Church, yea, will come to itself and be shorn of a great part of its pride, when it fully realizes that its real growth and prosperity are dependent upon the attention it pays to God's poor and God's neglected. Our churches will re-echo with the sentiment of that song, "God Will Take Care of You," but there must be a refreshing application of it, knowing that caretaking reaches further than ourselves and extends to our neglected brother, whom we, so oftentimes, have forgotten. If the Church is no stronger than it is to-day it is due chiefly to the neglect of the unfortunate *many* who have been unreached and need to be reached.

The Church of the future must humble its pride, buckle on its armor, and cease not in its labors until this great army of unreached is reached and helped, and impressed and convinced and saved. "Go ye into all the world and preach my Gospel," does not mean to distant people merely, but to people at home as well, many of whom know as little of the Gospel as many others in distant Africa. There must be, there will be, a religious awakening along this line, so that if the people do not go to the Church, then the Church must go to the people, and there will be thousands, in the next few years in answer to the question, "Who will go?" who will answer in language which cannot be misunderstood, "Here am I, send me."

The Church of the future will have to do with the greater problems of every day life. It will have to aid in teaching the people life and duty and how best to meet and battle with these. It will have to impress the importance of home-getting,—whether in city or on farm,—and the possessing of these in fee simple, by actual purchase, and we will become more valuable as citizens as we acquire more in our individual right in real and personal property.

* * * * *

The Church of the future will urge the starting of savings accounts with the youth, and the organization of savings banks among our people in all sections, and the opening, incidentally, of opportunities for our boys and girls to get in close touch with business life and business habits. We will thus make the Church an influence, as it has been in the past, in paving the way for the future financial and substantial importance of the race. The Negro Church of the future will be less fettered by denominational lines and possessed of a broader Christian spirit, recognizing denominational names of course, but laying greater stress on Christianity, than on any church allegiance. Methodists, Baptists, and Presbyterians, and Congregationalists, and Episcopalians will interchange pulpits and preach one Gospel in the name of our common Lord, Who is in all, and through all and over all. There will be inter-denominational Sunday-school unions, Church conventions and conferences, and the ministers and congregations will be in closer union, praying for the same spiritual power, the same common blessings, and the removal of the same great evils. Judah will not vex Ephraim, and Ephraim will not vex Judah. Under the mighty influence of this commingling and oneness of heart and purpose

"Error will decay and Truth grow strong
And right shall rule supreme and conquer wrong."

* * * * *

To Thee! God of our fathers, we render praise and thanksgiving for such abundant evidence of Thy guiding presence during these fifty years of freedom and civil liberty. We predict for the future on the basis of our achievement during the past; and since the Negro Church has been a great factor in lifting us up and enabling us to see the new light, in spite of many obstacles, we are confident that by following the same Omnipotent Hand, that never errs and never fails, we will, in the coming years, prove that no sacrifice, either in war or in peace, made in our behalf has been made in vain, and no service rendered us has been without its subsequent reward. We rejoice, and are glad in our gladness and rich in our wealth. In the midst of it all, the Negro Church survives and is steadily moving on.

THE NEGRO LAWYER; HIS OPPORTUNITY, HIS DUTY[52]

BY W. ASHBIE HAWKINS

Of the Baltimore Bar

Gentlemen:

The legal profession is without doubt in the lead. Its devotees outrank all others in service to the government and they come the closest in personal contact to the individual. This is denied of course, and always will be denied by men of all other professions, but when the roster of the world's lawyers who have faithfully and efficiently served humanity in every conceivable way is pitted against that of the others, the question is relieved of all doubt. The Negro lawyer is no longer an experiment. He has been severely tried from within and without, and he has proved his worth. His place in our economy is fixed. He has demonstrated his capacity to serve, and to serve well, and for all of this both the lawyer and the race he is helping to advance are under lasting obligations to Howard University. She has to her credit more men who are actively and successfully pursuing their calling than any other institution of learning in this land.

* * * * *

The Negro race is probably to-day in greater need of consecrated lawyers than it is of pious priests. The time has come for the lawyer to take his place in the lead. We are celebrating this year the 50th anniversary of our emancipation, and, paradoxical though it may be, we appear further from emancipation to-day than when Lincoln signed his Emancipation Proclamation, or when Lee surrendered at Appomattox. It is quite true that we have an immensely larger realty-holding to our credit, that our financial worth is constantly on the increase, that our illiteracy is rapidly reaching the vanishing-point, and that in all matters, spiritual as well as temporal, we seem to have improved, but the closer we approximate the standard of life and living of the dominant race, all the harder apparently have we to fight to maintain our self-respect, and preserve the rights and privileges which the letter of our American law guarantees. When we were slaves and had nothing except our muscles, there was no thought of separate-car laws. When we were ignorant and powerless to think coherently, there were no efforts at our disfranchisement. When we were poverty-stricken and satisfied if we might live in the alleys of our great American cities, there was no thought of segregation, whether in the matter of our residences, or in that of the employees of our much-heralded republican government. With every increase in accomplishment, or worth, or demand for the better things of life, comes the burden of wrongs, injustice, and rash discrimination. It would be idle here to attempt to recount in detail the grievances we justly have against the government in city, state and nation; to do so further than the purpose I have in view would be but to tell you what you full well know. The Negro race needs a change of viewpoint; another leadership is an absolute necessity, and I see no reason why men of our profession should not attain it. For years we have had in the ascendency the prophets of submission and silence, and we have been taught to declare for peace when we knew there was no peace. No other element in our great nation, except that of ourselves is content with things as they are, accepting without protest every new injustice, in the vain hope that some day would bring about a change for the better. We have lulled ourselves to sleep with this fatalism, and what is the result? We have noted the practical nullification of every act suggested or inspired by the changing conditions in the lives and property of freedmen brought about by the Civil War. Disfranchisement in every Southern State is as fixed and determinate, as the indifference of the Negroes of those sections, or the practises of all political parties can make it. Separate, and therefore inferior, accommodations on public conveyances are the rule, and we have endured these conditions so long that it would appear almost cruel now to undertake, or to ask a change. We have noted further, and this is the saddest of all, that our inactivity in claiming our rights, or our indifference about their recognition, has not only emboldened our enemies, but it has silenced our friends.

We have seen with increasing alarm the judicial construction of statutes and the Constitution itself, which all but vitiate and annul the basis of our citizenship; we have seen repeated attempts made to discredit the War amendments to the national Constitution, and some have in all seriousness gone so far even as to question their constitutionality. Every student of our common law has always been sure of the right to private property, and the corollaries thereto, but it is just in the present year that a court of last resort in a neighboring State, in an interpretation of one of these new conceptions, a segregation ordinance, declared that while the one under investigation was invalid, that the municipality enacting it might under its police powers make provision for the segregation of the races in the matter of their residences, schools, churches, and places of public assembly. The law is not a fixed science; it is more properly growth, a development. What is not regarded as law to-day may, by the inactivity or indifference of those most deeply concerned, become the law of the next decade. So we behold to-day our rights and liberties drifting away from us, and that regarded as the law which years ago we deemed impossible. What are we to do, you say? What can we do? The lawyers trained here and in other institutions of learning must answer these questions, and in finding their answers will be their opportunity. The adjudication of the conflicting interests of mankind, the interpretation of our statutes and our common law the determination of rights and privileges of all men, is a judicial function. What rights we enjoy to-day have come in the final analysis from the courts. What rights we find ourselves to-day deprived of, and which we hope to enjoy to-morrow, must come, if at all, from the same source. The courts have the last word, and it is to that instrument of government we must appeal, and to that last word we must look for our safety, or fear our doom. But courts are not self-acting institutions, and they are not engaged in academic discussions of abstractions. They are severely serious. It may be that, like so many Americans, we have lost faith in the courts, and Heaven knows we have had abundant reason for so doing, but there's hope. They have too often and too long listened to the clamors of public opinion, put too much faith and credit in the utterances of latter-day journalism, coloring their opinions to suit the one, or to escape the criticism of the other. Under the pernicious doctrine of public policy and in fortifying that undefined and indefinable legal notion of police power, courts have wiped aside Constitutional limitations, and disregarded what the profession at least had learned to consider as almost fixed precedents of the law, but even with all these defects admitted, there remains the startling truth that to these governmental agencies we must look for the righting of our wrongs and the redress of our grievances. We have shunned the courts too often in our temporal affairs, fearing, it seems, further adverse decisions, or waiting a proper adjustment at some other forum. In my own State it might now be compulsory upon you, or any other decent self-respecting person of the race, in travelling from here to New York or elsewhere in the North, to ride in the so-called "Jim-Crow" cars provided by an indulgent Maryland legislature for Negro patrons of its railroads, had it not have been for a member of the Faculty of this institution. William H. H. Hart knew that legislation of that character was an attempt to restrict interstate traffic, and the Court of Appeals of Maryland agreed with him. The case of State vs. Hart, reported in 100 Md. at page 595, is a landmark in our Maryland law, and under its influence "Jim-Crow" cars have almost disappeared from the railroads of our State. Another distinguished member of the Faculty of Howard University, but of another department, in travelling over the railroads in the eastern part of our State last fall, discovered that the compartments provided by the roads for their colored passengers, in point of cleanliness, appointment, and convenience, were notably inferior to those furnished others. He complained to the Public Service Commission and, after a full hearing, the Commission passed a decree requiring these railroads to furnish accommodations to its colored passengers equal in all respects to that furnished others. This is exactly what the Separate-Car Law provides, but it is exactly what the railroads had never intended to furnish and, without the complaint of Professor T. W. Turner, no other course would have been followed. Here are two, and there are numerous other concrete examples of what may be accomplished by sane and timely appeals to our judicial tribunals. Our government has three well defined departments separate and distinct, each operating in a manner as a check on the other, and all together working for the common good of the whole. We have resorted generally to the executive and have been satisfied with its appointment of a few men to office, and with its passive execution of the laws affecting us. In recent years we have arisen to the point of seeking legislation in the defense of our civil rights, and it is hoped that as the years pass more of this will be done. But in the judicial branch of the government is where, after all, we must place our reliance. We need a body of trained lawyers in full sympathy with our community life, eager, anxious, and capable, prepared at any emergency to present our cause fairly and intelligently before any tribunal; and with this accomplished, I have faith in the American people that justice will prevail, and right triumph over every wrong. I do not mean that the lawyer is to seek such service by the fomenting of litigation; far from it, but let him be prepared for it by study and devotion to racial ideals, and when the hour comes he will be called on to marshal its forces and take charge of the legal contests of a race. This will never be if he dreams only of his money, if he thinks only of present material gain, if he counts his successes in terms of houses and lands. He must be willing to serve for the sake of the service. The failures in our professional life come almost wholly from those who had no high ideals of their calling, and no devotion to the interests of their race or country. Country and race in this matter are synonymous; you can't serve one without at the same time serving the other. The lawyer who advocates the protection of the lives, the property, and the civic welfare of ten millions of Americans of whatever hue, or origin, is not a racial zealot, but a patriot of the highest character, and his worth in preserving the nation's ideals is beyond calculation.

Young men, you who are either about to leave these halls for the active life of the lawyer, or you who are just beginning the pursuit of your studies here looking to the same end, I bring you, I hope, no discouraging note. My aim is to do the contrary. The heavy burdens the race is bearing in the form of unjust laws and practises, in strained constructions of statutes, constitutions, and the common law; in the thousand ways which the ingenuity of the prejudiced find to bar us from the full enjoyment of American liberty and freedom, these will some day, along with those of us who are now at the bar, furnish your greatest opportunity. Your duty then, as now, will be to fortify yourselves with all the learning which this institution provides, with all that the libraries in your reach contain, with all that close and intimate association with others of your profession will secure, with sincere devotion to the ideals and traditions of our noble profession, and with no less devotion to the interest of your clients, and a determination faithfully and loyally and efficiently to serve your race, your nation and your God.

THE TRAINING OF NEGROES FOR SOCIAL REFORM[53]

BY W. E. BURGHARDT DU BOIS, PH. D.

Editor and Founder "The Crisis"

The responsibility for their own social regeneration ought to be placed largely upon the shoulders of the Negro people. But such responsibility must carry with it a grant of power; responsibility without power is a mockery and a farce. If, therefore, the American people are sincerely anxious that the Negro shall put forth his best efforts to help himself, they must see to it that he is not deprived of the freedom and power to strive. The responsibility for dispelling their own ignorance implies that the power to overcome ignorance is to be placed in black men's hands; the lessening of poverty calls for the power of effective work; and the responsibility for lessening crime calls for control over social forces which produce crime.

Such social power means, assuredly, the growth of initiative among Negroes, the spread of independent thought, the expanding consciousness of manhood; and these things to-day are looked upon by many with apprehension and distrust. Men openly declare their design to train these millions as a subject caste, as men to be thought for, but not to think; to be led, but not to lead themselves.

Those who advocate these things forget that such a solution flings them squarely on the other horn of the dilemma: such a subject child-race could never be held accountable for its own misdeeds and shortcomings; its ignorance would be part of the nation's design, its poverty would arise partly from the direct oppression of the strong and partly from thriftlessness which such oppression breeds; and, above all, its crime would be the legitimate child of that lack of self-respect which caste systems engender. Such a solution of the Negro problem is not one which the saner sense of the nation for a moment contemplates; it is utterly foreign to American institutions, and is unthinkable as a future for any self-respecting race of men. The sound afterthought of the American people must come to realize that the responsibility for dispelling ignorance and poverty, and uprooting crime among Negroes cannot be put upon their own shoulders unless they are given such independent leadership in intelligence, skill, and morality as will inevitably lead to an independent manhood which cannot and will not rest in bonds.

Let me illustrate my meaning particularly in the matter of educating Negro youth.

The Negro problem, it has often been said, is largely a problem of ignorance—not simply of illiteracy, but a deeper ignorance of the world and its ways, of the thought and experience of men; an ignorance of self and the possibilities of human souls. This can be gotten rid of only by training; and primarily such training must take the form of that sort of social leadership which we call education. To apply such leadership to themselves and to profit by it, means that Negroes would have among themselves men of careful training and broad culture, as teachers and teachers of teachers. There are always periods of educational evolution when it is deemed quite proper for pupils in the fourth reader to teach those in the third. But such a method, wasteful and ineffective at all times, is peculiarly dangerous when ignorance is widespread and when there are few homes and public institutions to supplement the work of the school. It is, therefore, of crying necessity among Negroes that the heads of their educational system—the teachers in the normal schools, the heads of high schools, the principals of public systems, should be unusually well trained men; men trained not simply in common-school branches, not simply in the technique of school management and normal methods, but trained beyond this, broadly and carefully, into the meaning of the age whose civilization it is their peculiar duty to interpret to the youth of a new race, to the minds of untrained people. Such educational leaders should be prepared by long and rigorous courses of study similar to those which the world over have been designed to strengthen the intellectual powers, fortify character, and facilitate the transmission from age to age of the stores of the world's knowledge.

Not all men—indeed, not the majority of men, only the exceptional few among American Negroes or among any other people—are adapted to this higher training, as, indeed, only the exceptional few are adapted to higher training in any line; but the significance of such men is not to be measured by their numbers, but rather by the numbers of their pupils and followers who are destined to see the world through their eyes, hear it through their trained ears, and speak to it through the music of their words.

Such men, teachers of teachers and leaders of the untaught, Atlanta University and similar colleges seek to train. We seek to do our work thoroughly and carefully. We have no predilections or prejudices as to particular studies or methods, but we do cling to those time-honored sorts of discipline which the experience of the world has long since proven to be of especial value. We sift as carefully as possible the student material which offers itself, and we try by every conscientious method to give to students who have character and ability such years of discipline as shall make them stronger, keener, and better for their peculiar mission. The history of civilization seems to prove that no group or nation which seeks advancement and true development can despise or neglect the power of well-trained minds; and this power of intellectual leadership must be given to the talented tenth among American Negroes before this race can seriously be asked to assume the responsibility of dispelling its own ignorance. Upon the foundation-stone of a few well-equipped Negro colleges of high and honest standards can be built a proper system of free common schools in the South for the masses of the Negro people; any attempt to found a system of public schools on anything less than this—on narrow ideals, limited or merely technical training—is to call blind leaders for the blind.

The very first step toward the settlement of the Negro problem is the spread of intelligence. The first step toward wider intelligence is a free public-school system; and the first and most important step toward a public-school system is the equipment and adequate support of a sufficient number of Negro colleges. These are first steps, and they involve great movements: first, the best of the existent colleges must not be abandoned to slow atrophy and death, as the tendency is to-day; secondly, systematic attempt must be made to organize secondary education. Below the colleges and connected with them must come the normal and high schools, judiciously distributed and carefully manned. In no essential particular should this system of common and secondary schools differ from educational systems the world over. Their chief function is the quickening and training of human intelligence; they can do much in the teaching of morals and manners incidentally, but they cannot and ought not to replace the home as the chief moral teacher; they can teach valuable lessons as to the meaning of work in the world, but they cannot replace technical schools and apprenticeship in actual life, which are the real schools of work. Manual training can and ought to be used in these schools, but as a means and not as an end—to quicken intelligence and self-knowledge and not to teach carpentry; just as arithmetic is used to train minds and not skilled accountants.

Whence, now, is the money coming for this educational system? For the common schools the support should come from local communities, the State governments, and the United States Government; for secondary education, support should come from local and State governments and private philanthropy; for the colleges, from private philanthropy and the United States Government. I make no apology for bringing the United States Government in thus conspicuously. The General Government must give aid to Southern education if illiteracy and ignorance are to cease threatening the very foundations of civilization within any reasonable time. Aid to common school education could be appropriated to the different States on the basis of illiteracy. The fund could be administered by State officials, and the results and needs reported upon by United States educational inspectors under the Bureau of Education. The States could easily distribute the funds so as to encourage local taxation and enterprise and not result in pauperizing the communities. As to higher training, it must be remembered that the cost of a single battle-ship like the Massachusetts would endow all the distinctively college work necessary for Negroes during the next half-century; and it is without doubt true that the unpaid balance from bounties withheld from Negroes in the Civil War would, with interest, easily supply this sum.

But spread of intelligence alone will not solve the Negro problem. If this problem is largely a question of ignorance, it is also scarcely less a problem of poverty. If Negroes are to assume the responsibility of raising the standards of living among themselves, the power of intelligent work and leadership toward proper industrial ideals must be placed in their hands. Economic efficiency depends on intelligence, skill and thrift. The public school system is designed to furnish the necessary intelligence for the ordinary worker, the secondary school for the more gifted workers, and the college for the exceptional few. Technical knowledge and manual dexterity in learning branches of the world's work are taught by industrial and trade schools, and such schools are of prime importance in the training of colored children. Trade-teaching can not be effectively combined with the work of the common schools because the primary curriculum is already too crowded, and thorough common-school training should precede trade-teaching. It is, however, quite possible to combine some of the work of the secondary schools with purely technical training, the necessary limitations being matters of time and cost: *e. g.*, the question whether the boy can afford to stay in school long enough to add parts of a high-school course to the trade course, and particularly the question whether the school can afford or ought to afford to give trade training to high-school students who do not intend to become artisans. A system of trade-schools, therefore, supported by State and private aid, should be added to the secondary school system.

An industrial school, however, does not merely teach technique. It is also a school—a center of moral influence and of mental discipline. As such it has peculiar problems in securing the proper teaching force. It demands broadly trained men: the teacher of carpentry must be more than a carpenter, and the teacher of the domestic arts more than a cook; for such teachers must instruct, not simply in manual dexterity, but in mental quickness and moral habits. In other words, they must be teachers as well as artisans. It thus happens that college-bred men and men from other higher schools have always been in demand in technical schools. If the college graduates were to-day withdrawn from the teaching force of the chief Negro industrial schools, nearly every one of them would have to close its doors. These facts are forgotten by such advocates of industrial training as oppose the higher schools. Strong as the argument for industrial schools is—and its strength is undeniable—its cogency simply increases the urgency of the plea for higher training-schools and colleges to furnish broadly educated teachers.

But intelligence and skill alone will not solve the Southern problem of poverty. With these must go that combination of homely habits and virtues which we may loosely call thrift. Something of thrift may be taught in school, more must be taught at home; but both these agencies are helpless when organized economic society denies to workers the just rewards of thrift and efficiency. And this has been true of black laborers in the South from the time of slavery down through the scandal of the Freedmen's Bank to the peonage and crop-lien system of to-day. If the Southern Negro is shiftless, it is primarily because over large areas a shiftless Negro can get on in the world about as well as an industrious black man. This is not universally true in the South, but it is true to so large an extent as to discourage striving in precisely that class of Negroes who most need encouragement. What is the remedy? Intelligence—not simply the ability to read and write or to sew—but the intelligence of a society permeated by that larger vision of life and broader tolerance which are fostered by the college and university. Not that all men must be college-bred, but that some men, black and white, must be, to leaven the ideals of the lump. Can any serious student of the economic South doubt that this to-day is her crying need?

Ignorance and poverty are the vastest of the Negro problems. But to these later years have added a third—the problem of Negro crime. That a great problem of social morality must have become eventually the central problem of emancipation is as clear as day to any student of history. In its grosser form as a problem of serious crime it is already upon us. Of course it is false and silly to represent that white women in the South are in daily danger of black assaulters. On the contrary, white womanhood in the South is absolutely safe in the hands of ninety-five per cent. of the black men—ten times safer than black womanhood is in the hands of white men. Nevertheless, there is a large and dangerous class of Negro criminals, paupers, and outcasts. The existence and growth of such a class far from causing surprise, should be recognized as the natural result of that social disease called the Negro problem; nearly every untoward circumstance known to human experience has united to increase Negro crime: the slavery of the past, the sudden emancipation, the narrowing of economic opportunity, the lawless environment of wide regions, the stifling of natural ambition, the curtailment of political privilege, the disregard of the sanctity of black men's homes, and, above all, a system of treatment for criminals calculated to breed crime far faster than all other available agencies could repress it. Such a combination of circumstances is as sure to increase the numbers of the vicious and outcast as the rain is to wet the earth. The phenomenon calls for no delicately drawn theories of race differences; it is a plain case of cause and effect.

But plain as the causes may be, the results are just as deplorable, and repeatedly to-day the criticism is made that Negroes do not recognize sufficiently their responsibility in this matter. Such critics forget how little power to-day Negroes have over their own lower classes. Before the black murderer who strikes his victim to-day, the average black man stands far more helpless than the average white, and, too, suffers ten times more from the effects of the deed. The white man has political power, accumulated wealth, and knowledge of social forces; the black man is practically disfranchised, poor, and unable to discriminate between the criminal and the martyr. The Negro needs the defense of the ballot, the conserving power of property, and, above all, the ability to cope intelligently with such vast questions of social regeneration and moral reform as confront him. If social reform among Negroes be without organization or trained leadership from within, if the administration of law is always for the avenging of the white victim and seldom for the reformation of the black criminal, if ignorant black men misunderstand the functions of government because they have had no decent instruction, and intelligent black men are denied a voice in government because they are black—under such circumstances to hold Negroes responsible for the suppression of crime among themselves is the cruelest of mockeries.

On the other hand, a sincere desire among the American people to help the Negroes undertake their own social regeneration means, first, that the Negro be given the ballot on the same terms as other men, to protect him against injustice and to safeguard his interests in the administration of law; secondly, that through education and social organization he be trained to work, and save, and earn a decent living. But these are not all: wealth is not the only thing worth accumulating; experience and knowledge can be accumulated and handed down, and no people can be truly rich without them. Can the Negro do without these? Can this training in work and thrift be truly effective without the guidance of trained intelligence and deep knowledge—without that same efficiency which has enabled modern peoples to grapple so successfully with the problems of the Submerged Tenth? There must surely be among Negro leaders the philanthropic impulse, the uprightness of character and strength of purpose, but there must be more than these; philanthropy and purpose among blacks as well as among whites must be guided and curbed by knowledge and mental discipline—knowledge of the forces of civilization that make for survival, ability to organize and guide those forces, and realization of the true meaning of those broader ideals of human betterment which may in time bring heaven and earth a little nearer. This is social power—it is gotten in many ways by experience, by social contact, by what we loosely call the chances of life. But the systematic method of acquiring and imparting it is by the training of youth to thought, power, and knowledge in the school and college. And that group of people whose mental grasp is by heredity weakest, and whose knowledge of the past is for historic reasons most imperfect, that group is the very one which needs above all, for the talented of its youth, this severe and careful course of training; especially if they are expected to take immediate part in modern competitive life, if they are to hasten the slower courses of human development, and if the responsibility for this is to be in their own hands.

Three things American slavery gave the Negro—the habit of work, the English language, and the Christian religion; but one priceless thing it debauched, destroyed, and took from him, and that was the organized home. For the sake of intelligence and thrift, for the sake of work and morality, this home-life must be restored and regenerated with newer ideals. How? The normal method would be by actual contact with a higher home-life among his neighbors, but this method the social separation of white and black precludes. A proposed method is by schools of domestic arts, but, valuable as these are, they are but subsidiary aids to the establishment of homes; for real homes are primarily centers of ideals and teaching and only incidentally centers of cooking. The restoration and raising of home ideals must, then, come from social life among Negroes themselves; and does that social life need no leadership? It needs the best possible leadership of pure hearts and trained heads, the highest leadership of carefully trained men.

Such are the arguments for the Negro college, and such is the work that Atlanta University and a few similar institutions seek to do. We believe that a rationally arranged college course of study for men and women able to pursue it is the best and only method of putting into the world Negroes with ability to use the social forces of their race so as to stamp out crime, strengthen the home, eliminate degenerates, and inspire and encourage the higher tendencies of the race not only in thought and aspiration but in every-day toil. And we believe this, not simply because we have argued that such training ought to have these effects, or merely because we hope for such results in some dim future, but because already for years we have seen in the work of our graduates precisely such results as I have mentioned: successful teachers of teachers, intelligent and upright ministers, skilled physicians, principals of industrial schools, business men, and above all, makers of model homes and leaders of social groups, out from which radiate subtle but tangible forces of uplift and inspiration. The proof of this lies scattered in every State of the South, and, above all, in the half-unwilling testimony of men disposed to decry our work.

Between the Negro college and industrial school there are the strongest grounds for co-operation and unity. It is not a matter of mere emphasis, for we would be glad to see ten industrial schools to every college. It is not a fact that there are to-day too few Negro colleges, but rather that there are too many institutions attempting to do college work. But the danger lies in the fact that the best of the Negro colleges are poorly equipped and are to-day losing support and countenance, and that, unless the nation awakens to its duty, ten years will see the annihilation of higher Negro training in the South. We need a few strong, well-equipped Negro colleges, and we need them now, not to-morrow; unless we can have them and have them decently supported, Negro education in the South, both common-school and industrial, is doomed to failure, and the forces of social regeneration will be fatally weakened, for the college to-day among Negroes is, just as truly as it was yesterday among whites, the beginning and not the end of human training, the foundation and not the cap-stone of popular education.

Strange is it not, my brothers, how often in America those great watchwords of human energy—"Be strong!" "Know thyself!" "Hitch your wagon to a star!"—how often these die away into dim whispers when we face these seething millions of black men? And yet do they not belong to them? Are they not their heritage as well as yours? Can they bear burdens without strength, know without learning, and aspire without ideals? Are you afraid to let them try? Fear rather, in this our common fatherland, lest we live to lose those great watchwords of Liberty and Opportunity which yonder in the eternal hills their fathers fought with your fathers to preserve.

FOOTNOTES:

[1] Extracts from an address delivered at the American Convention for Promoting the Abolition of Slavery and Improving the Condition of the African Race, Philadelphia, Pa., December 11, 1818.

[2] Extracts from a lecture delivered at the Stuyvesant Institute, New York, for the benefit of the Colored Orphan Asylum, February 26, 1841.

[3] A speech delivered in 1846, on the anniversary of the founding of the Republic of Liberia.

[4] Extract from an oration delivered by Frederick Douglass at Rochester, N. Y., July 5, 1852.

[5] Speech of Charles H. Langston before the United States District Court for the Northern District of Ohio, May 12, 1859. Delivered when about to be sentenced for rescuing a man from slavery.

[6] Extracts from a speech delivered in the House of Representatives, January 6, 1874.

[7] Lieber on Civil Liberty, page 25.

[8] Hamilton's History of the American Republic, Vol. I, page 70.

[9] A speech delivered in the House of Representatives, February 3, 1875.

[10] From "The Life of A. Dumas," by Arthur E. Davidson, (p. 356).

[11] Philadelphia, Wednesday, April 14, 1875.

[12] Philadelphia, Wednesday, April 14, 1875.

[13] Delivered in the Hall of the House of Representatives, Washington, D. C., at the request of the Chaplain, Rev. William H. Channing.

[14] Extracts from an address delivered before the Banneker Literary Club, of Boston, Mass., on the occasion of the commemoration of the "Boston Massacre," March 7, 1876.

[15] Oration delivered by Frederick Douglass on the occasion of the unveiling of the Freedmen's Monument, in memory of Abraham Lincoln, in Lincoln Park, Washington, D. C., April 14, 1876.

[16] "I am naturally anti-slavery. If slavery is not wrong, nothing is wrong. I cannot remember when I did not so think and feel."—Letter of Mr. Lincoln to Mr. Hodges of Kentucky, April 4, 1864.

[17] Delivered at Indianapolis, Indiana.

[18] Address before the "Freedman's Aid Society," Methodist Episcopal Church, Ocean Grove, N. J., August 15th, 1883.

[19] June, 1889.

[20] Extract from an address delivered at the Music Hall, Boston, Mass., October 4, 1894, before the Seventh Biennial Meeting of the Grand United Order of Odd Fellows of America.

[21] Atlanta, Georgia, September 18, 1895.

[22] Delivered at the Negro Congress, at the Cotton States and International Exposition, Atlanta Ga., November 11 to November 23, 1895.

[23] An address by Booker T. Washington, A. M., delivered on the occasion of the unveiling of the Robert Gould Shaw Monument, Boston, Mass., May 31, 1897.

[24] An address delivered before the Tennessee Centennial Exposition, Nashville, Tenn., June 5, 1897.

[25] Address delivered at the Lincoln Day Banquet, Dayton, Ohio, Feb. 11, 1899.

[26] From *Howard's American Magazine.*

[27] War with Spain.

[28] Extracts from a speech delivered in the House of Representatives, January 29, 1901.

[29] Delivered at Cape Town, South Africa, February 1902.

[30] Delivered at a fair in Philadelphia, held in the interest of the *Christian Recorder.*

[31] From "The Negro and the White Man," 1897.

[32] Extracts from a speech made at a banquet given in his honor by native Africans at Holborn, England, August 15, 1903.

[33] Extract from an Address delivered before the Eureka Literary Society at Penbrooke, Pa., December 16, 1904.

[34] Delivered before General Conference, Chicago, Ill., 1904.

[35] Delivered at the International, Interdenominational Sunday-school Convention, Massey Hall, Toronto, Canada, June 27, 1905.

[36] Delivered on the occasion of the Citizen's Celebration of 100th Anniversary of the birth of William Lloyd Garrison, held under the auspices

of the Boston Suffrage League, in Faneuil Hall, Boston, Mass., U.S.A., Dec. 11, 1905.

[37] Speech delivered on the Centenary of his birth, February 12, 1909.

[38] Extract from address given at Carnegie Hall, New York, February 12, 1909.

[39] Delivered, in appreciation of his service on behalf of the members of Companies A, B and C, 25th Infantry, March 6th, 1909, at Metropolitan A. M. E. Church, Washington, D. C.

[40] A discourse delivered in the Fifteenth Street Presbyterian Church, Washington, D. C., Sunday, March 7, 1909.

[41] An address delivered before the young men of the National Religious Training School, Durham, N. C.

[42] An address delivered at the Tuskegee Commencement, May, 1912.

[43] An address delivered at a banquet given in his honor, May 21, 1912.

[44] Delivered at Cooper Institute, New York, 1912.

[45] An address delivered before the Wilmington District Epworth League Convention.

[46] Boston, Massachusetts, Wednesday, February 12, 1913.

[47] Delivered at Lincoln University, Pennsylvania, on the occasion of the Centenary of the birth of David Livingstone, March 7, 1913.

[48] Reprinted from *Kelly Miller's Monographic Magazine*, April, 1913.

[49] Extracts from Commencement address delivered at Tuskegee Institute, May 29, 1913.

[50] An address delivered upon the invitation of the citizens of Brownsville, Pa., on the occasion of the Fiftieth Anniversary of the Emancipation Proclamation and also to celebrate the event of Decoration Day, May 30, 1913.

[51] Delivered at the Celebration of the Emancipation Proclamation, Philadelphia, September, 1913.

[52] An address at the opening of Howard University Law School, Washington, D. C., Oct. 1st, 1913.

[53] From the New York *Outlook*.

CPSIA information can be obtained
at www.ICGtesting.com
Printed in the USA
LVHW040949020323
740706LV00007B/628

9 789356 902268